Imperial German Uniforms and Equipment 1907-1918

Imperial German Uniforms and Equipment 1907-1918

Field Equipment
Optical Instruments
Body Armor
Mine and Chemical Warfare
Communications Equipment
Weapons
Cloth Headgear

Johan Somers

Schiffer Military History
Atglen, PA

Dedication

I dedicate this book to
my wonderful daughter *Anneke* and
my love and best friend *Linda*

Book design by Ian Robertson.

Library of Congress Control Number: 2005931918

Printed in China.
ISBN: 0-7643-2261-3

We are interested in hearing from authors with book ideas on related topics.

Published by Schiffer Publishing Ltd.
4880 Lower Valley Road
Atglen, PA 19310
Phone: (610) 593-1777
FAX: (610) 593-2002
E-mail: Info@schifferbooks.com.
Visit our web site at: www.schifferbooks.com
Please write for a free catalog.
This book may be purchased from the publisher.
Please include $3.95 postage.
Try your bookstore first.

In Europe, Schiffer books are distributed by:
Bushwood Books
6 Marksbury Avenue
Kew Gardens
Surrey TW9 4JF
England
Phone: 44 (0) 20 8392-8585
FAX: 44 (0) 20 8392-9876
E-mail: Info@bushwoodbooks.co.uk.
Free postage in the UK. Europe: air mail at cost.
Try your bookstore first.

Contents

Foreword

"Und wenn der Kuckuck rufen tut, Wird alles wieder gut, Wird alles, alles, alles wieder gut."

Soldiers song: *"When the cuckoo sings, everything will be alright, everything, everything, will be alright." Meaning that better and happier times will return eventually.*

Foreword

This pictorial reference work provides a detailed overview of the uniforms, weapons and equipment used by the bulk of the Imperial German Army before and during the First World War, without claiming to be comprehensive.

The European armies of the 19th and early 20th century were still dressed in brightly colored uniforms and used equipment essentially unchanged in design for since the middle of the 1800s. The French soldiers of 1914 faced the German Army in dark blue overcoats and striking red trousers, while the Belgian infantry appeared in a completely outdated dark blue-grey overcoat and curious hat. In Germany, a new field grey uniform was proposed in 1907 and most parts of the army had already received new uniforms when the war broke out in 1914. However, several units were still dressed in uniforms of dark blue, red, green, brown, during the first months of the conflict – and for many more years with Reserve and *Landwehr* troops in the home country. Specialized forces, like the military post or the military police continued to wear dark blue or dark green uniforms in the occupied territories. Therefore some attention is paid to these uniforms as well as they were used during the conflict. An understanding of the colored appearance of the German Army prior to 1907 is also useful in order to understand the design of the field-grey future peace-time uniform (*Friedensrock*), which was introduced in 1915. Its basic design was very much like the old traditional tunics and field caps. For a complete history of pre-1907 uniforms and equipment one can find many interesting reference books in the literature list.

The uniform section will cover the main types of tunics (*Waffenrock*) and trousers in use with regular infantry, artillery, cavalry and marine. In particular, cavalry troops had attractive uniforms, which were often very unique in design. Uhlan, Hussar, *Jäger-zu-Pferde* (Mounted rifles), Dragoon, Cuirassier and *Cheveauleger* units formed the backbone of the German mounted contingents. Another important part of the war machine was the military officials or *Beamte*. *Beamte* were responsible for administrative duties in the Army clothing depots and other departments, and wore a field-grey *Waffenrock* during the war. The tunic and field caps were mostly identical to the regular officers field-grey garment, apart from differences in colored piping, shoulder boards or special insignia. It's important to be able to distinguish an Army tunic or cap from one used in the administrative branches.

The field equipment section will cover most of the material used by the regular foot soldier. Only a little attention is paid to specific officers equipment. Communications were critical during the war and messages and reports needed to be sent between first line troops and more permanent command positions. The German Army possessed a wide range of instruments and communication devices, ranging from optical signals, flare pistols and telephone equipment of which several examples are described in this book.

The weapons chapter will provide a general overview of the most common rifles, pistols, revolvers, grenades, knives and machine guns. Some attention is also given to the different types of flame-throwers and trench mortars. There are again many outstanding books available which cover in detail the vast topic of weaponry and arms used by the Imperial German Army.

This work would not have been complete without the many period illustrations and photographs from museums and collections showing a particular uniform or piece of equipment 'in action'. This way, I hope that this work can also serve as a pictorial reference guide for the novice or advanced military enthusiast, collector, modeller and re-enactor.

A work of this size is bound to have several errors and mistakes. I have tried to keep these to an absolute minimum and I hope to have achieved this task. However, many descriptions just give a general idea of the evolution of a certain piece of equipment, and exceptions to these rules or unmentioned details will no doubt exist. All sizes and dimensions of artifacts quoted in this book are only approximate and variations between individual pieces can occur - depending on the manufacturer, date of production, etc. It appears as well that substitute materials and methods of construction were tolerated, often due to temporary shortages of components or materials.

Finally, this book honors all the men and women, regardless of nationality, who gave their lives during the Great War nearly 100 years ago. The suffering and grief of their loved ones is unimaginable. Let us remember them and never forget their sacrifice.

Acknowledgments

Acknowledgments
This book would not have been possible without the healthy criticism, ideas and advice of so many enthusiasts and the availability of high quality reference works. First of all, my sincere appreciation goes to those who have volunteered to review the draft version of the manuscript. It was a real global experience for me as collecting friends from France, U.S., U.K. and Canada volunteered to write specialized chapters and to improve the text, spelling and grammar of the manuscript.

Arnaud Lejaille (France) wrote the entire chapter on the gas mask filters and mine warfare sections and supplied many photographs, so that the gas warfare section of this book is very detailed and well illustrated. Arnaud regularly publishes articles in *Militaria Magazine* and runs an excellent website which covers French and German gas masks.

Dr. *Brian Ludwig* (U.S.) photographed over 100 items from his own collection, wrote the chapter on flare pistols and reviewed and edited the complete text, giving essential feedback. Brian is a professional archaeologist living near Lake Tahoe, California, whose family history can be traced back to at least sixteenth century Germany. One grandfather served in the American military during the Great War but three uncles, all young brothers, enlisted in the Kaiser's army in 1914. This personal connection to the war has inspired an active interest in Imperial German militaria for over fifteen years.

Chip Minx (U.S.) reviewed large parts of the manuscript, wrote several chapters related to communication devices and provided several pictures from his collection. His advice and knowledge proved to be of great value and saved me from sometimes presenting inconsistent or incorrect information. Chip has studied World War I militaria for over forty years and his interest in the subject is due to his grandfather's stories of the Great War, in which he participated as a Master Signal Electrician in the 314. Field Signal Battalion of the 89th Division, AEF.

Faris Siwadi (UK) offered to find period photographs, contacted friends in a search for even more material, shared pictures from his own collection and reviewed and corrected the complete manuscript. Faris is employed in the legal profession and has been a World War I enthusiast for the past twenty years, an interest that was sparked off from listening to the recollections of his Grandfather who served in the 2/10th Bn London Regt during World War I. Whenever possible he manages to sneak off to the Western Front to visit the battlefields, and like the author, has a very understanding wife.

Finally, I would like to thank *Gordon Wilson* (Canada) for reviewing parts of the text as well. The frequent email traffic between my collecting friends and myself really gave me the motivation to carry on with this project.

This book only came about because of the work invested by many authors in previous publications and reference works. Three publications gave me a lot of inspiration and critical information. The first work is the video created by *Marshall Daut*. Marshall presents an extensive collection of field-grey uniforms from 1907 to 1918. He clearly and in detail describes the evolution of the *Waffenrock* in the German Army, while the camera captures an amazing number of tunics and other uniforms. The second work "*Die formations- Und Uniformierungsgeschichte des Preuflischen Heeres*" was written by *Paul Von Pietsch* and published in 1963 by *Helmut Gerhard Schultz*. These two out-of-print volumes describe Prussian uniform history from 1808 to 1914. Finally, "*Die Feldgraue Uniformierung des deutschen Heeres 1907-1918*" was published by Dr. *Jürgen Kraus* in 1999. The work consists of two heavy volumes packed with black & white and color drawings of uniforms and field equipment, and was published by *Biblio Verlag* to celebrate the 100th anniversary of the *Deutschen Gesellschaft für Heereskunde e.V.* A lot of facts found in these excellent books – which are highly recommended for further reading – were used in this work as well and I want to thank *Biblio Verlag* and the *Deutschen Gesellschaft für Heereskunde e.V* for allowing me to use this information.

Nearly all the photographs came from fellow collectors and museums that allowed me to use pictures from items in their collections, and I would especially like to thank *Alex Deseyne*, curator of *Domein Raversijde* in *Ostend* (http://www.domeinraversijde.be), the staff of the *Royal Army and Military History Museum* in *Brussels* and *Franky Bostuyn*, curator of *Memorial Museum Passchendaele 1917, Zonnebeke*. A special word of thanks goes to *Eric Siegel* (France) and *Sven Kuczyk* (Germany) for sending me many excellent photographs of rare items in their collection. I would also like to thank:

Belgium
Freddy Raepsaet
Julien Stroobants, *Museum "Slag der Zilveren Helmen"*, Halen
Dirk Theunissen
Ben Torfs

Canada
Gordon Wilson

Finland
Jukka Juutilainen

France
Arnaud Lejaille
David Kittler
Eric Siegel

Germany
Biblio Verlag
Sven Kuczyk
Rolf Noeske, *Deutschen Gesellschaft für Heereskunde e V*

Malta
Robert Attard

UK
Stephen Chambers
Mike Brennan
Faris Siwadi

U.S.
George Anderson
Christopher Engel
Kenneth Greenfield
Bruce Jarvis
Brian Ludwig
Chip Minx
John P. Price
Remy Schaal
Tony Schnurr, Kaiser's Bunker
John Strott
Randy Trawnik
Ronald Watson
Thomas Wictor

Spain
Alberto Flórez

...and all the others who preferred to remain anonymous.

I would like to express my gratitude for my publisher Peter B. Schiffer and my editor Bob Biondi, for making this book possible. Many thanks also for my mother and for her interest and enthusiasm while I was working on this project and my father for running to the post office each time a registered shipment arrived with a new item to be photographed for the book. This book would never have been published without the many years of support from my wife *Linda*. It was not always easy for her to endure my passion for collecting. Finally, it's great to have a thirteen-year-old daughter *Anneke*, who is always listening with patience and interest when her daddy talks enthusiastically about a new acquisition.

Johan Somers
January 2005

Chapter One

Introduction

The Army Corps System

On January 18, 1871, following the end of the Franco-Prussian War, the German Empire was founded. The new empire was composed of:

The Kingdoms of Preuflen, Bavaria, Sachsen and Württemberg.

The Grand Dukedoms of Baden, Hesse, Oldenburg, Mecklenburg-Schwerin, Mecklenburg-Strelitz, and Sachsen-Weimar.

The Dukedoms of Anhalt, Brunswick, Sachsen-Altenburg, Sachsen-Coburg-Gotha, and Sachsen-Meiningen.

The Earldoms of Lippe, Reuss-Greiz, Reuss-Schleiz-Gera, Schaumburg-Lippe, Schwarzburg-Rudolfstadt, Schwarzburg-Sonderhausen, and Waldeck-Pyrmont.

The Free Cities of Bremen, Hamburg, and Lübeck.

The German Empire was divided into 24 regions (including three Bavarian), and their corresponding "Army corps" were identified using Roman numerals. The purpose of the Army corps was to function as an administrative body to support the recruitment and training of soldiers. Only the XV, XVI and part of XXI army corps recruited from other districts. Except the XVIII, XX, XXI and III Bavarian, each army corps had a *Bekleidungsamt*, responsible for the equipment needs and outfitting of the troops in that area as well as providing garrisoning facilities.

The army corp was a completely self-supporting entity, which had a large degree of independence. The commander of the army corp took orders from the Kaiser or the King of Bavaria. Note that of the 24 army corps, 21 reported to the Kaiser while the three Bavarian army corps reported to the King of Bavaria. Each army corp normally consisted of two divisions, each composed of:

A divisional staff.

Two or three infantry brigades, each made up of two infantry regiments of three battalions each and one machine-gun company.

A cavalry brigade of one or two regiments (Cuirassiers, Dragoons, Hussars, Uhlans or Mounted Rifles). As an exception, the Guard corps had four cavalry brigades in one cavalry division.

A field artillery brigade of two regiments, each composed of two *Abteilungen* of three batteries. Some *Abteilungen* were equipped with light field howitzers. A number of regiments had *Abteilungen* of only two batteries. Each battery had 6 horse drawn guns and several ammunition carriages (*Munitionswagen*).

In addition to non-combatant units such as military officials in administrative work (*Militärbeamte*) and medical units, special formations were also allocated to an army corps, with some variations. These were:

Jäger battalions which were composed of four companies
Machine-gun company.
Cyclist company.
Foot artillery regiment.
Pioneer regiment or battalion.
Searchlight unit.
Train unit.
Telegraph battalion.
Eisenbahn battalion.
Luftschiffer and *Flieger* battalions.
Kraftfahrer battalions.

The following list gives an overview of the different Army corps, their district and the cities where the headquarters of the Army corps were located. These headquarters were called *Stellvertretende Generalkommandos* (acting Army corps headquarters) during the war:

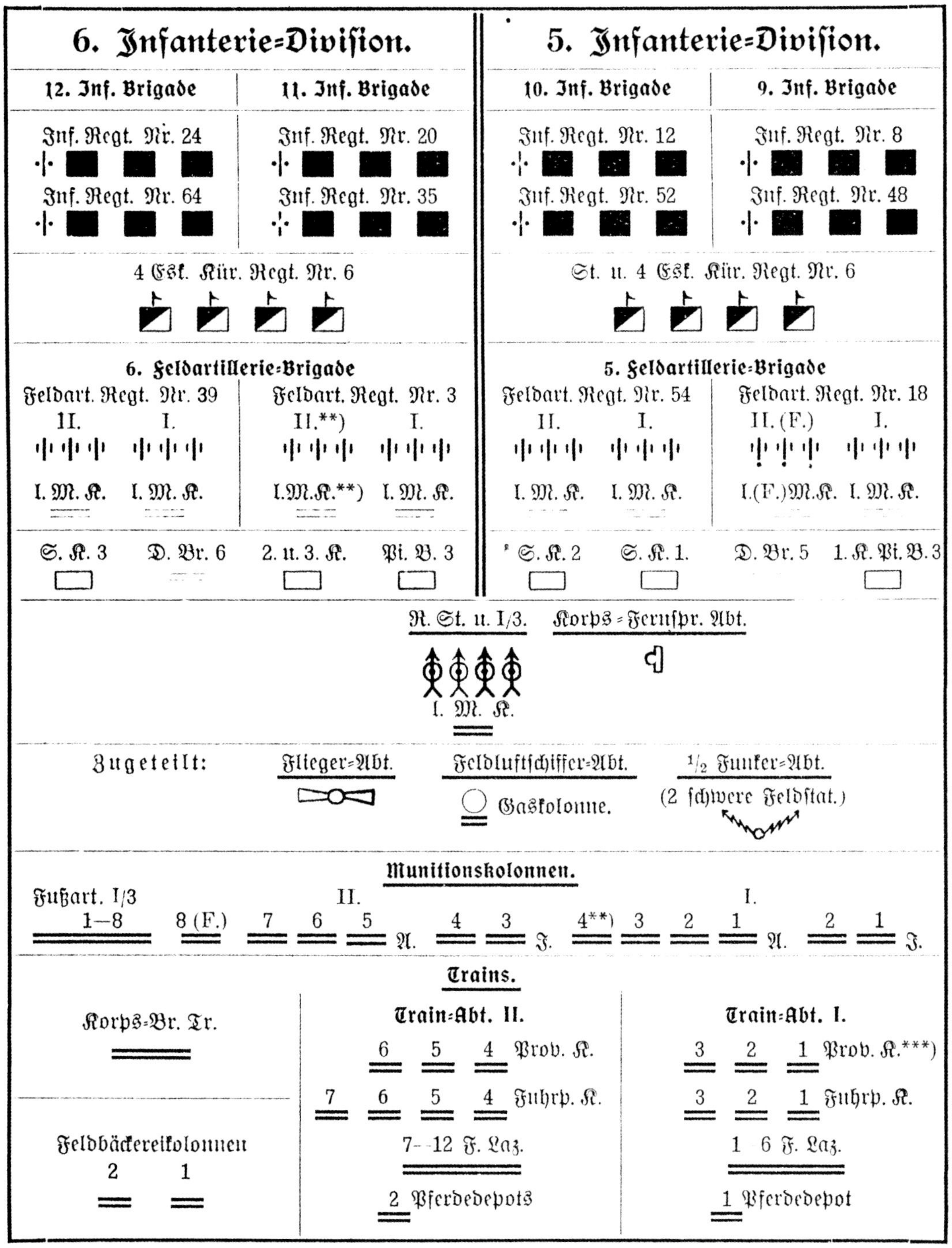

Tafel 3.

Beispiel der Kriegsgliederung eines Armeekorps.*)

III. Armeekorps. 24. 8. 24. 4.

*) Nach v. Moser „Führung des Armeekorps im Feldkriege". 2. Aufl. 1913.
**) „F." sobald jede J. D. eine l. Feldhaub. Abt. besitzt.
***) Darunter zwei besonders bewegliche „leichte" Prov. Kolonnen.

Diagram showing the organization of the III Army Corps during the war. The corps was made up of the 6th and the 5th Infantry Divisions. The 6th Division was composed of the 12th and the 11th Infantry Brigades. As an example, the 12th Infantry Brigade contained two infantry regiments, the 24th and the 64th. The 6th Cuirassier Regiments belonged to the III Army Corps as well. Each division had two Field Artillery Brigades. The 6th Brigade is attached to the 6th Infantry Division and composed of the 3rd and the 39th Field Artillery Regiments. The lower half of the drawing shows the different special troop formations allocated to the Army Corps. These include bakeries, two Train *Abteilungen*, munitions supply columns, a telegraph unit and several airborne units. *Reproduced from "Der Einjährige Freiwillige der Infanterie, Berlin 1916".*

Army Corps	**District**	**Headquarters of the district**
Guard (G.K : Garde Korps)	Prussia & Alsace-Lorraine	Primarily located in Berlin, although Potsdam, Spandau & Charlottenburg also had a Guard Corps.
I	East Prussia	Königsberg
II	Pomerania	Stettin
III	Brandenburg	Berlin
IV	Prussian Saxony	Magdeburg
V	Duchy of Posen	Posen
VI	Silesia	Breslau
VII	Westphalia	Munster
VIII	Rhineland	Koblenz
IX	Schleswig-Holstein	Altona
X	Hanover	Hanover
XI	Thuringia & Hesse-Nassau	Kassel
XII (Sax)	Eastern Saxony	Dresden
XIII (Würt)	Württemberg	Stuttgart
XIV (Baden)	Baden	Karlsruhe
XV	Alsace	Strassburg
XVI	Western Lorraine	Metz
XVII	West Prussia	Danzig
XVIII	Hessen	Frankfurt a/M
XIX	Western Saxony	Leipzig
XX	South East Prussia	Allenstein
XXI	Eastern Lorraine	Saarbrücken
I Bavarian	Southern Bavaria	Munich
II Bavarian	Lower Franconia and Palatinate	Würzburg
III Bavarian	Northern Bavaria	Nürnberg

Regimental Numbering

Most units had both an Imperial numbering sequence as well as their original unit number in the state army they originated from. Units created after the unification received both an Imperial unit number, but also a new number of their state of origin. These numbers reflected the seniority of the regiment. The official name of the regiment often included the name of a famous commander or distinction. Saxon and Bavarian troops carried the prefix "*kgl Saxon*" (or Royal Saxon) or "*kgl*" respectively before the unit name. An example:

> The "*Infanterie-Regiment Graf Schwerin (3. Pommersches) Nr.14*" is the 14th Infantry Regiment of the Imperial Army, but when originally raised in 1.7.1813 carried the seniority number "3" in Pommern. "*Graf Schwerin*" is part of the title of the regiment.

An infantry regiment in peacetime consisted of three battalions, numbered I, II and III and a machine gun company. Each battalion had four companies of three platoons (*Zuge*). A platoon was made up of four sections (*Korporalschaften*) each consisting of two groups (*Gruppe*). The companies were considered to be the smallest tactical unit, and were numbered consecutively as follows:

- *Battalion I*
  - *Company nr. 1*
    - *Platoon nr. 1*
      - *Korporalschaft nr. 1*
        - *Gruppe (8 men plus a lance corporal)*
        - *Gruppe*
      - *Korporalschaft nr. 2*
      - *Korporalschaft nr. 3*
      - *Korporalschaft nr. 4*
    - *Platoon nr. 2*
      - *Korporalschaft nr. 5*
      - *Korporalschaft nr. 6*
      - *Korporalschaft nr. 7*
      - *Korporalschaft nr. 8*
    - *Platoon nr. 3*
      - *Korporalschaft nr. 9*
      - *Korporalschaft nr. 10*
      - *Korporalschaft nr. 11*
      - *Korporalschaft nr. 12*
  - *Company nr. 2*
    - *Platoon nr. 1*
    - *Platoon nr. 2*
    - *Platoon nr. 3*
  - *Company nr. 3*
  - *Company nr. 4*
- *Battalion II*
  - *Company nr. 5*
  - *Company nr. 6*
  - *Company nr. 7*
  - *Company nr. 8*
- *Battalion III*
  - *Company nr. 9*
  - *Company nr. 10*
  - *Company nr. 11*
  - *Company nr. 12*
- *Machine Gun Company nr. 13*
- *Fortress Machine-gun Abteilung nr. 14 (optional)*

Each infantry regiment would thus have 12 line companies. Between 1887 and 1897, infantry regiments had 16 companies. Before the war, the German army consisted of 217 infantry regiments, 18 *Jäger* battalions and 11 machine gun detachments. The mobilization and war effort required new units to be formed. Apart from one new active infantry regiment (the *Infanterie-Lehr-Regiment*), 113 Reserve infantry regiments, 96 *Landwehr* infantry regiments, 86 *Ersatz* battalions and 18 Reserve *Jäger* regiments were created. A Reserve infantry regiment had between two and four battalions. The unit abbreviation used was R.I.R (sometimes R.J.R.) or "*Reserve-Infanterie-Regiment*". About a third of the regiments had been formed through the participation of the active infantry regiment of the same number, which created *Landwehr* infantry and Reserve *Jäger* regiments.

During the war, further reserve regiments were formed, such as the *Reserve-Brigade-Ersatzbataillone*, *Landwehr-Brigade-Ersatz-Bataillone*, *Mobile Ersatz-Bataillone* etc.

Army Depot and Unit Markings

Many issue caps, tunics and trousers have depot markings, and it is of interest to provide some background information on these. Stamps are usually in black ink although brown, blue or red shades are also seen. Most markings in tunics are on the left side of the liner just above the pocket. The army depot markings normally consist of the army corps number (*Bekleidungsamt*), i.e. the letters "B.A." followed by a roman numeral. The year of issue can sometimes be present as part of the BA depot marking. Apart from these, the size of the tunic or trousers, regimental markings, battalion and company numbers, and the *Garnitur* number are usually present as well.

Tunics and trousers can display very detailed markings to indicate the size of the garment. Tunics are marked as follows:

waist length	breast size	collar width
	body length	sleeve length

If the B.A number is I or II or III, the possibility exists that this piece of clothing was stamped by one of the two Bavarian army depots. In accordance with the 1871 Unification Agreement, Bavaria was allowed to retain it's own army corps system and regimental numbering sequence.

The *Garnitur* Roman number indicated the condition of the tunic or trousers. "I" was brand new condition and after a certain period of use and wear, up to four additional "I"s were stamped over time into the liner. In addition to the *Bekleidungsamt* stamp and year of issue, various other regimental markings can be found. To understand these depot markings it is useful to comprehend the different regimental numbering schemes. The book *The Imperial German Regimental Markings* from Jeff Noll provides an excellent overview of cloth and weapon markings used by the German Army. Nevertheless, here are some examples of markings often seen of cloth gear:

Marking	***Unit***
10 J.R.	10th Bavarian infantry regiment
10 I.R.	16th Bavarian infantry regiment

Liner with unit and size markings on a model 1909 *Cheveauleger* tunic. In this case the B.A. designation and the year of issue are each stamped within a separate rectangle. When separated they can be boxed, without a border or a combination of the two.

10E	10th squadron
10Esc.	10th squadron
1 R.J.R.	1st Bavarian reserve infantry regiment
5 R.I.R.	5th Bavarian reserve infantry regiment
5. G.R	5th Guard regiment
4 Comp	4th company
2 K	2nd company
2 Chev	2nd Cheveauleger regiment
1.Tel.-Batl	1st Telegraph battalion
B.J.A.G.	Repair clothing depot Guard (*Bekleidungs-Instandsetzungssamt des Gardekorps*)
B.J.A.	Repair clothing depot
B.2.s.R.	2nd Bavarian Schwere Reiter regiment
Ch	Cheveauleger
D.R.	Dragoon regiment
F.A.R.	Field artillery regiment
G.F.A.R.	Guard field artillery regiment
G.F.R.	Guard Fusilier regiment
G.G.R.	Guard grenadier regiment
G.J.B.	Guard Jäger battalion
G.Sch.B.	Guard Rifles (*Schützen*) battalion
H.R.	Husaren regiment
I.R. 5	5th Infantry regiment
J.R. 9	9th Infantry regiment
K.B.A.G.	Clothing depot Guard (*Kriegs-Bekleidungsamt Guard*)
K.R.	Cuirassier regiment
M.D.	Matrosen division
M.G.K.	Infantry machine gun company
R.J.R. 40	40th Reserve infantry regiment
R.I.R. 20	20th Reserve infantry regiment
T.2.	2nd Train battalion

Rare telegraph battalion stamp, dated 1915. *Courtesy of Dirk Theunissen.*

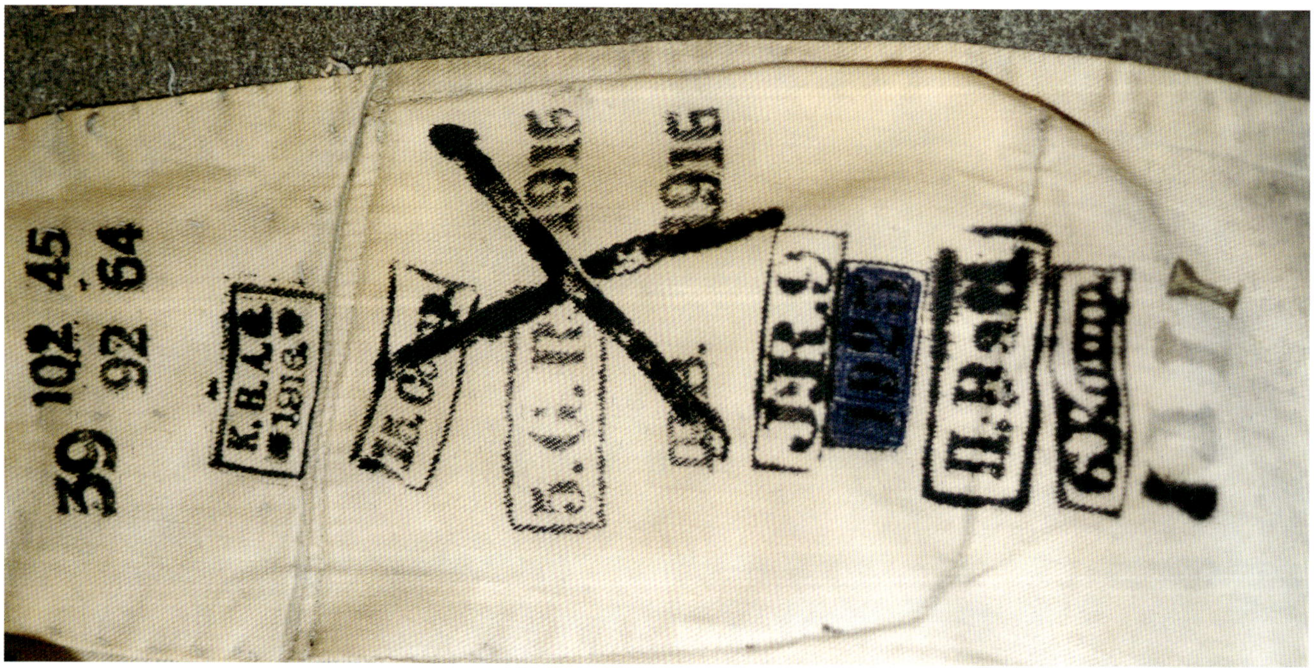

This mod 1915 tunic has seen an amazing number of owners. It carries both World War I era markings, but also dates which proved its use in the *Reichswehr*. It belonged to a Guard regiment, as can be seen by the K.B.A.G black stamp and the 9th Infantry Regiment A date of 1923 can just be seen in the black box below J.R.9. *Author's early collection.*

Markings seen on the rear visor Brunswick spiked helmet of the 92nd Infantry Regiment "*92. R 1B*", 1st Battalion.

Above: A tent pole bag dated from 1916 with markings for the *Guard Bekleidungsamt.*

Right: 14th Bavarian infantry regiment marking.

Military Service in Germany

The military service in Germany started at the age of 17 and ended after reaching the age of 45. During this time, the soldiers served in the Regular Army, *Reserve*, *Ersatz*, *Landwehr or Landsturm*. After performing the obligations in the *Landwehr I* between the ages of 17 to 20, a medical examination determined if the individual had to follow a 'career' path in the Regular Army, followed by the Reserve, *Landwehr I* and *Landsturm II*, or if he was moved to the Ersatz Reserve division. The *Landsturm* was the normal "home defense force" and the *Landsturm II* the second rank "home defense force". All soldiers ended up in the second rank *Landsturm II* at the age of 39.[1] All military obligations ended at the age of 45.

Military Ranks

The following table shows the ranking and command structure of the German Army in 1914, together with an English translation:

Officer Corps:		
Kaiser Wilhelm II		
General Feldmarschall	Field Marshal	Army Group (An Army Corps is comprised of two or more Armies)
Generaloberst	Senior General	Army (2 or more Corps)
General der Infanterie	General	Corps
Generalleutnant	Lieut. General	Division
Generalmajor	Major General	Brigade
Stabsoffiziere (Field officers)		
Oberst	Colonel	Regiment
Oberstleutnant	Lieutenant Colonel	Regiment
Major	Major	Battalion
Hauptleute (Company officer)		
Hauptmann	Captain	Company
Rittmeister in cavalry and supply units		Company
Oberleutnant	Lieutenant	Platoon
Leutnant	2nd Lieutenant	Platoon
Feldwebel-Leutnant	Sergeant Major-Lieut.	During the war functioning as platoon and company commanders
Offizier-Stellvertreter	Acting Officer	During the war functioning as platoon and company commanders

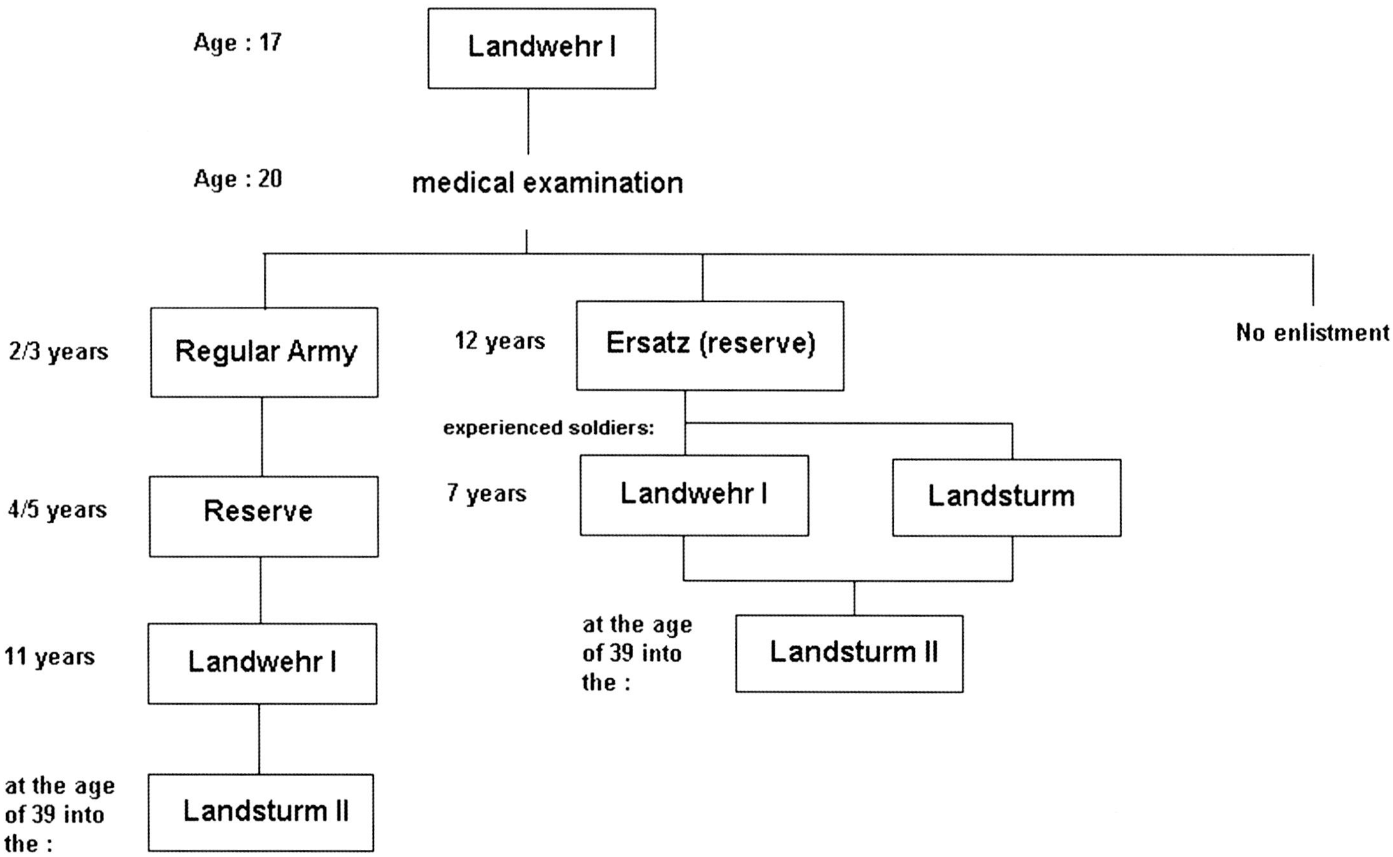

Military service

Non-Commissioned officers

Etatmäflige Feldwebel	Regimental Sergeant-Major	
Feldwebel	Company Sergeant Major	
Vizefeldwebel	Staff Sergeant	
Sergeant	Corporal	Korporalschaft

Enlisted men

Unteroffizier	Lance Corporal	Gruppe
Obergefreiter (Foot artillery regiments)		
Gefreiter	Private	
Gemeine	Soldier	

Depending on the branch of service or sometimes state, the *Gemeine* of active units were also called:

Dragoner	Dragoon regiment
Fahrer	Driver (of a *Kraftfahrer* unit, for example)
Füsilier	Fusilier regiment
Gardist	Foot Guard regiment
Grenadier	Grenadier regiment
Husar	Hussar regiment
Jäger	*Jäger* battalion
Kanonier	Gunner
Kürassier	Cuirassier regiment
Militärkrankenwärter	Medical unit
Musketier	Line infantry regiment
Pionier	Sapper from a pioneer unit
Sanitätssoldaten	Medical unit
Schütze	*Schützen* regiment or MG unit
Ulan	Uhlan regiment

Equivalent ranks were used within other branches of service.

Imperial Navy
Flag officers: Grofl-Admiral, Admiral, Vize-Admiral, Kapitän z. See, Konter-Admiral
Staff officers: Kapitän zur See, Fregattenkapitän, Korvettenkapitän
Lower officers: Kapitänleutnant
Subaltern officers: Oberleutnant zur See, Leutnant zur See
Deckoffiziere with Portepee (NCO): Oberdeckoffiziere, Deckoffiziere, Fähnriche zur See
Deckoffiziere without Portepee(NCO): Obermaate, Maate

Medical service
Sanitätsoffiziere: Generalstabarzt der Armee, Generalärzte, Generaloberärzte, Oberstabärzte, Stabärzte, Oberärzte, Assistenzärzte
Sanitätsoffiziere with Portepee (NCO): Unterärzte, Einjährige Freiwillige Ärzte, Sanitätsfeldwebel
Sanitätsoffiziere without Portepee (NCO): Sanitätssergeanten, Sanitätsunteroffiziere

Veterinary service
Veterinäroffiziere: Generalveterinär, Korpsstabveterinär, Oberstabsveterinäre, Stabsveterinäre, Oberveterinären Veterinäre
Veterinäroffiziere with Portepee (NCO): Unterveterinäre

Army Formations
Numerous army and civilian formations were active during the Great War and are referred to in the remainder of the book. It is therefore useful to quickly describe the purpose of each one of them.

Military Personnel
Infantry: The infantry composed of Line and Guard infantry and infantry machine gun troops.

Jäger and Schützen: Light infantry formations organized in battalions. They performed scouting tactics often together with cavalry formations. During the war, they were also involved in static trench warfare as normal infantry. A *Jäger* battalion also had an MG and cyclist company.

MG-Scharfschützen-Abteilungen: These machine gun detachments were raised as reserve machine-gun units for the division/General Headquarters. The men received one months' in-depth training, becoming experts in the assembly and disassembly of the machine gun, releasing of blockages in the mechanism, and learning how to use captured guns and to fire at static or moving targets.

Train: The train soldiers provided transport facilities, drivers of motor vehicles and horse attendants to individual army formations.

Pioneers (*Pioniere*): Responsible for the design and construction of fortified or fortress positions. In addition pioneers were also engaged in building tunnels and mining (*Pionier-Mineuren-Kompanien*), bridging, searchlight (*Scheinwerfer*) and trench mortar (*Minenwerfer*) duties, flame-throwing (*Flammenwerfer*) and the exploitation of gas warfare.

Air Service (*Luftschiffer*): The air force was made up of technical and flying personnel for airplanes and Zeppelin, as well as soldiers responsible for barrage and observation balloons (*Ballonzuge*).

Transportation troops (*Verkehrstruppen*)
Eisenbahn: This was the railway service of the German Army, responsible for the loading of trains, maintenance of the railway system and constructing new railways for supply purposes.
Kraftfahrer: The mechanical transport service operated trucks and other mechanical vehicles, mainly for supply purposes or staff cars.

Medical services
Sanitätswesen: This was the German Army medical service and composed of officers (doctors), stretcher-bearers and hospital orderlies.
Veterinärswesen: The Veterinary service consisted of officers and surgeons whose duties where mainly focused on horses and dogs.

Technical formations
Festungsbau: Officers responsible for the design and construction of fortified or fortress positions
Zeugpersonal: *Zeugpersonal* took care of the maintenance and administration of artillery pieces, weapons, etc. when these were not allocated to the troops.

Signal Service (*Telegraphentruppen*): Were responsible for all communication. They were reorganized into *Nachrichtentruppen* during 1917.

Artillery
Foot artillery: The Foot artillery was initially armed with 5.9" (15cm) howitzers and 8.3" (21cm) mortars, but heavier artillery pieces were used as the war progressed.
Mountain artillery: This artillery formation was working with lighter field guns in mountainous areas.
Field artillery: Field artillery was very mobile and also contained Horse artillery batteries. They were armed with 3" (7.7cm) field guns or the 4.1" (10.5cm) light howitzers.

Cavalry
Cuirassiers (*Kürassiere*): A highly prestigious cavalry arm, composed of volunteers. Many families were proud to have a member serving in a cuirassier regiment. Cuirassier troopers were using big and strong horses and were intended to serve as heavy cavalry (*Schlachtenkavallerie* to decide the outcome of the battle with heavy attacks). A metal cuirass was worn until 1888[2] for field service and later only for parades.
Dragoons (*Dragoner*): The largest part of the German cavalry was made up of Dragoon regiments. Their uniforms were very similar to the infantry, which had a historical reason. In the 15th century, armies used to employ foot soldiers on horses, which were called *Dragoner*. Dragoons were employed as light cavalry.
Hussars (*Husaren*): The Hussar formations found their origin in Eastern Europe, especially in Hungary. They were used as light cavalry operating behind enemy lines to cause disruption. The deaths head Hussar regiments with fur hats are still famous and well known, even today.
Uhlans (*Ulanen*): Uhlans or "horsemen in Tartar dress"[3] appeared in Prussia as of 1741. They were armed with lances and wore a helmet with a mortarboard on top. Uhlan regiments were equipped with heavy horses and were used as heavy cavalry, similar to the Cuirassiers.
Mounted rifles (*Jäger-zu-Pferde*): The main responsibilities of the *Jäger-zu-Pferde* regiments were to observe unknown territory. Young men were recruited who could perform these duties and sit on the horse for a prolonged period of time. In addition they were used a light cavalry as well.
Heavy Cavalry (*Schwere Reiter or Karabinier*): Originally Cuirassier regiments, the Saxon (*Karabinier*) and Bavarian *Schwere Reiter* Regiments had the same responsibilities as the Prussian Cuirassier and were used as *Schlachtenkavallerie*.
Cheveualegers: This light cavalry formation existed only in Bavaria, and had the same duties as the Dragoons, performing patrolling and reconnaissance duties.

Military and Civilian Officials (*Beamte*)
Military officials (*Militärbeamte*) were not categorized with the status of 'soldier', but still received a military rank. The *Obere Beamte* had an officer's rank, while the other officials were called *Untere Beamte*. Apart from the *Militärbeamte*, civilian officials (*Zivilbeamte der Militärverwaltung*) were also actively assigned to certain functions, including the War Ministries, Army Corps, etc. The following specialties existed:

Armee-Musikerinspizienten: Assisted the War Ministry in all matters related to military music. Inspected military musicians and were involved with relevant musical training.
Bekleidungsämter: In each army depot, a number of civilians performed administration duties. They coordinated the delivery of raw material, clothing and uniforms for the army corps.
Blutuntersuchstellen: The members of the *Blutuntersuchstellen* were responsible for performing blood tests on horses to prevent or investigate the outbreak of diseases.
Garnisonverwaltung: The *Garnisonverwaltung* was responsible for the administration of military real estate and operated within the garrison.
Geheime Feldpolizei and Zentralpolizei: Secret military police.
Generalstabes: It employed military as well as administrative civilian personnel working in the General headquarters.
Kassenwesen: Administered all accounting aspects related to cash registers of the Army.
Kriegministerium: Prussia, Bavaria, Saxony and Württemberg had a Ministry of War. The Prussian Ministry of War was made the center of authority during the war. It consisted out of eight departments, i.e. central department, general war department, army administration, quartering, pensions and law, remount inspections, medical department and the war bureau.[4]
Lazarettverwaltung: Performed administration duties for the garrison hospitals.
Militärjustizverwaltung: The military court. They went into the field and were active on Division or Army Corps level. In addition, several courts were attached to the War Ministry as well.
Militär-Bau: Civilian personnel involved in military construction works and operating in the home country.
Militärbildungsanstalten: A number of institutes which were responsible for the training and education of soldiers, NCOs and officers. These were called the *Militärbildungsanstalten* in which civilians had administrative or operational duties.
Militärapotheker: A limited number of civilian administrative personnel were involved in the administration of pharmaceutical supplies and research. They operated on corps or garrison level.

Militärdolmetscher: The *Dolmetscher* provided translation services for prisoners of war. They supported language translation during questioning and controlled incoming and outgoing post.
Proviantsamt and *Feldmagazin:* Operating from larger garrisons, the *Proviantsamt* (supply office) and *Feldmagazin* provided supplies and food to the troops. A number of civilians went to the front areas and coordinated the food supply from Germany to the front line.
Remontedepots: A *Remontedepot* took care of young horses before sending them to the front.
Technische Verkehrtruppen: The inspection and maintenance of machinery, airplanes, and air ship installations, etc. was supported by a number of technical civilians working for the technical traffic units.
Technische Institute: Technical institutes providing technical personnel, inspectors and weapons auditors.
Waffenmeister: Persons working on regimental level to maintain the weapons of the unit.
Zahlmeister: Operating on regimental level, the paymaster (*Zahlmeister)* was responsible for the administration, clothing, care and payment of the troops.
Zahnärzte: There were no military dentists before the war; so a number of civilian dentists operated within the military.
Zivil & Militärverwaltung der besetzten Gebiete: The occupied territories fell under a civilian or military administration in which civilians operated as well.

Notes
[1]John Walter, *Central Powers Small Arms of WW1.*
[2]Until 1876 for Bavarian Cuirassiers.
[3]European Military Uniforms, a short history, Paul Martin, Spring Books 1967, page 39.
[4]The German Army Handbook, p.36.

Chapter Two

Field Equipment

Introduction

Apart from a uniform, one or more weapons and ammunition, every soldier was kitted out with a backpack and bread bag to carry his personal equipment, either stored inside the pack or strapped around it. This equipment provided shelter and additional comfort during periods of rest, like a tent, drinking cup or a camp kettle to warm up food and drinks. Half of the men carried a small portable tool, a spade, hatchet or pick. 1st line transport or train carried the other tools belonging to the regiment. Small and large spades, picks and pickaxes were used for building earth works and axes, hatchets, hand and crosscut saws and wire cutters for timberwork and clearing barbed wire.[1] The basic model 1895 issue military equipment for foot troops in use at the beginning of the First World War, consisted of a:

Backpack (*Tornister*)
Belt (*Leibriemen*) with belt buckle
Bayonet and bayonet frog (*Seitengewehr*)
Two cartridge boxes (*Patronentaschen*)
Bread bag (*Brotbeutel*)
Cup (*Trinkbecher*)
Individual tent (*Zelt Ausrüstung*)
Tent pegs (*Zeltstock*)
Individual camp kettle (*Kochgeschirr*)
Individual canteen (*Feldflasche*)
Portable tool. Each infantry company had about 115 portable tools, i.e. five hatchets (*Beil*), 100 small spades (*Kleine Spaten*), 5 hatchets and 10 pick hatchets (*Beilpike*).

In the book *Field Equipment of the European Foot Soldier, 1900-1914*, the following nomenclature and weights of the effects are given, composing the field equipment of the German Foot Soldier around 1895:

Backpack and its load

Item	*Weight in kg*
Clothing	
Overcoat	1.9
Headdress	
Field cap	0.094
Equipment	
Knapsack	1.570
Overcoat Straps	.110
Small articles of equipment	
Toothbrush	.020
Socks or foot linen	.080
Easy shoes	1.050
Shirt	.275
Knife and spoon	.095
Soldiers handbook	.076
Handkerchief	.050
Sewing and brush case	.230
Camp equipment	
Camp kettle and straps	.459
Tent shelter and accessories	1.620
Arms	
Cartridges (30)	.944
Rations	
Reserve (3 days)	2.388
Tobacco and cigars	.150
Tools[2]	
Total	**11.163 kg**

On the man

Item	*Weight in kg*
Clothing	
Tunic	1.450
Trousers	.970
Headdress	
Helmet and ornaments	.360
Helmet cover	.030
Equipment	
Two cartridge boxes	.540
Belt and plate	.330

Small articles of equipment	
Boots	1.990
Trouser bracers	.115
Drawers	.450
Socks or foot linen	.080
Shirt	.275
Cravat	.034
Strap	.027
Breadbag	.350
Aluminium drinking cup	.055
Handkerchief	.050
Pocketbook	.030
Camp equipment	
Canteen	.243
Contents of canteen	.580

Arms	
Rifle	4.100
Bayonet	.580
Ammunition	
Cartridges (90)	2.831
Rations	
Days ration	.350
First aid package	.034
Identification card	.009
Total	**15.543 kg**
Grand total	**26.706 kg**

Sewing material. *Author's collection.*

Soap manufactured in Brussels in 1917. *Courtesy of BT.*

As a matter of interest, here is the total weight carried per foot soldier for different nations at the end of the 19th century[3]:

Austria	28.161 kg
Belgium	24.255 kg
Denmark	29.470 kg
France	24.767 kg
Germany	26.706 kg
Holland	22.771 kg
Italy	26.350 kg
Norway	24.531 kg
Russia	26.430 kg
Spain	27.264 kg
Sweden	27.360 kg
Switzerland	25.710 kg
United States	28.505 kg

Carrying the Equipment

Pre-war regulations prescribed that each foot soldier was equipped with a belt and belt buckle, two ammo pouches at each side of the belt, a bayonet in a leather carrier at the left side, while a bread bag with a water bottle was hanging at the back of the belt. The backpack was worn and two backpack straps hooked into the ammo pouches to reduce the weight on the belt. An individual tool, like a spade or axe was carried on the left side as well and connected to the bayonet. A bayonet knot (*Troddel* or *Portepee*) was wrapped around the bayonet to identity the battalion of the soldier. The tent half and/or overcoat was wrapped around the backpack and attached to it with three leather straps. A mess kit was carried on top of the *Tornister* and fixed with two leather straps. During the first months of the war, when mobility was still key, most of the infantry soldiers were carrying their equipment this way.

Assault Pack (*Stürmgepäck*)

During the war, a more convenient way of carrying essential equipment was introduced. Static trench warfare was becoming the norm and the *Tornister* was often left behind during attacks. The *Stürmgepäck* consisted of a tent half, which was rolled around the mess tin, forming a smaller and lighter pack. Sometimes, the overcoat or a blanket was wrapped inside the tent shelter. Leather straps (*Tornisterriemen*) were used to tightly fix the mess kit to the tent half. One or two bread bag straps were passed through the *Tornisterriemen* holding the *Stürmgepäck* roll together and served as the shoulder straps, allowing the pack to be carried on the back. With the *Tornister* shoulder straps no longer needed, the weight of the ammo pouches was supported with a bread bag strap slung over the back of the neck and clipping onto the loops on the back of each box. The bayonet, individual tool and the bread bag with one and later two water bottles were still worn, but the *Troddel* often disappeared from the field equipment. The *Tornisters* were used only behind the front line or left in depots. A third method of carrying the equipment existed before the war, where the shelter half was rolled and ran diagonally from the left shoulder to the right hip. The mess kit was attached with leather straps to the tent half. All other equipment was worn on the belt.

Colored postcard with soldiers, NCOs, and officers observing the scene. Most men wear a bayonet, bread bag, water bottle and brown jackboots. The spiked helmets have helmet covers. Note the cyclist at the left who has large *Litzen* on his tunic collar.

Pre-war arrangement. *Courtesy of BT.*

Rear view.

Storm troop formations often carried an impressive number of grenades. Especially after the introduction of the stick grenade in 1915, additional equipment straps were used sometimes to cover the chest and back with as many grenades as possible. In addition, a set of two stick grenade bags slung around the neck can be seen as well on period photographs.

Belt and Buckle

Enlisted Men's Belt and Buckle (*Trageriemen und Koppel*)

The belt was made from brown or black leather. *Jäger* wore black, while other contingents used the brown belt as ordered in 1909. This practice was changed in 1915[4] when regulations prescribed black belts for all troops. For parade, a white lacquered belt was used[5], often with a white bayonet frog. Different types of belt buckles were in use for officers and enlisted men and a distinction was made between mounted and dismounted troops and the state of origin. Pre-war dismounted EM buckles were made from a brass or bronze backing and a nickel center and had a length of 2.4" (6.3cm) and a height of 1.9" (4.8cm). As an exception, Saxon regiments with nickel buttons were equipped with a nickel buckle having a brass center. Starting in 1916 stamped steel was used which was painted field-grey or sometimes earth brown. Other

Assault pack.

alloys were used in limited quantities as well. Dismounted men had a belt buckle plate embossed with the state motif and motto. These could be:

"Gott mit uns"	Prussia
"Fruchtloss und Trew"	Württemberg
"In Treue Fest"	Bavaria
"Providentiae Memor"	Saxony[6]
"JG"	107 Saxon Fusilier Regiments[7]
"GG"	108 Saxon Fusilier Regiments[8]
crown	Hessen
state motif	Mecklenburg-Schwerin
state motif	Mecklenburg-Strelitz

Cavalry Belt (*Säbelkoppel*)

The model 1895 cavalry belt buckle (*Schlossschalle*) was made of cast brass with a rear hook to accommodate the clip of the standard issue model 1895 belt. Similar to the dismounted belt buckle, the buckle was manufactured from grey painted steel and the belts were blackened during the war. This type of belt was worn until 1915.

Model 1909 natural brown leather belt dated 1915 and 1916. The belt is marked for the 173rd Infantry Regiment. *Courtesy of Michael Brennan.*

Unit marking.

Above: It was not uncommon for *Landwehr* and *Landsturm* units to use obsolete equipment, and the same was true for the belt buckle. This is a model 1870/71 Prussian buckle, larger in size that the later pattern, 2.5" (6.5cm) by 2" (5.2cm). *Courtesy of BT.*

Left: Pre-war Bavarian belt buckle with motto "*In Treue Fest*". Size: 2.5" (6.4cm) by 2" (5cm). *Courtesy of BT.*

Above: Late war field-grey painted Prussian buckle. *Courtesy of BT.*

Left: *Schutztruppen* belt buckle bearing the Imperial crown. Apart from the Marine Corps, the buckles with Imperial crowns were used by German colonial troops in Africa, China & the Pacific. Native troops tended to be issued with a plain brass buckle. *Courtesy of Michael Brennan.*

Württemberg brown belt and buckle. *Courtesy of BT.*

Above: These two Hessen buckles are bearing the crown of Hessen. Both are 1895 pattern brass examples, but one is an issue item and the other is a privately purchased walking out uniform version with a separately affixed gilt crown and a better quality buckle body. Most Hessen buckles are made from brass, except for the Leib Garde Regiment and the Hessen Dragoon Regiments 23 and 24 who had white metal buckles. *Courtesy of Michael Brennan.*

Top: Mecklenburg-Schwerin. Bottom: Mecklenburg-Strelitz. The buckle design for these two Grand Dukedoms is divided in two upper, three middle and two lower motifs, each of them representing on of the smaller states in Mecklenburg. These are from top to bottom and left to right: Mecklenburg, Wenden, Schwerin, Stargard, Ratzeburg, Earldom Schwerin and Rostock. *Courtesy of Michael Brennan.*

Top: early Württemberg buckle. Bottom: field-grey painted wartime buckle. *Courtesy of Michael Brennan.*

Top: Saxon buckle for regiments with nickel tunic buttons. Bottom: Saxon version for regiments with messing tunic buttons. *Courtesy of Michael Brennan.*

Rear view of the Saxon buckles. *Courtesy of Michael Brennan.*

Pre-war telegraphers belt buckle with the Imperial Crown, used, amongst others, by marine infantry formations. *Courtesy of Domein Raversijde -Ostend.*

Late war field-grey painted Prussian telegrapher's buckle. Telegraphers could carry a wire drum to lay telephone cables by using a special device (*Aufspuler*) attached to the two clips of their belt buckle. *Author's collection.*

Reverse detail.

Belt buckle made from zinc. *Courtesy of Sven Kuczyk.*

Rear view.

Buckles are rarely unit marked. This set is marked "*P.B.15*" (15th Pioneer Battalion), "*22.P.B*" (22nd Pioneer Battalion), "*28.R*" (28th Regiment), "*179.R.*" (179th Regiment) and "*122.R.*" (122nd Regiment). *Courtesy of Michael Brennan.*

This soldier of the 108 *Schützen* regiment (*Freiberg*) wears a telegrapher's belt buckle.

This is an example of the white lacquered parade belt (originally in brown), marked "*25 F.A.R BA. XVIII*". This corresponds with the *1. Großherzoglich-Hessisches Feld-Artillerie-Regiment Nr.25* (Army Corps XVIII). *Courtesy of BT.*

An enlisted soldier in a pre-1907 parade dress with a white belt, bayonet carrier and gloves. The cap has a particular stiff round form. The soldier wears a signalers patch at his right upper sleeve with two crossed flags. In 1892, some infantry regiments were still equipped with a white belt, like the *Grenadier-Bataillone der Garde Infanterie* and the Grenadier Regiment Nr 1 to 12.[9] *Courtesy of BT.*

Officers Belt and Buckle (*Feldbinde* and *Feldkoppel*)

Officers received a 4.3cm wide *Feldbinde,* composed of silver cords stiffened with a cloth or velvet backing. The belt had two 0.2" (0.5cm) colored stripes, each 0.4" (1cm) from the outer edges. The piping color was black for Prussia, green for Saxony, light blue for Bavaria, and a combination of dark-blue/carmine/gold for Mecklenburg. The golden or silver buckle was embossed with the state monogram, "*W II* "enclosed within a laurel leaf wreath for Prussian contingents. The monogram "*FF*" was used in Mecklenburg, "*FL*" in Hessen, "*FW*" in Mecklenburg-Strelitz, "*W*" in Württemberg, a death head for Brunswick, "*FA*" in Saxony and the Royal *Wittelsbach* crown in Bavaria. Medical officers (*Sanitätsoffiziere*) received in 1914 a *Feldbinde* with a state monogram surrounded with two *Aesculape* symbols, a practice which was discontinued in 1918.[10] Naval officers had a different design of buckle, with the W monogram and anchor below the imperial crown. The belt had two rows of black and one middle row of red piping. The colonial officers belt buckle had a center with the *Hohenzollern* Crown as opposed to a Wilhelm cipher on an Army officer or the fouled anchor and crown, which we see on a Naval officer examples.

The *Feldbinde* was easy to observe during manoeuvres or in the field and the need emerged to introduce a less noticeable *Feldkoppel* for officers in 1915. The wartime design was made from brown or black leather.

Footwear (*Schuhzeug*)

Footwear is an essential part of the soldier's equipment. A good shoe must provide protection against the weather, mud, dust, and must be rugged yet relatively light, and be easy to put on and take off, even when the soldier is burdened with his equipment. The German soldiers received two main types of footwear. The high "jack" boot ("jack" referring the method of manufacturing the sole and lower part of the boot) with side-seam stitching and the lower shoes worn with gaiters or leggings. These leggings protected the wearer against water and mud, and also reduced wear on the lower parts of the trousers.

Mounted troops, like cavalry, field artillery, etc wore a plain metal buckle until 1915.

A grey painted steel cavalry buckle and a pre-war Messing buckle. *Courtesy of Michael Brennan.*

Officer with the model 1915 *Feldkoppel. Courtesy of BT.*

Officer's model 1915 *Feldkoppel* with leather belt instead of silver cord. The yellow buckle was replaced with field-grey painted steel later in the war. *Courtesy of BT.*

Jack Boots Model 1866 (*Infanteriestiefel*)

Since 1910 (1908 for cavalry troops), jack boots were made of a natural brown leather. The 1915 regulations, prescribed the use of black boots instead of brown. The total height of the infantry boot was between 11.8" (30cm) and 13.8" (35cm)[11] and had stitching at the sides. Two 4.7" (12cm) long straps were attached inside the boot. These straps were made made from *Gurt* (fabric) or other materials as of 1916 (leather). The sole of the boot contained between 30 and 45 hobnails. The 1.2" (3cm) high heel was reinforced with steel, a bit like a little "horseshoe". Later in the war, leather shortages let to the demand for heels to be manufactured from several layers of wood.[12] Initially only troops in the *Heimat* were equipped with these economy boots, but later on they also appeared with front line troops. The model 1866 boots were used well into the Reichswehr period.

One of the *Gurt* straps.

Pre-1915 brown infantry boots with side lace. One of the *Gurt* straps has a nametag and unit *"Musketier Hellmeister 4. Ersatzkomp. 168". Courtesy of BT.*

Officer Boots (*Offizierstiefel*)

Officer boots, except those of mounted units, were usually made of natural brown leather. Higher in design than the enlisted mans boots, they reached up to the knee. The boot at the back was approximately 1.6" (4cm) lower than at the front. The heel was 0.8" (2cm) to 1.2" (3cm) high. After 1915, officers were issued with the new cavalry boots (*Einheitskavalleriestiefel*).

Ankle Boot Model 1901 and Model 1914 (*Schnürschuhe*)

Alongside with jackboots, a pair of leather ankle boots was available as well. The model 1901 had a shoelace at the left side with two rows of six eyes. During 1914-1915[13], a new model was introduced with shoelace at the front and also two rows of six eyes. The heel was 0.8" (2cm) high and initially had no nails. During the war[14], hobnails were introduced to protect the shoe heel. Similar to the jackboots, heels made from different layers of wood appeared in 1916. The boots were worn with putties or leather leg caps.

Ersatz Boots (*Ersatzschnürschuh*)

Due to an increased shortage of leather, ankle boots made from ersatz material were produced as of 1917.[15] The most common material used was a paper (*Papierstoff*) body with a wooden heel reinforced with nails. A leather strap provided more strength to the boot.

Issue bicycle troops leggings. Although these are probably of civilian manufacture, the ocher canvas is identical in quality and construction to that typically used in pre-war and early-war equipment. Stamped into the leather on one legging is the mark "B.10.R." *Courtesy of Brian Ludwig.*

A group of marines pose in front of a shelter. The hobnails and the horseshoe type metal reinforcement around the heel of the jackboots can clearly be seen. *Courtesy of Stephen Chambers.*

Brown leather model 1914 pattern ankle boots with two rows of six eyes at the front. A combination of three rows of eyes and three rows of hooks can be seen as well. The boots are size "2", indicated on the sole. *Courtesy of BT.*

Overshoe (*Filzschuhe, Filzwachtpostenstiefel*)

The *Filzschuhe* were worn over the normal shoes to provide extended protection against the cold. They were manufactured without any special regulation until March 1918, so variations in height and design can be seen. The thick sole was made from wood and the upper part from felt. They were either closed with one or two buckles at the back for mounted troops or at the front for dismounted units.

Putties (*Wickelgamaschen*)

Sand, small stones, snow, etc. would often get into the high jackboots and provided a serious lack of comfort to the wearer. Putties were very popular with the troops, and were worn by storm troopers (*Sturm-Abteilungen*), mountain troops (*Gebirgsjäger*) and flying personnel.[16]

An ersatz boot made from different materials. *Royal Army and Military History Museum, Brussels.*

Filzschuhe or Filzwachtpostenstiefel. Royal Army and Military History Museum, Brussels.

Cavalry Boots (*Kavalleriestiefel*)

Cavalry boots were worn by all mounted troops, including cavalry, field artillery and train units. They were introduced in 1908[17] and made from natural brown leather. The boot reached up to the knee and was 2.4" (6cm) lower at the back. The inside was lined with leather. Each boot had two straps 5" (13cm) in length sewn into the shaft. The boots had no hobnails and were worn with spurs. New cavalry jackboots (*Einheits-Kavalleriestiefel*) were adopted in 1915.[18] The boot had to be worn by all mounted contingents, which previously had their own design, for example the Hussars, Cuirassiers, *Schwere Reiter*, Mounted rifles and *Stabsordonnanzen*. The main difference of the model 1915 boots was a reduction in height between the front and back of the shaft to 2" (5cm). Inside the boot, a 1" (2.5cm) wide leather reinforcement ran at the back seem of the shaft. The height of the boot was between 10.6" (27cm) and 17" (43cm) depending on the size. Bavaria decided to adopt a slightly different design in 1915[19] and made the boot of equal height at the front and back. The Bavarian version has the same boot reinforcement as the Prussian one.

Hussar Jackboots (*Dienststiefel*)

Hussars had a very distinctive boot with white or yellow (silver or gold for officers) lace running around the top of the boot. The color was according the uniform lace and button color. The boots were introduced in 1867.[20] Officer's boots featured a metal rosette at the front of the boot, while NCOs often had a cloth rosette.

Cuirassier Boots (*Brandenburger Stiefel* and *Stülpstiefel*)

Cuirassier wore brown leather "*Brandenburger Stiefel*" with nails and spurs (*Anschnallspuren*) until late 1800. These boots were sewn at the rear and reinforced with a small leather strap at the inside of the boot running down the seam. The 1.6" (4cm) wide *fabric* straps

Storm troopers were usually equipped with ankle boots and putties instead of the traditional jackboots. These putties are in perfect condition. Note the buckles at the straps. *Courtesy of BT.*

Model 1915 cavalry boots with leather reinforcement at the back seam. *Author's early collection.*

Lace with a metal rosette.

had a length of 15" (38cm) and were sewn over an area of 3.7" (9.5cm) onto the leather. Both the Guard Cuirassier Regiment and the 3rd Regiment abolished their *Brandenburger Stiefel* in 1886[21] and replaced them with *Stülpstiefel*. The other Cuirassier regiments followed in 1888.[22] It is therefore very unlikely that the old *Brandenburger Stiefel* were used during the First World War.

Stülpstiefel were introduced for Cuirassiers in 1886. The brown leather boots reached 2" (5cm) over the knee. The front boot was nearly 5.5" (14cm) higher at the front. *Stülpstiefel* were replaced in 1915 by the *Einheits-Kavalleriestiefel*. Some ersatz regiments were still using the *Stülpstiefel* in 1917 and were ordered[23] to modify these by cutting off the front part of the boot (*Stulp*), which covered the knee. Saxon *Schwere Reiter* (heavy cavalry) were issued with *Stülpstiefel* as well, but the front of the boot was only 4.7" (12cm) higher at the front.[24]

Mountain Boots (*Bergschuh*)

Mountain boots were issued from 1915. The demand for boots rose significantly when more and more mountain troops, like the *Alpenkorps* were raised. They had a stronger sole and a row of special nails (*Bergnadeln*) running around

Shiny black leather Hussar officer jackboots with the special golden lace around the top of the boot and a rosette in metal at the front. *Courtesy of BT.*

Cuirassier *Brandenburger Stiefel*. Courtesy of BT.

Cuirassier *Stülpstiefel*. *Royal Army and Military History Museum, Brussels.*

A postcard dated May 17th 1909 showing men from *Füsilier-Regiment Prinz Heinrich von Preuflen (1. Brandenburgisches)* nr. 35. The two cuirassiers to the left and right are probably from the 6th cuirassier regiment and are wearing the white *Koller* or grey Litewka and the high *Stülpstiefel*.

the sides of the heel and tip of the boot. Initially only a limited number of boots were manufactured and civilian stocks and re-worked ankle shoes were issued to the troops as well. A new pattern was officially introduced in 1917.[25] The boot was 8.2" (21cm) high at the back and 6.7" (17cm) at the front and was closed with three series of eyes, three or four series of hooks and one pair of eyes at the top. Approximately 20 special nails ran around the tip and 25-26 nails around the heel of the shoe, which were clearly visible when wearing the boot.

These Bavarian mountain boots are marked *"B.A.II.1917"*. *Courtesy of Chip Minx.*

Special nails (*Bergnädeln*) ran around the sides of the heel and tip of the boot. *Courtesy of Chip Minx.*

Portable Tools (*Kleines Schanzzeug and Schanzzeug 96*)

Portable tools were used to build strong trench walls, bunkers, raise telegraph lines, to dig in and generally adapt the terrain to the needs of warfare. Using saws or axes, trees were felled across roads to block enemy advances or used to reinforce trenches. Picks would have been used to dig for cover and wire cutters would have aided in laying barbed wire or cutting through the wire laid by the enemy. Apart from the larger hand-held tools such as full-sized shovels, picks, and axes, the typical German soldier carried smaller tools attached to their belts. This meant that the small infantry shovel, folding saw or axe, could easily be reached, compared with other countries (e.g. France), which carried the tools on top or inside the knapsack.[26]

Two sets of tools were available. The smaller tools were used by the infantry and *Jäger* (*Kleines Schanzzeug*) and the larger tools introduced in 1897 (*Grosses Schanzzeug 96*) were used by pioneer and *Eisenbahn* battalions. The smaller tools included among others the spade (*Spaten*) model 1874 or model 1899, the hatchet (*Beil*) model 1888, the Axe (*Beilpicke*) model 1899 or model 1909, the saw (*Säge*) model 1905 and the wire cutter (*Kleine Drahtschere*) model 1911 or model 1915. The large tools were a spade (*Spaten*), axe, hand axe and a wire cutter model 1907. Pioneers or units performing pioneer assignments had many more tools, like handsaws, etc. and machine-gun troops were issued with a scaled-down version of the spade in 1901. The following table shows the pre-war (1911) allocation of tools within several types of units. Note that this table – reproduced from the instruction book *Feld-Pionierdienst aller Waffen, Berlin 1911* – does not yet take into account the distribution of the 1911 introduced wire cutters. Allocation of equipment would be adapted to the requirements of the war in the years to come. The individual soldier either carried these tools or they were transported in the unit's luggage carriages.

Unit	*Location*	*Earth works*					*Wood works*		
		Small spade	Large spade	Pick	Axe	Hatchet	Handsaw	Crosscut saw	Wire cutter
Infantry regiment	Portable	1200			120	60			
	Luggage		260	80		45	6	14	
MG company	Luggage	18	24	3	9	12	4		
MG *Abteilung*	Luggage	18	28	14	6	20	11		
Cavalry regiment (4 Sq.)	Portable	32				32		16	
	Luggage		14	4	16	21		2	
Field artillery battery			38	31		33	1		
Heavy Field Howitzer battery			93	43		19	4	2	
Mortar battery			112	52		31	4	2	
Pioneer company	Portable		99	57		21			6
	Luggage		8	4		4	9	6	30
Pioneer Abt. of a Cavalry Div.			15	7		4	2	2	

Saw Model 1905

Cavalry units were issued with a folding saw with two separate wooden handles in 1905. The saw and other items were stored in a special brown leather case. These included a file (*Feile*), awl (*Ahle*) and a gimlet (*Nagelbohrer*). In 1915, the saw was issued to infantry formations as well, as it proved to be extremely useful in the trenches. Cases made from ersatz materials such as canvas or paper cloth were also manufactured during the war.

Hatchet (*Beil model 1888*)

A small axe was introduced in 1888. It weighed almost 1 kg and had a wood handle of 13.6" (35cm) and a 6.6" (17cm) high blade. The leather axe pouch (*Beiltasche*) was initially issued with one leather loop (*Trageschlaufe*) to attach it to the belt. A new type with two leather loops was designed in 1914. The pouch has a strap and buckle to close it and a second strap and buckle, which held the bayonet in place.

This picture shows some pioneer troops posing with the tools of the trade. *Courtesy of Brian Ludwig.*

Contents of the folding saw case including the saw, handles, spare thread for case repair, various cleaning picks, and a sharpening file. *Courtesy of Brian Ludwig.*

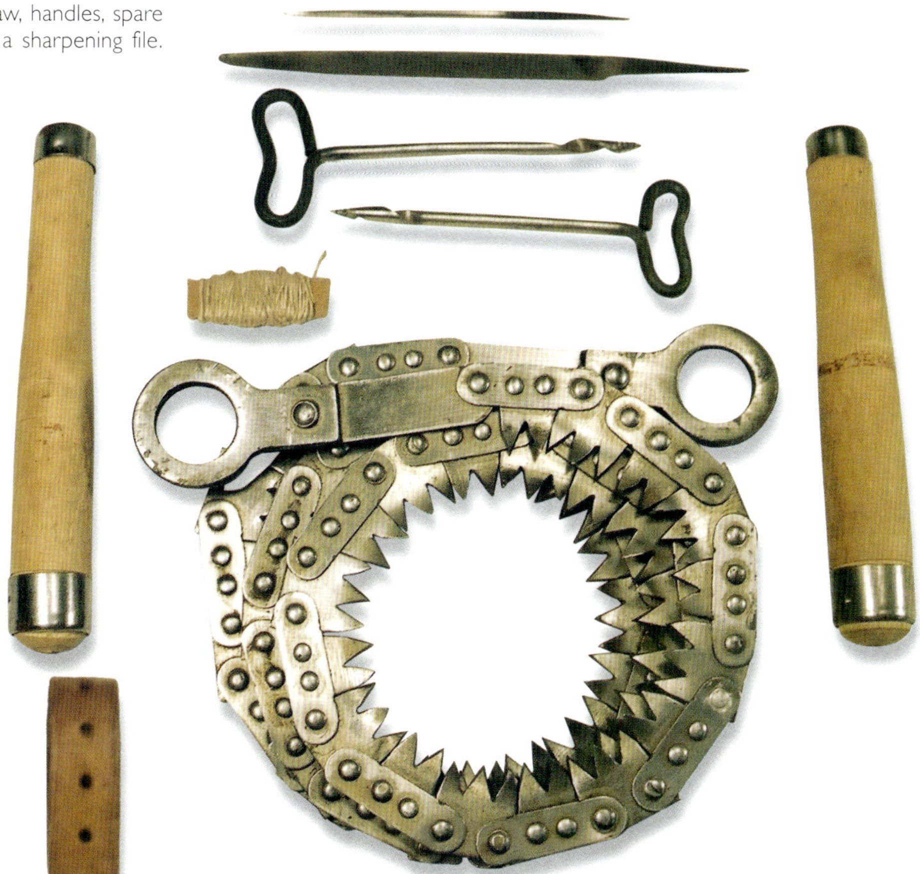

Brown leather folding saw leather case. Manufactured by "*Industriegruppe I, Stuttgart, 1917*". *Courtesy of Brian Ludwig.*

Reverse.

Detail of markings.

Paper cloth folding saw case. Manufactured by *"Heinrich Terstegge, Bocholt"*. *Courtesy of Brian Ludwig.*

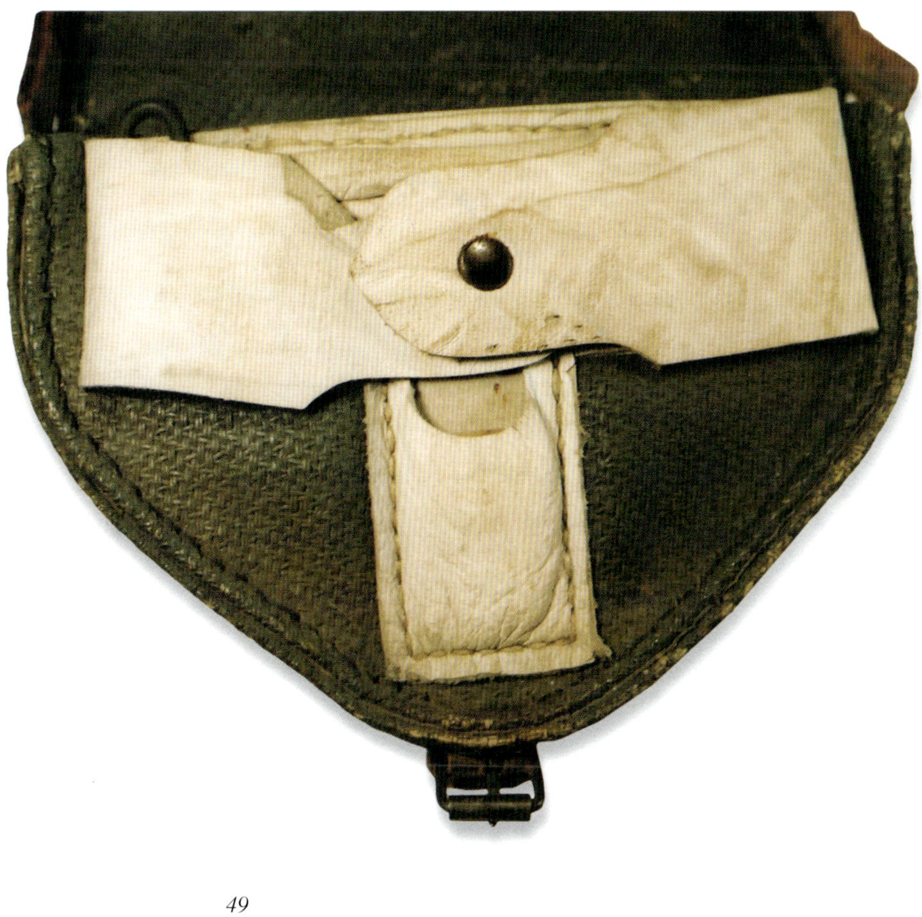

Axe (*Beil*) model 1888. *Author's early collection.*

First type axe carrier with one belt loop. *Courtesy of BT.*

Reverse detail.

Pickaxe (*Beilpicke - Kleines Schanzzeug*)

The pickaxe introduced in 1899 (*Beilpicke 98*) was 18.9" (48cm) long and had a 10" (25.5cm) long blade with a flat end one side and a sharp-ended point the other. A 1.2" (3cm) steel ring attached the axe to the shaft. It weighted 1400g. A lighter model was introduced in 1909 (*Beilpicke 09*)[27] and once again in 1912 (*Beilpicke 12*).[28] The latter had a sharp point slightly bent inwards.[29]

Rear view of pick hatchet carrier with "*Shulz & Co Lederwarenfabrik Augsburg*" manufacturing markings. *Courtesy of BT.*

Rear view of pick hatchet carrier. The carrier was manufactured by "*Hans Romer of Neu Ulm*" in 1917 who also made other leather gear including bayonet frogs, cartridge boxes, and *Tornister* straps. *Courtesy of Brain Ludwig.*

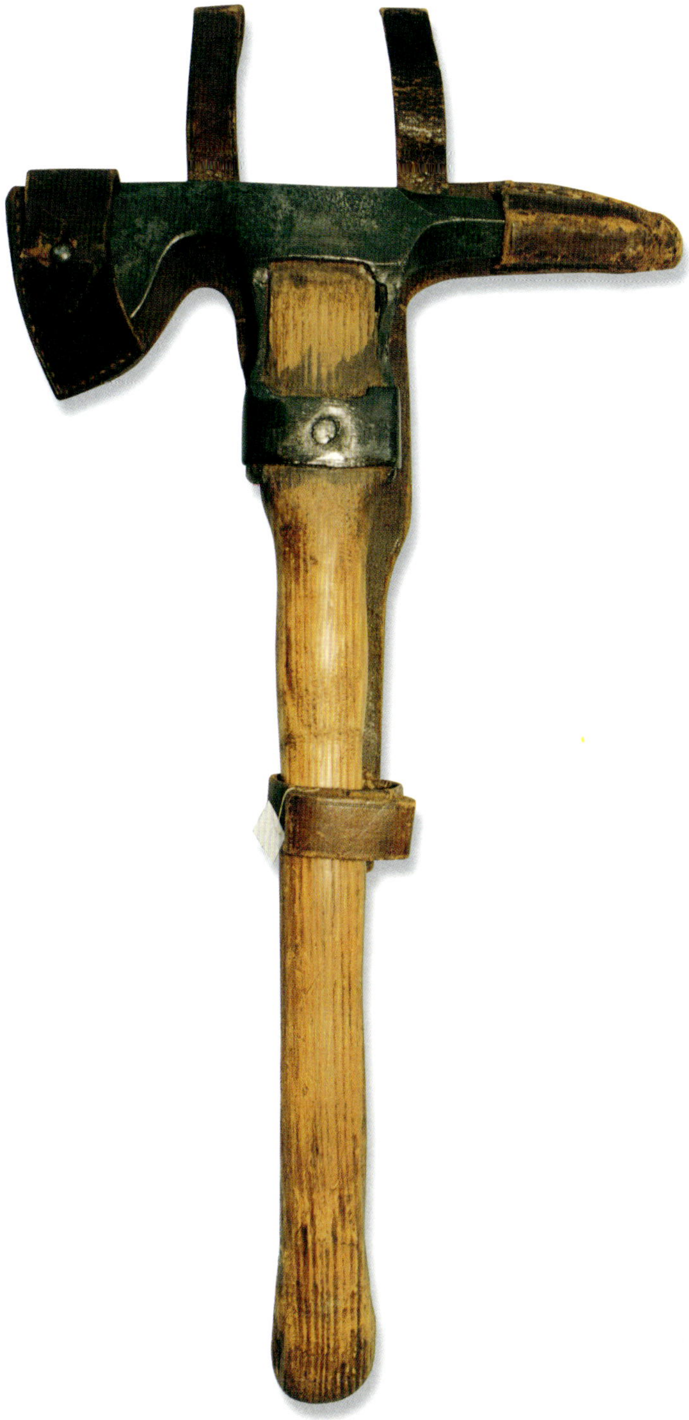

Pick hatchet (*Beilpicke*) model 1909 with a wooden handle. It is carried in a brown leather holder. The leather is marked: "*Shulz & Co Lederwarenfabrik Augsburg*". A small crown is stamped below the manufacturers name. On the front, the leather is marked: "*T.B.L. 17*". The iron is marked "*HERMAN*". *Courtesy of BT.*

Pick hatchet. The axe handle bears an Imperial mark, which is unusual as these are rarely stamped. Imperial marks such as this are the only way to differentiate between actual World War I era *Beilpickes* and those manufactured after the war. *Courtesy of Brian Ludwig.*

Short handled *Beilpicke* manufactured by "*Hermann Dahlman*". Other examples of *Dahlmann's* work include pioneer shovels, infantry shovels, and wire-cutters. *Courtesy of Brian Ludwig.*

Below: Model 1898 spade with first type single loop shovel carrier. The name of the owner can just be seen on the leather. *Courtesy of BT.*

Spade (*Spaten m*odel 1874, model 1898/99, model 1898/1909)
The most common tool carried by the German soldier was a spade carried on the belt in a leather carrier. When advancing, it was sometimes necessary to dig in quickly. On the command "*Spaten heraus, einzeln eingraben*", soldiers had to dig in themselves. Usually, two soldiers were lying next to each other. The first one started to dig a hole, while the second one kept firing at the enemy. When the hole was deep enough, the spade was given to the second soldier and the first one started to fire.

The model 1874 spade had a wooden shaft of about 15" (38cm) and a 7.4" (19cm) by 6" (15cm) steel blade. A large 1.2" (3cm) steel ring attached the blade to the shaft (see photograph). It was a fairly heavy tool with a weight of 890g.[30] A new model was introduced in 1898, which was lighter and had a better means of attaching the blade to the shaft without the steel ring. Because the sharp ends of the blade were damaging the equipment and uniforms, the blade tips were bend towards the inside[31] and riveted (model 1898/1909). The spade was attached to the belt using a leather carrier with one leather strap. Carriers with two leather straps were introduced starting in 1909.[32] Cavalry shovel carriers were identical in design, but the carrier was made longer as of 1916 to prevent the sharp shovel corners damaging the equipment and carbine.[33] The attachment strap for the belt was different as well as a single long leather strap fastened with a buckle replaced the simple loops.

As the war progressed, other materials were used in the manufacture of shovel cases, including *Papierstoff* as from 1916, canvas, white cloth or even a combination of wood and leather in Bavaria.[34] Ersatz spades made entirely from steel appeared during the war as well. These and regular shovels as well were sometimes sharpened to make them useful in hand-to-hand combat. As the spade proved to be a successful design a nearly identical model was used after World War I. These shovels can be easily recognized as they lack the rivets on the blade, which were replaced by nine weld points. A completely new model (*Klappspaten*) was finally introduced in 1938.

Reverse detail of Model 1898 spade (see p 52).

Left: Shovel cover model 1909 manufactured by an *Artillerie Werkstatt* in 1913. Right: Rear view. *Courtesy of Brian Ludwig.*

Left: Example of an ersatz pouch, produced during the war. Right: Rear view. *Courtesy of BT.*

Ersatz paper cloth infantry shovel carrier. With the exception of the belt loops, the leather parts are of very thin, poor-quality leather and sewn with large, quickly applied stitching. *Courtesy of Brian Ludwig.*

Ersatz entrenching tool carrier made from white and red-striped canvas webbing. Although of wartime manufacture, this carrier is patterned after the earlier model carrier with a single belt loop. *Courtesy of Brian Ludwig.*

Ersatz infantry shovel carrier made from white webbing; some portions bearing a narrow red stripe as seen on some munition crate handles of the World War I period. The only leather used on this piece is the keeper on the buckle strap. *Courtesy of Brian Ludwig.*

This photograph clearly shows the differences between the 1898 spade (left) and 1874 pattern (right). *Courtesy of BT.*

All-steel ersatz shovel with original field-gray paint and marked to the 96th Infantry Regiment. This pattern of shovel is made from four separate pieces welded together: the ball end, the handle shaft, the blade, and the rear riveted reinforcement. These shovels typically have ears folded at a 90-degree angle although examples with the typical German folded and riveted ears have been noted. *Courtesy of BT.*

Machine Gunners Spade Model 1901 (*MG Spaten 01*)

Machine gun troops were equipped with a shorter and smaller spade as from 1901 and is therefore not really part of the *Kleines Schanzzeug*. The shovel had a very short wooden handle and the overall dimensions of the blade are smaller than the regular infantry issue shovel. The overall length of the MG shovel blade is about 18cm, width about 12cm, the overall socket length is approximately 11cm, socket diameter about 2.8cm, and the maximum width of the triangular support section on the back of the blade is about 7.5cm. Unlike the infantry shovels, there is no reinforcing band on the socket and the ears of the blade are bent at a 90 degree angle, not bend over and riveted. In addition, MG shovels are nearly always maker-marked whereas infantry pattern shovels are rarely stamped. The MG shovel also had it's own distinctive pattern leather carrier with a single belt loop and a loop for attaching the bayonet.

Model 1901 machine gunners spade, front and rear views.
Courtesy of BT.

Machine-gunner's shovel carrier. This cover was manufactured at the *Artillerie Werksatt Dr*(esden), by work group 18, in 1917. *Courtesy of Brian Ludwig.*

Pioneer Spade (*Schanzeug 96 Spaten*)

Pioneers and *Eisenbahn* troops were equipped with larger tools (*Grosses Schanzeug 96*), including spades, axes and wire cutters. The spade had a length of 47" (120cm). The steel blade was 9.4" (24cm) by 9.4" (24cm) in overall dimension and had inward-bending upper edges. The wooden shaft was 39.3" (100cm) long.[35] To the author's knowledge, no WWI-era or earlier pioneer spade had folded and riveted ears like those on the smaller infantry shovel. This is the main difference between WWI-era and later patterns. The leather or later reinforced canvas spade carrier had a ring or triangle with a spring clip (*Karabinerhaken*) attached, similar to those found on canteens, which clipped onto a ring at the bottom left side of the pioneer backpack (*Tornister*), while the wood handle was held in place by an adjustable double loop leather strap fastened through a loop at the top left of the pack. If the backpack did not have this steel ring, it was possible to wear a small leather chape (*Schutzleder*) with a steel ring on the belt. The spade carrier was then attached to this ring. The leather chape had a length of 7" (18cm) and a width between 1.5" (4cm) (lower part) and 3.1" (8cm) (upper part). Other large pioneer tools, like the axe, were attached in a similar way to the backpack. A period photograph has been seen as well where a soldier is pictured carrying a water bottle attached to the *Schutzleder*. Regular foot troops also received the spade[36] in 1914 and their backpacks were modified with the same ring and strap as the pioneer *Tornisters*.

A group of soldiers with various woodworking and digging tools posed above the entrance to a dugout with a 30-man capacity. *Courtesy of Brian Ludwig.*

Large pioneer spade. *Courtesy of BT.*

Post-war pioneer spade with folded and riveted ears. *Courtesy of BT.*

Well-used short-handled pioneer shovel with 13-inch handle. The steel blade and socket are the same as used on the regular issue long-handled shovel. *Courtesy of Brian Ludwig.*

Leather chape/loop (*Schutzleder*) for attaching the pioneer shovel, axe, or pick carrier to the belt. Berlin marked. *Courtesy of Brian Ludwig.*

Double-loop utility straps for attaching the long-handled pioneer tools (shovel, axe, or pick) to the *Tornister*. The smaller strap is marked BA III. *Courtesy of Brian Ludwig.*

The two flaps of the pioneer spade carrier have a small leather straps and went through the buckles at each side of the spade carrier. *Courtesy of BT.*

This pioneer unit is wearing a mixture of the model 1907/10 and model 1915 simplified tunics. The colored cap bands are covered for both the field caps and the peaked cap. On the right is the large pioneer spade. The spade ends are folded but not riveted. *Courtesy of Stephen Chambers.*

Wire Cutters (*Drahtschere*) Model 1911 and 1915

Model 1911 Wire Cutters

When the war broke out, the German infantry was equipped with 10.2" (26cm) long wire cutters, which were introduced in 1911. A strap at the rear allowed the pouch to be carried on the belt. Issue to infantry companies, cavalry squadrons and artillery batteries were four, two and two, respectively. Trench warfare conditions required doubling these numbers during the war. The model 1911 wire cutter was manufactured in two different types depending on the manufacturer. The cutting jaws were made from tool steel, while the handles were forged and could be held closed with a small leather loop. A larger 50cm long pioneer model 1911 wire cutter with wooden grips existed as well. Each infantry company received 48 of those. The model 1911 wire cutters were mostly painted black or field-gray.[37] During the war, carriers were issued for the model 1911 wire cutters using different materials, including leather, ocher or gray canvas, *papierstoff*, or canvas reinforced with leather. The author has even seen several examples of carriers made in white clothe.

Model 1915 Wire Cutters

Two new models for both infantry and pioneer formations were introduced during 1915. The infantry wire cutter increased in length to approx. 13" (33cm) to 13.8" (35cm). Several variations of these wire cutters have been seen, but all closely resembling each other. It was carried in a canvas bag with leather reinforced lower and upper sections. A single leather strap at the back permitted the wearing of the tool on the belt. During 1917 and 1918, a carrier entirely made from canvas appeared as well, which was weaker in design. A flap and one button closed these late war bags, instead of the buckle closure on the model 1915 bags.

The pioneer model 1915 cutters followed the same trend as the infantry cutters and were increased in size from 19.7" (50cm) to 25.6" (65cm). The cutting jaws had the same design as the pre-war model, but the handles were larger and lacked the wooden grips. Similar to the late war infantry bags, a large canvas bag was designed for the pioneer wire cutters as well. These had two straps at the back to attach it to the belt.

Spring handled model 1911 wire cutters and leather carrying case. These were sometimes used by telegraph troops for cutting heavy communications and electrical wire. Cutters are approximately 11" (28cm) in overall length. *Courtesy of BT.*

Wire cutter.

Ersatz carrying case of ocher-colored canvas and leather for 11" (28cm) spring handled cutters. *Courtesy of Brian Ludwig.*

Model 1911 infantry wire cutter in 10.6" (27cm) long canvas carrying case. The total weight of the case and cutter is 620g. *Courtesy of BT.*

Reverse of the 1911 case.

Model 1911 pioneer wire cutter. These wire cutters were supplied initially without a carrying case and were simply inserted under the belt or attached to the belt using a metal carrying clip. *Courtesy of BT.*

Steel belt clip for carrying the long pioneer wire cutters. *Courtesy of Brian Ludwig.*

This storm trooper is equipped with a large pioneer wire cutter model 1911. The tool is carried on the belt with a metal clips. The soldier wears a gas mask (*Gummimaske* model 1915) in alert position and is armed with a carbine and an early stick grenade model 1915. The two bags slung around the neck contain stick grenades as well. *Courtesy of Faris Siwadi.*

Wire cutters with stamped and rolled steel handles, marked "*DRGM*", and manufactured by "*Adolf Coorts, Remscheid*". Overall length approximately 13" (33cm). *Courtesy of Brian Ludwig.*

Black-painted cast-steel handled wire cutters with wire guide. Marked with "*CA*" company logo and stamped "*DRGM*". The overall length is approximately 13" (33cm). *Courtesy of Brian Ludwig.*

Tubular steel 8-inch handled wire cutters marked "*TD III*", 1915 and manufactured by "*Hugo Linder, Delta Werk, Solingen*". The overall length is approximately 13" (33cm). *Courtesy of Brian Ludwig.*

Close-up of markings.

Fabric and leather carrying case for 13" (33cm) wire cutters. Marked "*TD XVIII*" and manufactured by *J.S. Bursche. Courtesy of Brian Ludwig.*

Poor quality canvas bag introduced in 1917 for the model 1915 infantry wire cutter. *Courtesy of BT.*

Model 1915 pioneer wire cutters. *Courtesy of BT.*

This close-up of the model 1915 pioneer wire cutters shows the manufacturer markings "*Deltawerk Solingen*". *Courtesy of BT.*

Wire cutters model 1915 with tubular steel handles manufactured by *Karl Mesenholler*, overall length approximately 23" (58cm). This pair retains most of its original black paint and was carried in the sheet metal clip or bag. *Courtesy of Brian Ludwig.*

Backpack (*Tornister*)

Infantry Backpack Model 1895 (*Tornister 95* or *Tornister 96* in Bavaria)

The backpack was light brown in color, bordered with tan leather and covered with fur covered calf skin or horse hide. The framework was made from wood and lined with waterproof canvas. The backpack flap could also contain equipment, as well as the central frame, which was fastened with two flaps. There were several compartments for storing clothes (*Wäschebeutel*), cartridges (*Patronenbehälter*), ration pocket (*Lebensmittelbeutel*) and tent accessories (*Zeltzubehörbeutel*). In the middle of the knapsack was a shelf used to store personal accessories like a toothbrush, sewing and washing kit and a meat tin. The use of compartments ensured a correct distribution of the weight and the contents ran less risk of becoming damaged. A *Tornister*, packed according to regulations would contain the following items:

Rations (*Eiserne Portion*) for two days will be stored in the ration compartment and in the *Tornister* itself and consist of:

One package with two rations of canned vegetables (300gr) (stored in the upper end of the backpack).
Two bags of rusk (500gr).
Two cans of coffee (50gr).
Bag of salt (50gr).
One package with two rations of canned meat (400gr) (stored on the middle shelf of the backpack).

Foot wear, as follows:

A pair of ankle boots (*Schnürschuhe*) stored along the sides of the *Tornister*, the right boot on the right side, the left boot on the left side.

Rifle cleaning material stored in a bag (*Gewehrreinigungsbeutel*) and stored on top of the canned meat ration:

One can with dubbin (*Lederfett*), a dull, waterproofing wax compound for leather equipment.
One can of rifle grease (*Gewehrfett*).
Duster (*Putzlappen*).
Bristle.

Other cleaning material (*Putzzeug*) was stored in the backpack as well, usually divided between a group of five men:

Clothes brush (*Kleiderbürste*).
Shoe brush (*Stiefelbürste*).
Sewing kit (*Nähzeug*).
Messing cleaning material (*Messingputz*).

Linen and underwear stored in the cloth compartment in the backpack flap:

One shirt.
One pair of socks (*Strumpfe*) or footcloths (*Fuflappen*).
One handkerchief (*Taschentuch*).
Underpants (*Unterhose*), only in winter.

Other equipment stored in the cloth compartment:

Military pass (*Soldbuch*).
Song book (*Feldgesangbuch*).
Spoon (*Löffel*).
Knife (*Messer*).
Toiletry items (*Waschzeug*).
Spare cartridges are stored in the cartridge compartment.

Tent accessories (*Zeltgeräte*) were stored in a bag (*Zeltzubehörbeutel*) which was strapped inside the backpack with leather loops, on top of the closed central frame. The opening-flap of this bag should be on the left side. The *Zeltzubehörbeutel* contained:

Three tent poles (*Zeltpflöcke*).
Three tent pegs (*Zeltstöcke*).
Rope (*Zeltleine*).

A field cap was stored below the tent accessories bag on top of the closed central frame of the backpack.

The backpack was carried using two main leather suspension straps, which were attached with screw nuts on top of the backpack. They ran over the shoulders, down to the belt and united with the ammo pouches using a brass hook. Each leather strap contained a smaller strap, fixed on a movable pivot. These smaller straps ran under the armpits and hooked to the lower part of the backpack. The backpack could be adjusted by shortening or lengthening the main suspension straps. To do so, the screw nuts could be removed and the strap moved upwards or downwards. An overcoat was folded or wrapped up in a tent half (*Zeltbahn*) and attached to the backpack with three leather straps (*Mantelriemen*) of 20" (43cm). These straps increased to 20.9" (53cm) in 1915. Both types of straps had an additional smaller strap sewn in the middle of the base straps, pointing towards the buckle and attached by means of a stud. Finally, a mess kit was attached to the front flap of the backpack with two straps (*Kochgeschirrriemen*) of 21.7" (55cm) in length.

German regulations prescribed that the backpack should be in close fit with the man's back. It was therefore delivered in three sizes, having heights of 11.6" (29.5cm), 12.4" (31.5cm) and 13.1" (33.5cm). This had certain disadvantages, as during the summer, it produces excessive heat and in the winter, there was a possibility that – during rests – the back of the backpack became wet and the soldier could catch a cold or get sick.[38]

Above: This backpack is marked *"J.R.15 16K"* (Infantry Regiment 15, 16th Company) with dates 1916, 1917, 1927 and 1937. These dates show that this type of equipment was also in use during the *Reichswehr* era (note that during the war, infantry regiment sometimes had a 15th and 16th company). The exterior is marked *"Oskar Scheyhing Gassel 1914"*.

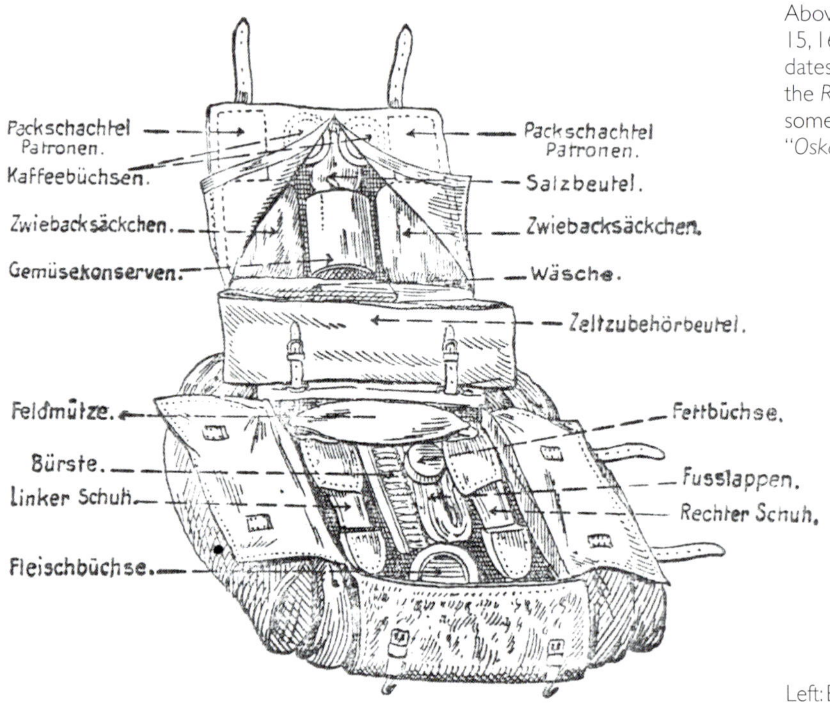

Gepackter Tornister.

Left: Backpack content, reproduced from *"Der Feldgraue" Leitfaden für den Dienstunterricht des Infanteristen (Ausgabe für Württemberg).*

Infantry Backpack Model 1907 and 1907/13
(*Tornister 07 and Tornister 07/13*)
A somewhat lighter version of the *Tornister* 1895 was approved in 1907 made from the same material. Ersatz and civilian backpacks appeared in 1914 when the demand outstripped the supply of backpacks.

While the infantry was using the standard model 1895 backpack, specialty formations like pioneers, medical troops, telephone units and artillery were using an adapted version. The *Tornister* for telegraph troops is discussed in a separate chapter. Lower ranking officers used a backpack, which was a bit smaller than the enlisted men's version. It featured identical straps.

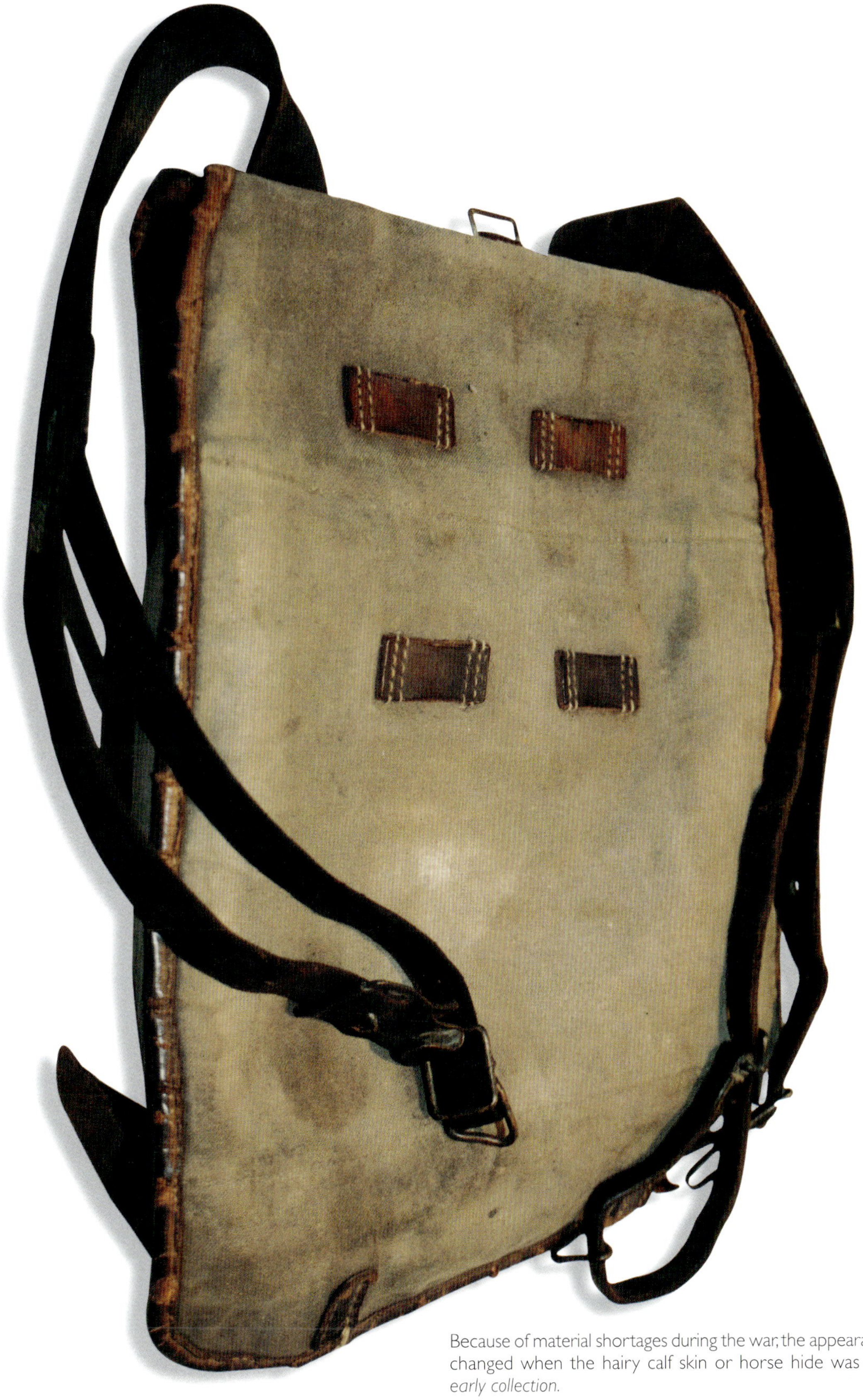

Because of material shortages during the war, the appearance of the backpack changed when the hairy calf skin or horse hide was eliminated. *Author's early collection.*

Bavarian ersatz backpack (*Rucksacktornister*) as issued at the end of 1914 to compensate for the shortage of standard issue backpacks. It has a slighter larger capacity than the normal *Tornister*. The Bavarian War Ministry placed orders for these backpacks with several private companies. This example has a height of 15.6" (40cm) and a width of 12.5" (33cm). *Courtesy of Sven Kuczyk.*

Prussian ersatz backpack as issued at the end of 1914. The reserve ammunition could be stored in the outer compartment. The *Tornister* is marked KBAG 1914. It has a height of 16.7" (43cm) and a width of 12.1" (31cm). *Courtesy of Sven Kuczyk.*

1918 ersatz backpack. The cover is made from dog skin. *Courtesy of Sven Kuczyk*

Side view.

Rear view.

Ersatz backpack made from *Papierstoff. Courtesy of Sven Kuczyk.*

Jäger and Schützen Backpack

The model 1895 *Tornister* used by *Jäger* and *Schützen* battalions was made of black leather and covered with black calf hide.

Cyclist Backpack

The small and very simple cyclist *Tornister* was made of a plain reddish-brown or grey canvas. The cyclist backpack had very simple strap arrangements that did not support cartridge boxes like the model 1895 or 1907 backpacks. The leather shoulder straps only hooked to the bottom of the *Tornister*, allowing for the greater freedom of movement bicycle troops needed for mounting and dismounting their bikes. The pack is also very simple and contains only a single large interior compartment with no provision for attachment of the mess kit or tent half (*Zeltbahn*). Bicycle troops often rolled their overcoats and *Zeltbahns* into a tight bundle and strapped them to the handlebars. Mess kits were carried on a small rack attached behind the bicycle seat. Dispatch cases and handlebar mounted bicycle tool case were available as well for the cyclists.

Field Artillery Backpack

Field artillery units were equipped with a backpack, which closely resembled the old infantry model 1887 backpack. Similar to the cyclist's *Tornister*, the field artillery *Tornister* had no means for attaching it to the ammo pouches. Two simple straps ran around the shoulder and under the arms. There were no additional straps on the outside of the backpack to attach the overcoat, mess tin or any other equipment. Because Field artillery was very mobile, most

Jäger *Tornister. Courtesy of Eric Siegel.*

Bicycle troops *Tornister* in gray canvas and dated 1915. The construction is very simple with there being only one large interior pocket. Dimensions are about 14x7x5" (36x18x13cm). *Courtesy of Brian Ludwig.*

First type cyclist *Tornistor (Radfahrertasche), Alter Art. Courtesy of Sven Kuczyk*

Second type cyclist *Tornistor. Courtesy of Sven Kuczyk.*

Brown leather bicycle dispatch case. *Courtesy of Brian Ludwig.*

Pre-war military handle-bar mounted bicycle tool case. *Courtesy of Brian Ludwig.*

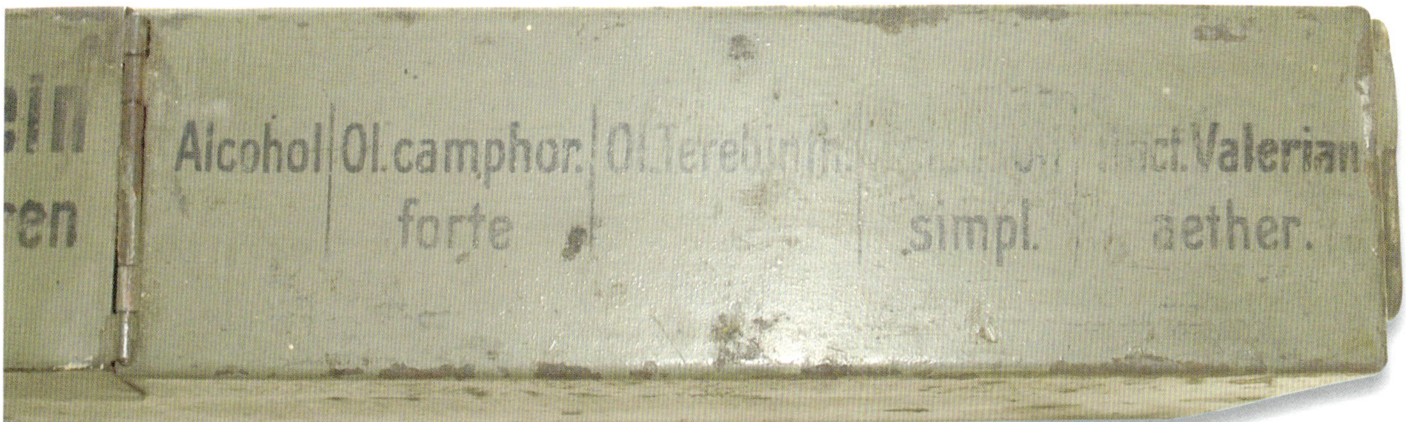

Above and next page: Box stored in the red cross backpack.

Above and following: Medical orderlie's *Tornister*. Courtesy of Eric Siegel.

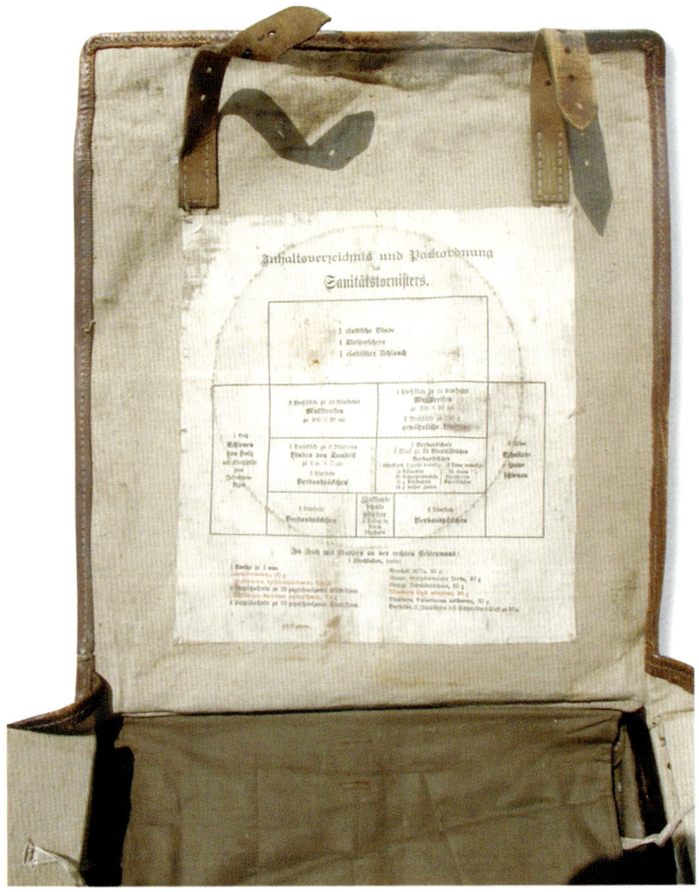

equipment was carried in the supply wagons and were not carried by the soldier, hence the simplified backpack. The inside of the *Tornister* had one large compartment closed with two flaps. A dark colored cows skin covered the early issue models, although this was suppressed on the late war ersatz backpacks. The bag was 12.2" (31cm) in height, 13.4" (34cm) in length and had a depth of 3.5" (9cm) to 4.7" (12cm).[39]

Medical Troops Backpack

Medical orderlies – two men in each infantry battalion or one person in each pioneer or artillery unit – attached to regular regiments were equipped with a larger model backpack, which had a height of 15.7" (40cm), a length of 14.6" (37cm) and a depth of 4" (10cm).[40] A large red cross in a white circle made the backpack easily recognizable. It was packed with bandages and other first aid material. Similar to the Field artillery backpack, no outside attachment straps were available, nor could the backpack be attached to the ammo pouches with the additional straps found on the infantry model.

Telegraph Units Backpack (*Fernsprechtornister*)

See chapter on special telegraph equipment.

Rucksack

The lack of sufficient numbers of backpacks to equip the troops required the use of both civilian acquired *Rucksack's* and other issue models.[41] These packs were mainly issued to mountain troops, ersatz units, *Landwehr*, cavalry, train, etc. so that the infantry had enough supplies to equip all soldiers with the backpack. A white cover (*Rucksacküberzug*) to hide the pack was issued in 1915 for mountain troops. Many variations of the *Rucksack* existed, until in 1916 a standard model was proposed (*Einheitsmünster für Rucksacke*). The *Rucksack* measured 22.8" (58cm) by 18.9" (48cm) and has a thickness of 4" (10cm) at the bottom. It had two large compartments of 15.7" (40cm) by 13.8" (35cm) and 11.8" (30cm) by 0.8" (2cm) respectively. A flap with leather reinforcements closed the pack.

A *Rucksack* with a small pocket closed with a strap and buckle.

Rucksack marked "*B.A.X. 1915*" with two additional pockets. *Courtesy of BT.*

Cartridge Boxes

The German army changed the design and pattern of their basic cartridge pouches five times, from 1870 to 1914. Many obsolete models were still in use by *Landwehr* and *Landsturm* formations, so they deserve some attention. The evolution of the ammo pouches saw, among others, the following models:

Model 1850
Model 1874
Model 1887, enlisted men
Model 1887, pioneer, foot artillery and traffic troops
Model 1887, reserve pouch
Model 1889, enlisted men
Model 1889, reserve cartridge pouch
Model 1889, NCO
Model 1895, enlisted men
Model 1895, NCO
Model 1909, infantry
Model 1911, mounted troops
Model 1901, machine-gun Model 1901, cyclist

Apart from the above base models, several other variants existed, like the colonial troops (*Schutztruppen*) cartridge belt. The German occupation troops in China were already equipped with a very similar design of cartridge pouches, the model 1901. It was later used with cyclist's troops and finally in 1909 further developed for the regular troops. The *Württemberg Ski Kompanie* was given special ammunition sacks, called *Bilgeritaschen*, named after their inventor. As they were too difficult to be worn under the anorak (*Windbluse*), they were soon abandoned.

Model 1874 and 1874/87 for Enlisted Men

At the outbreak of the war, some troops, especially *Landwehr* were still wearing these older types of ammo pouches.

Model 1887 for Pioneer, Foot Artillery and Traffic Troops

Pioneer, Foot artillery and traffic troop EM had a pair of smaller ammo pouches. The rectangular brown leather box originally contained 11mm ammunition, but was modified during the war to hold 15 rounds of 7.9mm. A pair contained thus 30 rounds of ammunition.

A soldier of the 3rd Reserve Infantry Regiment, wearing one model 1909 cartridge pouch on the right side and a binoculars case at the left. The picture was taken in 1917.

German ammo pouches model 1874/87, 48 I.R. This was the *Infanterie-Regiment von Stülpnagel (5. Brandenburgisches) Nr.48* with garrison in *Custrin. Courtesy of BT.*

NCO ammo pouches model 1887 made in brown leather. Marked: "*TIMAR & Co Berlin 1915*" and "*F.W.Gammersbach 1915*". *Courtesy of BT.*

Three soldiers outfitted with the model 1887 pouches. *Courtesy of Stephen Chambers.*

Model 1889 for Enlisted Men

The model 1889 ammo pouches were made of black leather and were worn in pairs at each side of the belt. Each pouch was made of a single section containing 30 rounds.

Model 1895 for Enlisted Men

Model 1895 ammo pouches were similar to the previous type and were also made from a large rectangular leather box leather containing 45 instead of 30 rounds. A metal loop at the top was used to attach the backpack straps, similar to the later model 1909.

Model 1895 ammo pouches. *Courtesy of BT.*

Model 1901, Machine-Gun

The model 01 single clip cartridge pouch for MG *Abteilungen* were worn in sets of four, two on each side of the buckle. In this respect, they were similar to the navy and cyclists pouches, in that they were worn as separate pieces. They held one clip of rifle ammunition. The pouches were made from four pieces of medium to light brown colored smooth leather, with the closure flap made from smooth or pebbled leather. The back was 3.5" (9cm) tall and tapered from top to bottom, 2.7"(6.9cm) at the top down to 2.4"(6.2cm) at the bottom. Sewn to top of the back was the flap that folds over and buttons to the front of the pouch by means of a brass stud that was pushed through an eyelet cut in the flap. The flap was 3"(7.8cm) long and 2.6"(6.8cm) wide. The front of the pouch had the same dimensions as the back piece, to which it is sewn. Centered on the back was a leather belt loop that was 1.5"(3.8cm) wide and 2.7"(7cm) tall. There was no need for "D" rings, because of the relatively lightweight of the pouches and the fact that the knapsack of the MG *Abteilungen* did not require them. It was stamped with the manufacturer's markings. The thickness from front to back was 0.7"(1.9cm). Two makers observed are "*A.Ph.Hoffmann - Berlin - 1915*" and "*Trenner - Berlin - 1915*".

Model 1909

The model 1909 were the most commonly worn model during the First World War and was issued in February 1910. This model was to be used together with the new field-grey model 1907/10 uniforms. Each of the two pouches was divided into three 2.4" (6cm) wide sections each containing 20 cartridges. In addition, a further 60 rounds were carried inside the backpack. Soldiers could thus carry a total of 180 cartridges. In pre-war years, additional ammunition was stored in a company carriage (*Kompanie-Patronenwagen*), which contained approximately 80 rounds per gun for a company of 200 rifles. The *Kompanie-Patronenwagen* would travel to the infantry ammunition supply columns (*Infanterie-Munitionskolonnen*) when all ammunition supplies had been exhausted. There were four of these *Infanterie-Munitionskolonnen* per army corps, each carrying 140 rounds per rifle. It was assumed that the available number of rounds was sufficient for a campaign or battle of two to three days. Just before a battle, the entire stock of a company carriage was distributed to the soldiers, and individually stored in their bread bags, tunic pockets and cloth ammunition belts (*Patronengurt*). Local ammunition supplies were stored in the trenches as well. During a battle, the soldier had to first use all ammunition carried in the bread bag and tunic pockets and the left ammo pouch. Only when all rounds had been fired, or when rapid fire had to be maintained, could the rounds from the right pouch be used. Similar pouches consisting of one section instead of three were already on order by June 1901 for cyclist units (*Pietsch*). After the war, the model 1909 pouches were re-used by the Finnish army and stamped with the markings "*SA*".

Ersatz ammunition pouches model 1909. Leather shortages required that all sorts of equipment were made from replacement materials, like felt, paper, cloth, etc.[42] *Royal Army and Military History Museum, Brussels.*

This artillery NCO is equipped with the model 1887 ammo pouches. The picture was taken in Russia. The spiked helmet has a ball and is covered with a helmet cover bearing the red number "19". These types of covers were issued as of 1915. The number is the regimental number, i.e. the 19th Foot or Field artillery regiment. The model 1907/10 *Waffenrock* has Saxon (German) cuffs, which were only used by Saxon Foot and Saxon Field artillery regiments. Finally, it can be concluded that this person belonged to the *Kgl. Sächs. 2. Fußartillerie-Regiment Nr.19* (Army Corps XII), because the shoulder straps have no flaming grenade, as seen on Saxon Field artillery shoulder straps. *Courtesy of BT.*

Mint brown mod 1909 ammo marked : *"WILKEP & Bielefeld 1916 II. B.A . 18"* and *"J.S. Bauerr Frankfurt A.M. 1915"*. The large ring art the rear is used to attach the pouch to the backpack strap or the bread bag. *Courtesy of BT.*

Rarely found today are the blackened version of the model 1909 ammo pouches. By order of the High Command, all brown leather equipment, like jackboots, belt and ammunition pouches had to be blackened. This was very difficult to do on the shiny brown leather surface. *Courtesy of BT.*

Ersatz ammo pouches made from field-grey felt, produced around 1915. *Courtesy of Eric Siegel.*

Ersatz ammo pouches made from cancas. *Courtesy of Eric Siegel.*

The three studs to close each pouch were 0.6" (1.5cm) in length. The outer studs being more pointed than the middle one. A change was adopted in 1915 and the two outer buttons made 0.1" (0.3cm) longer. As of 1915, the material the studs were made of changed from brass to steel or iron.

Model 1911, Mounted Troops

The cavalry pouches were similar in design to the model 1909 for the infantry, but each 1.2" (3cm) wide section could only contain 10 cartridges. This type of pouch would become the standard model of the German soldier during the Second World War.

Cavalry ammo pouches were supported with three leather straps, called the "*Trageriemen für Patronentaschen*" model 1911. Two leather straps of 23.6" (60cm) hooked onto the ammo pouch ring and ran over the shoulders. At the back, they joined together in a large metal ring and a third strap of 12.2" (31cm) ran down and hooked onto the belt. The straps were made from leather and had a natural light brown color or were dark brown for *Jäger-zu-Pferde* and *Stabsordonnanzen*.[43]

Saddlebag Cartridge Pouch

Mounted soldiers were using saddlebags (*Packtaschen*) to carry personal equipment. Two usually brown bags were connected to each other with a wide leather strap. Each bag had a height of 12.2" (31cm), a width of 7" (18cm) and a depth of 3.5" (9cm) and was closed by a flap with rounded edges. The left bag was equipped with a 6.2" (16cm) by 5.5" (14cm) additional horseshoe case, which could be closed by a strap. A 4" (10cm) by 2.8" (7cm) cartridge pouch was sewn onto the right side of the bag. Each bag was strapped around the saddle with leather straps. Train and mounted officers were using a slightly different design, as well as Cuirassier and *Jäger-zu-Pferde* units, who used a larger version of the bags. When the mounted units had to give up their horses to fight in the trenches, they had to take the saddlebags with them, as they weren't equipped with backpacks.

Ammunition pouches for mounted troops, model 1911, marked "*1916 Neu-Ulm*" and on the inside "*BA X.II f*". *Courtesy of BT.*

Y-strap named "*Trageriemen für Patronentaschen*" stamped "*5.AR 2*" with label "*Kanonier Kallenberger Stabspersonal I./A.R.5*". This was the *Feld-Artillerie-Regiment von Podbielski (1. Niederschlesiches) Nr.5* with garrison in *Sprottau/Sagan* and army corps V. *Courtesy of BT.*

Owner's label.

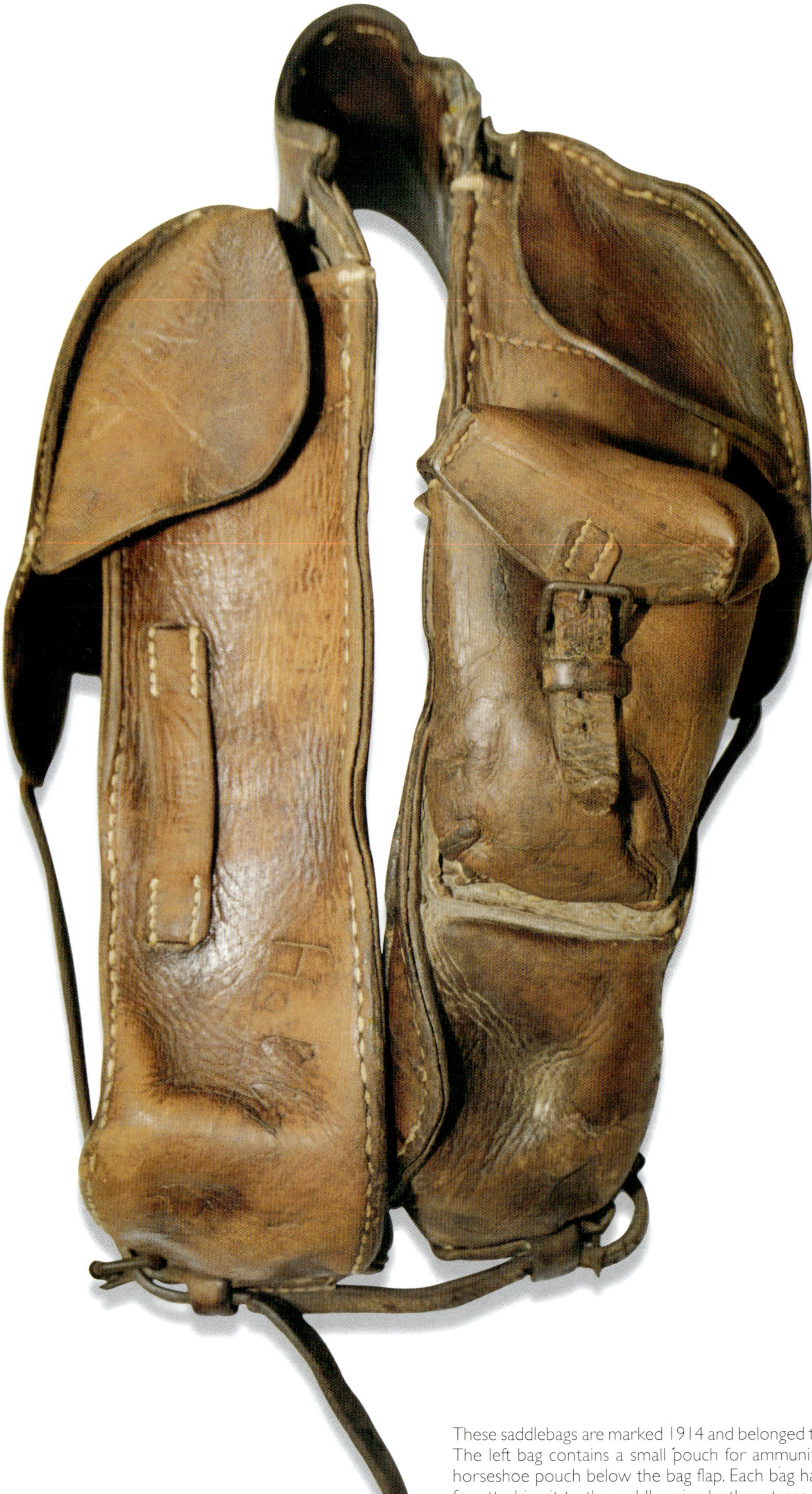

These saddlebags are marked 1914 and belonged to a Hussar regiment. The left bag contains a small pouch for ammunition in addition to a horseshoe pouch below the bag flap. Each bag has four leather loops for attaching it to the saddle using leather straps. *Courtesy of BT.*

Ammo Belt (*Patronentragegurte*)
Storm troop formations often preferred the 220 rounds cloth ammo belt (*Patronentragegurte*). This belt has two rows of five pockets and was worn around the neck.

Patronentragegurte. Courtesy of BT.

Bread Bags (*Brotbeutel*)

The bread bag (*Brotbeutel*) model 1893 was made of waterproof canvas and had two compartments. It was carried on the right hip by means of three suspenders attached to the belt. A button closed the two outer straps, while the middle one was a simple hook. The bread bag could also be suspended from the shoulder with a canvas belt (bread bag strap) with two spring clips at each end. These clips were attached to rings sewn at the back of the bread bag. When no backpack was worn, the bread bag strap could also be used to support the cartridge boxes. It was then attached to each cartridge pouch ring and went around the neck. Different color variations of bread bags and straps can be found. Starting with reddish brown to a very light grey material.

Its design, although slightly altered was still in use during the Second World War. The bread bag contains a daily ration, a spare set of 30 rounds and the drinking cup. A metal ring and a loop allowed the water bottle to be attached to the bread bag.

Unmarked *Brotbeutel* with shoulder strap. *Courtesy of BT.*

An early reddish brown bag. *Courtesy of BT.*

Rear view. The hooks to attach the bag to the belt are cut off, a practice sometimes done by storm troop formations, which preferred to carry the bag with the shoulder strap only.

Interior view with markings "*B.A.XV 1915*".

Marine troops were equipped with a special design of bread bag, which was fastened from the outside with one leather strap. *Courtesy of Domein Raversijde -Ostend.*

A reddish brown version of the marine bread bag. *Courtesy of Domein Raversijde -Ostend.*

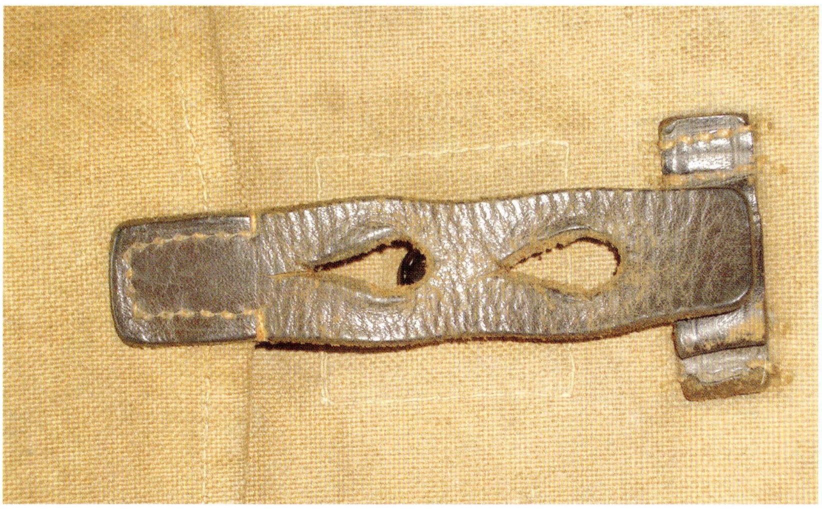

Tent Shelter (*Zeltbahn*) and Accessories

Tent shelters were introduced in Germany in 1892. The reason for its introduction was explained by the War Ministry as follows: "*By reason of the increase of the masses which will compose the field armies in the future, the cantonnement will be the exception while the bivouac will become the rule for troops in the theater of operations. The necessity then imposes itself of guaranteeing the health and vigor of the men sheltering them against cold and humidity.*"[44]

The tent shelter (*Zeltbahn*) was a square piece of canvas, 65"x65" (165x165cm). It was furnished with buttons and eyelets of zinc or aluminum. Ground sheets of material identical to the *Zeltbahn* were also issued of about the same size as the tent shelter but without buttons or grommets. The earlier versions of the *Zeltbahn* were usually made of the red-brown canvas with later produced models being grey (since 1911[45]). However, an 1897-dated and unit marked tent shelter in grey canvas has been observed as well.

Three tent poles (*Zeltstock*), three tent pegs (*Zeltpflöcke*) and tent rope (*Zeltleine*) were carried in a 14.8" (38cm) long earth brown or later grey bag (*Zeltzubehörbeutel*) and placed under the cover flap of the backpack. The three tent poles were inserted into each other to form the supporting pole. The bag was attached to the *Tornister* with two leather straps and closed at one side with two zinc buttons. The two leather straps were either closed with two buckles (standard issue) or with two buttons (variation). Examples have been observed as well where the two leather straps were replaced with two cloth straps closed with buckles.

The wooden tent pegs (*Zeltpflock 01*) in use during WW1 with the Austrian-Hungarian and German Army very closely resemble each other and deserve further explanation. German tent pegs were 10.2" (26cm) to 10.4" (26.5cm) long, had a rectangular form: 0.74" (1.9cm) x 0.55" (1.4cm) and a 1.6" (4.1cm) long black iron reinforcement (cap) at the end. Through this metal cap, a 0.62" (1.6cm) long iron pin was fixed into the wood to attach the tent rope. The Austrian pegs were almost the same as the German ones with a dimension of 0.74" (1.9cm) by 0.55" (1.4cm). The main difference is the size of the metal cap at the end of the peg. The metal pin goes directly into the wood and the cap was much shorter, i.e. 0.8" (2cm) instead of 1.6" (4.1cm).

It was found that the wooden pegs broke very often and trials[46] were made with a new tent peg, made entirely from steel. In 1915, the steel *'Zeltpflock 15'* were introduced with a length of 10" (25.5cm) into the German army.

The tent poles (*Zeltstock 01*) were 14.4" (37cm) long. Three of these were carried and inserted into each other to make a long supporting pole. A different version appeared in 1918 (*Zeltstock 18*), which saw a reduction in the use of metal parts of the tent pole.

An ingenious system was developed to allow the backpack, shoes and uniform to be carried across a river without it getting wet, using the tent half. The backpack, tunic, trousers and other equipment were placed on the tent half, which was completely filled with straw, reed or small branches, then strapped together to form a sort of buoyant cushion. The rifle was strapped on top of this cushion and the soldier could swim across the river, pulling this cushion after him. Several cushions could be strapped together to create a small raft. Soldiers who couldn't swim could hold onto the raft or sit on it when crossing the river.

A larger portable raft could be made with 12 tent halves, making six cushions. The cushions were instead filled entirely with a buoyant material like straw. When the tent half was strapped together a second tent half was strapped around it to seal the open side. Two rows of three cushions connected to each other with boards, lances or poles formed the raft.

The shelter which was initially ocher, was later made from grey canvas, and carried, strapped around the outer edges of the pack and often on top of the greatcoat. This piece is in near mint condition and dated 1915. It is marked: "*J.R.31*" and "*B.A.IX*". *Courtesy of BT.*

Tent pegs and poles were carried in a canvas bag and stored within the backpack. They contained three pegs and three pole segments and were closed with 2 straps and buckles or buttons. One bag is marked *"Steinmann & Comp. 1915"* and the second one has markings for a Guard unit "*K.B.A.G 1916*". *Courtesy of BT.*

This photograph shows clearly the difference between the German (top) and Austrian (bottom) tent pegs.

The three tent pole segments could be inserted into each other to make one large pole. *Courtesy of BT.*

This photograph illustrates the early wooden *"Zeltpflock 01"* and the 1915 introduced *"Zeltpflock 15"* made entirely from steel. *Courtesy of BT.*

This soldier with flowers is ready to go to the battlefield. He wears his blanket on top of the backpack and tent shelter. *Courtesy of BT.*

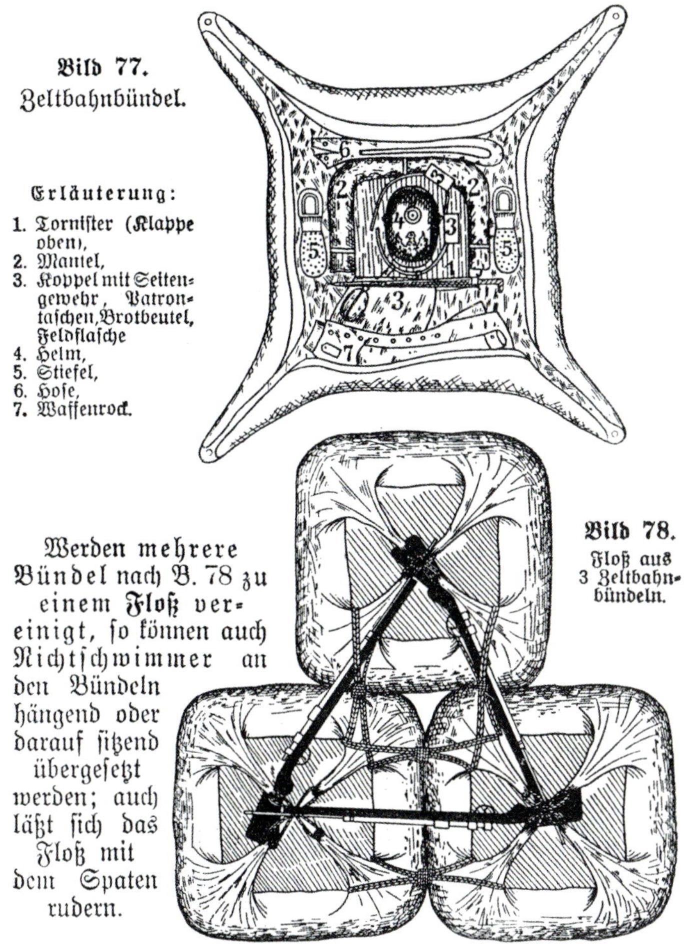

The top drawing shows the arrangement of equipment within the tent half before it is strapped together to make a buoyant cushion. 1. backpack with flap on top, 2. overcoat, 3. belt with bayonet, ammo pouches, bread bag and water bottle, 4. spiked helmet, 5. boots, 6. trousers and 7. *Waffenrock*. The lower drawing shows three tent halves strapped together to create a small raft. The three rifles are forming a triangle. *Reproduced from Feld-Pionierdienst aller Waffen*, Berlin, 1911.

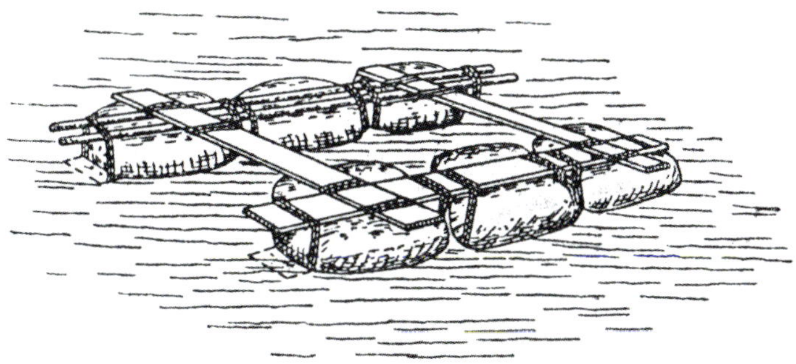

A larger raft made of two rows of three cushions. *Reproduced from Feld-Pionierdienst aller Waffen*, Berlin, 1911.

Individual Mess Kit (*Kochgeschirr*)

Soldiers had to be able to cook their food during periods of rest and lightweight individual boilers were issued in most European countries, although France, Austria and Norway were using larger collective boilers. The disadvantages were that if the soldier carrying the larger boiler got lost, a small group of soldiers had no cooking boiler to use.

The model 1887 *Kochgeschirr*, which was used prior to 1910, was made of aluminum and had a capacity of 2 1/2 liters. It was blackened for foot troops and left in aluminum finish for mounted units. The handle could be attached or detached from the lid of the canteen. Detached, it was carried in the backpack. It contained an opening to insert a wooden stick in case the handle became too hot when the contents were heated. The weight of the canteen was 380g for foot troops and 400g for mounted troops who had a version made of thicker aluminum. Markings on the outside/inside of the mess kit divide it into five sections of 1/2 liters. The *Kochgeschirr* was always carried attached to the backpack.

In January 1910[47], the Prussian War Ministry decided to adopt a new model for dismounted troops. Mounted troops were still to use the old model. This new model was reduced in size and could only contain 2 liters. The lid measured 2.1" (5.8cm) in height, 6.7" (17cm) in length and was 4.1" (10.4cm) deep and the lid handle was now permanently fixed. It was found that the detachable handle on the previously used camp kettle was often lost. The fork and spoon, attached to each other, was stored inside the mess kit. These could be unpainted or blackened.

The fork and spoon was attached to each other and had a tin plating over steel finish. They were carried inside the mess kit. *Courtesy of BT.*

Pattern of 1887 aluminum mess kit with its original detachable handle. This example was manufactured by *Wilhelm Berg* in 1907 and is marked "*D.18.10 5.E.I.*". *Courtesy of Brian Ludwig.*

Left: A model 1910 camp kettle, blackened with strong T shaped handle. Right: Simplified mess kit model 1915. *Courtesy of BT.*

July 1915. A collection of mess kits can be seen at the front. Trench shields are installed between the sand bags. *Courtesy of Stephen Chambers.*

The mess kit was attached on the backpack or, when no backpack was worn, often between the folded tent shelter during the later part of the war.

After the start of hostilities, the camp kettle was supplied with field-grey matt paint and was made from sheet metal "*Weissblech*" or "*Stahlbelch*" instead of aluminum[50], which was becoming more and more scarce[51]. Other wartime kettles[52] could be made from double tin *"Stahlblech"* with a field-grey exterior finish, a green enameled finish interior and exterior[48], a tinned finish interior and enameled with a field-grey painted exterior, or a tinned finish exterior and field-grey painted exterior.

The handle was simplified by changing its form from a T to a flat shape, thus eliminating the reinforcement. This model was not only issued to foot troops, but also saw its introduction for the first time to mounted units. A last change was finally introduced during 1917. The point of the triangular plate attached to the lid, used to pivot the lid handle was bent upwards, thus providing a better means to fix the canteen with leather straps (*Kochgeschirr-Riemen*) to the backpack. These straps were 0.7" (1.8cm) in width and 21.6" (55cm) long.

Hindenburg-Armee-Feldkocher

The *Hindenburg-Armee-Feldkocher* was used as a cooking device to heat the mess kit, a small oven or a lamp. Only the firm *Werner & Mertz, Mainz u. Wien*, manufactured it. It was a popular small device, which could make life in the trenches a bit more conformable.

According to the manufacturer, the cooker was able to heat up cold food and liquids in a matter of minutes and was weather and dust proof. Apart from cooking food, it was also used to create light equivalent to two large candles or when it was cold, to warm the hands. The burner (*Brenner*) and the cooking platform (*Kochaufsatz*) were small enough to be stored inside the canteen, while the spare fuel cartridges were kept in the backpack or bread bag. The burner could operate for 50 to 55 hours with one cartridge (*Füllung*) and four spare supplies (*Ersatz-Wachs-Patronen*).

Hindenburg-Armee-Feldkocher. Royal Army and Military History Museum, Brussels.

Individual Water Bottle (*Feldflasche*)

Model 1867

The ovoid model 1867 bottle was entirely made from thick glass and covered with black leather. It could contain 75cl and had a height of 7" (18cm) and a width of 4.3" (11cm). Filled, it weighted 1250g. It was carried around the shoulder with a long black leather strap. Bavaria had a very similar bottle, which was smaller at the bottom and increased in width going upwards. A change in regulation in 1887 prescribed that all equipment had to be worn on the belt and the water bottles received a bayonet hook to attach them to the bread bag. Many existing water bottles were modified and still used in 1914. It has been reported[53] that a glass bottle model 1867 was dug up in France near the sector of *Bois-le-Prete*, which proves this point.

Model 1893

The model 1893 water bottle (*Feldflasche*) could contain 0.8l and was made of an oval aluminum vessel with a flat back and a convex front. The height of the bottle was 8" (20cm), depth 2.4" (6cm) and width 5.1" (13cm). The neck had a length of 1.8" (4.5cm) and was closed with a simple cork.

Model 1907

When the war broke out, most of the army was equipped with the model 1907 water bottle. It had a smaller neck compared with the

Heavy tin-plated steel cup (*Trinkbecher*) model 1893, with double folding handles manufactured by *FCB FULDA* and dated 1915. The handle bracket appears to be soldered or spot-welded to the cup body. The cup was stored in the bread bag and had a height of 3.5" (9cm), a length of 3.1" (8cm) and a width of 2" (5cm).[54] It was replaced in 1916 with a new model. *Courtesy of Brian Ludwig.*

Two double model 1893 folding handle cups manufactured by *Wilhelm Berg* of Berlin. The regimentally marked cup on the left does not have a pouring spout. The example on the right, dated 1908, does have the spout. Pre-war and World War I era cups of this pattern always have six rivets attaching the bracket to the cup body. Later patterns only have three rivets. *Courtesy of Brian Ludwig.*

model 1893 of only 0.8" (2cm) in length[55] and it was closed with a metal cap and a cork, which could be screwed onto the neck. The bottle was covered with a brown cloth closed at one side with four push buttons. The cloth cover prevented unwanted noises as the metal of the bottle could come in contact with other equipment items. At the bottom was a larger button, which the bottle strap was attached to. A leather strap went around the neck and one strap ran across the body of the bottle. The *Feldflasche* could be attached to the large ring of the bread bag using a spring clip (*Karabinierhaken*), while an additional strap went through the leather strap of the bread bag. Starting in October 1914, aluminum was replaced by double tinned sheet metal.

When the war broke out, most of the troops used the model 1907 water bottle. *Courtesy of BT.*

Model 1915

A new model made from field-grey painted tinned sheet metal was adopted in 1915.[56] The neck was made larger again to 1.3" (3.3cm) and was closed with a cork and metal cap. A field-grey waterproof cloth, felt or other ersatz material covered the water bottle and the additional strap for the bread bag was suppressed. A new strap of 5.9" (15cm) went from the middle of the main strap, through the spring clip and was attached to the cork. The 1916 one-year volunteer instruction book recommended to fill the bottles with thee.

This is a model 1915 water bottle with full length carrying strap. An additional strap went from the middle of the main strap to the cork. *Courtesy of BT.*

Bottle model 1915 with grey cover and green/blue cup. The enameled cup model 1916 is marked: *"R.A.S. 17"*. This bottle features an even more simplified strap attachment, which just goes around the neck of the bottle. *Courtesy of BT.*

Left: bottle "model 1915 with simplified strap" and light brown cover marked *"Ullrich 16"*, middle: bottle model 1915 with felt cover, right: bottle model 1915 with dark brown cover. *Courtesy of BT.*

Glass Water Bottles

Glass bottles were introduced in 1917[57] and distributed as of 1918.[58] They were 8.7" (22cm) high, 3.5" (9cm) wide and 2" (5cm) deep. These bottles could contain 0.8l of liquid. A 1.6" (4cm) long bottleneck was closed with a 1.8" (4.5cm) long cork with a metal cap. Straps were almost 0.8" (2cm) wide, and a 4.9" (12.5cm) long strap ran around the neck and was fixed to a spring clip. The field-grey paper-based cover was closed with a 23.6" (60cm) long cord, which ran through five eyes.

Left: Light green enameled water bottle without its cover. Most bottles are often marked with the manufacturers name and a date. Here *"Gebr. Prestfeld 18 Vach"*.

Right: Very rare nowadays: a water bottle made from glass, complete with cover and cork. Left: Close-up of upper part and cork. *Courtesy of BT.*

Water Bottle for Medical Troops (*Labeflasche mit Trinkbecher*)
This water bottle had the same form as the normal model (*Feldflasche*), but was larger in size and could contain one liter of water. It had a length of 9" (23cm) and a width of 6.2" (16cm). The aluminum bottle was carried using a 51.2" (130cm) brown leather strap, which went around the canvas cover. If needed, a large brass hook was used to attach the bottle onto the belt for dismounted troops, while mounted troop bottles had a *Karabinerhaken*. A change was made in 1915. The bottle was now made from steel and had a volume of 1.2 liter.[59] The attachment straps were simplified and the back strap with the attachment hook made stronger. A small aluminum (pre-1915) or steel (model 1915) cup was fixed on top of the bottle. The carrying strap was extended from 51.2" (130cm) to 59" (150cm).

1.2 I *Labeflasche* for dismounted troops (pre-1915). *Courtesy of BT.*

Rear view.

Above: Model 1915 medic's canteen with tinned cup and leather and fabric shoulder harness. Cup and cover marked *Bellino*, 1916. *Courtesy of Brian Ludwig.*

Labeflasche model 1915. *Courtesy of Eric Siegel.*

First Aid Pouches (*Sanitätstaschen*)

Medical orderlies have two special leather pouches with first aid bandages and medicine. The right pouch was marked with the letter R (*Rechter*) and the left one with the letter L (*Linker*). Originally made from light brown leather, ersatz versions appeared made from different materials.

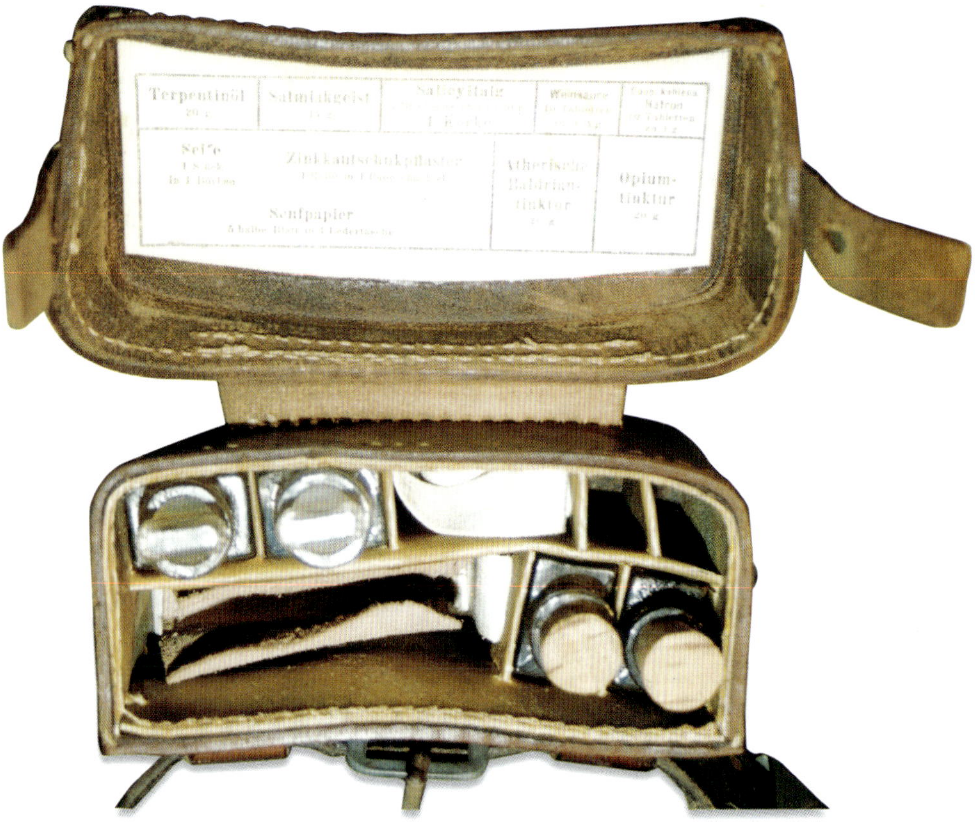

Right: pouch used by medical orderlies, containing small medical bottles: *1 bottle Terpentinöl 20g, Salmiakgeist 15g, ƒtherische Baldriantinktür 20g, Opiumtinktur 20g,* and one small leather bag. The pouch is marked *"R" (Rechter* or right side*). Courtesy of BT.*

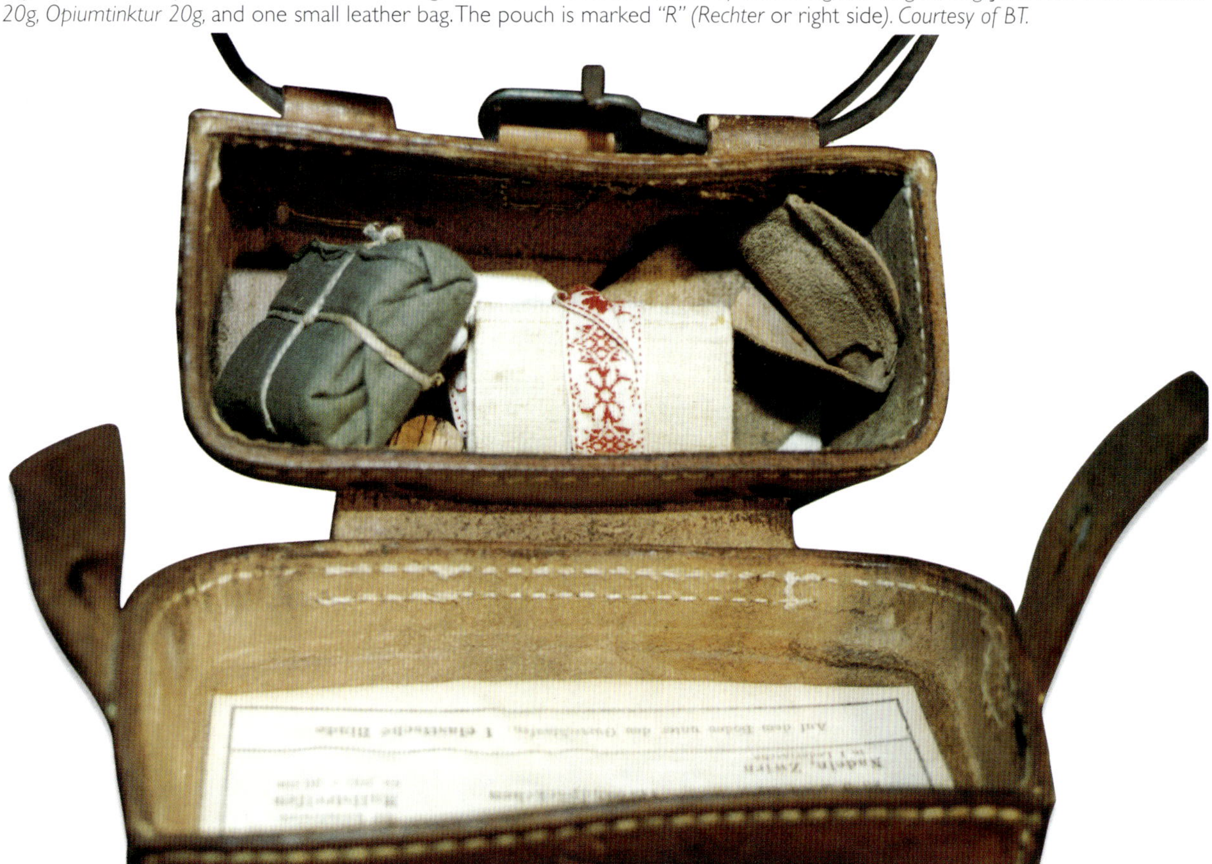

The left pouch contains one small leather bag, one bandage that was usually worn in the tunic inside pocket and one other bandage. It is marked *"L" (Linker* or left side*). Courtesy of BT.*

It was difficult to find any period photographs of the medical pouches. Here are two people in what probably was a post war sport manifestation. The person at the left wears the twin medical pouches. *Courtesy of BT.*

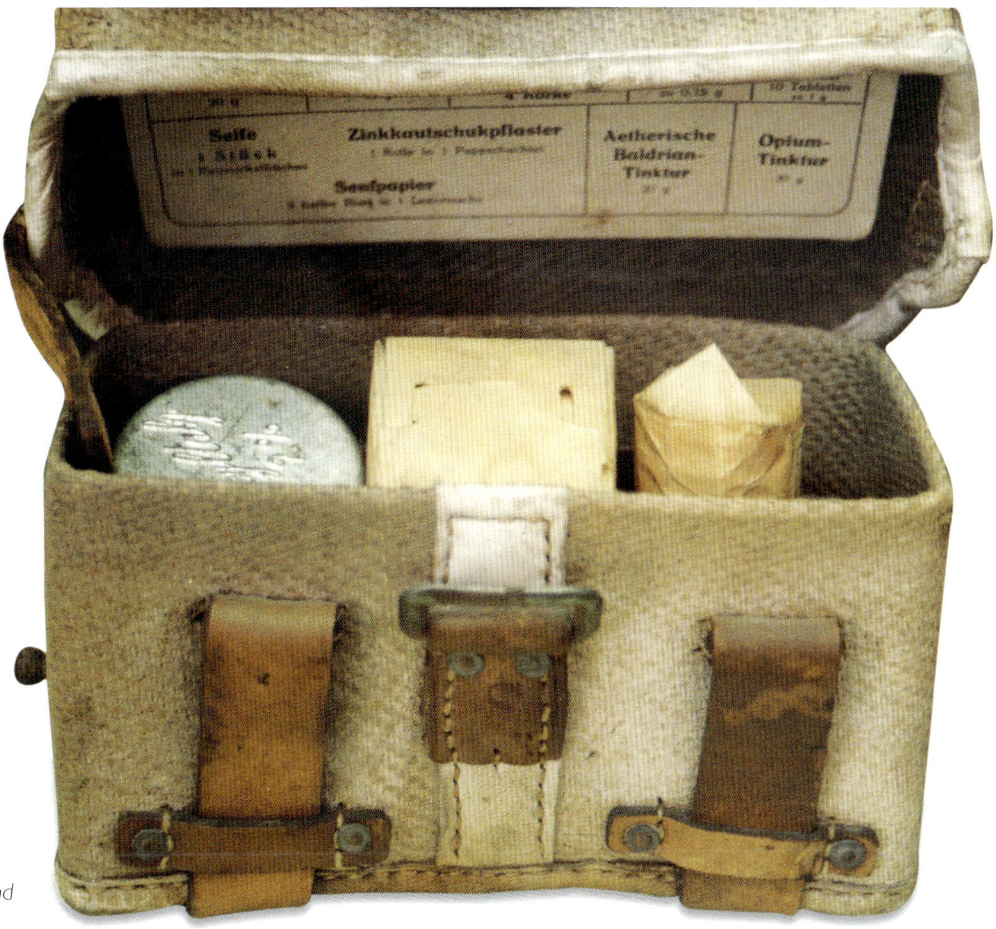

Late war ersatz type pouch. *Royal Army and Military History Museum, Brussels.*

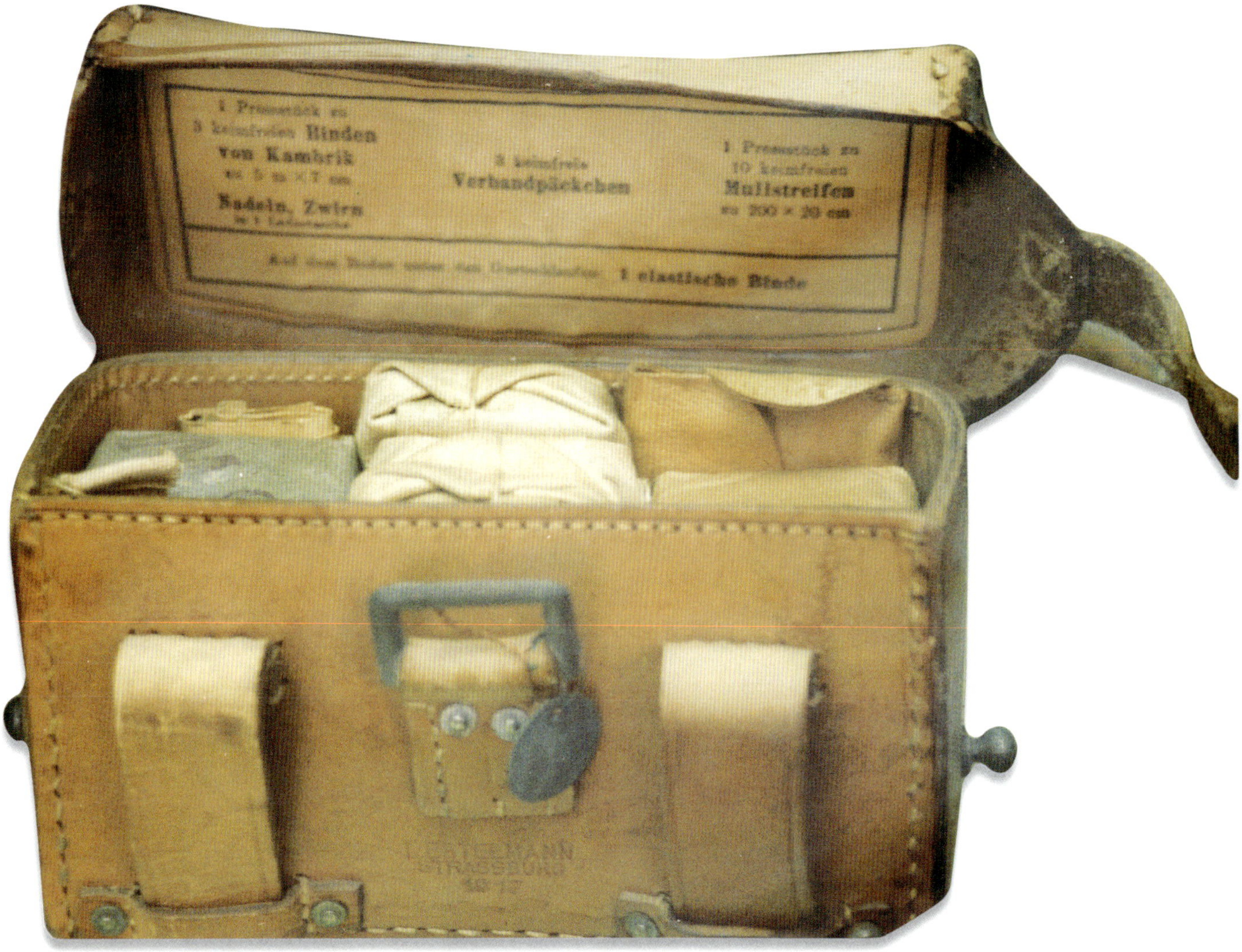

Another example in a very light shade of brown leather. *Royal Army and Military History Museum, Brussels.*

Bandages. *Courtesy of Eric Siegel.*

Medical orderlie's accessories. *Courtesy of Sven Kuczyk.*

Cavalry units received special pouches, which were attached to the saddle.
Royal Army and Military History Museum, Brussels.

Notes

1 German Army handbook, 1918.
2 Spade (100 per company, weight 0.890), pickax (10 per company, weight 1.480), ax (5 per company, weight 1.080).
3 Field Equipment of the European Foot Soldier, 1900-1914.
4 J. Kraus, page 295: Belts were changed in black in September 1915.
5 Stephen Bull, page 25.
6 The motto of the royal Wettin family: "*Providentiae Memor*" meaning "Mindful of Providence".
7 *König Johann* became an honorary colonel of the 107th Saxon Fusilier Regiment after the victory in France in 1871.
8 *Kronprinz Georg*, became honorary colonel of the 108th Saxon Fusilier Regiment after the victory in France in 1871.
9 *Das deutsche Reichsheer in Seiner neuesten Bekleidung und Ausrüstung* 1892, page 8.
10 The *Aesculape for Sanitätsoffiziere* was introduced in Prussia in February 1914 and discontinued in August 1918. The other states followed soon.
11 Eric Siegel, Militaria Magazine 200: Saxon boots had additional leather reinforcement on the upper part of the shaft.
12 J. Kraus: Leather and material shortages led to the demanded for heels to be manufactured from several layers of wood: December 1916 in Prussia, January 1917 Bavaria.
13 P. Pietsch, page 106: A new ankle boot was introduced with shoelace at the front and also two rows of six eyes Prussia December 1914, Bavaria April 1915, Saxony February 1915.
14 Hobnails were introduced to protect the shoe heel: Prussia April 1917, Bavaria June 1917.
15 J. Kraus: Ankle boots made from ersatz material were produced as from 1917: Prussia November 1917, Bavaria December 1917.
16 Drury, Ian & Embleton, Gerry. *German Stormtrooper* and J. Kraus.
17 J. Kraus: Cavalry boots were introduced in 1908: Prussia March 1908, Bavaria May 1908, Saxony July 1908.
18 J.Kraus: The *Einheits-Kavalleriestiefel* jackboots were adopted in 1915: Prussia January 1915, Saxony February 1915, Württemberg January 1915.
19 Bavaria adopted a different design of cavalry boot on February 1915.
20 *Das deutsche Reichsheer in Seiner neuesten Bekleidung und Ausrüstung* 1892: Hussar *Dienststiefel* were introduced for enlisted men on 21.7.1867 and for officers on 5.10.1867.
21 *Das deutsche Reichsheer in Seiner neuesten Bekleidung und Ausrüstung* 1892, page 66 : Cuirassier *Stulpstiefel* were introduced for both the Guard regiment and the 3rd Regiment on May 6th 1886.
22 *Das deutsche Reichsheer in Seiner neuesten Bekleidung und Ausrüstung* 1892, page 66 : Cuirassier *Stulpstiefel* were introduced for the remaining regiments on October, 15th 1888.
23 J. Kraus, page 528: Prussia January 1917.
24 J. Kraus, page 532: Saxon *Schwere Reiter* (Heavy Cavalry) were issued with *Stulpstiefel* as well, but the front shaft was only 12 cm higher at the front.
25 J. Kraus, page 217: A new pattern of mountain boot was officially introduced in 1917: Prussia and Bavaria in November 1917.
26 More info: Field Equipment of the European Foot Soldier, 1900-1914.
27 The *Beilpicke 09 was introduced:* Prussia May 1909, Bavaria October 1909.
28 The *Beilpicke 12 was introduced:* Prussia August 1912, Bavaria October 1912.
29 J. Kraus, page 360: The point of the *Beilpicke 12* was bend toward the inside.
30 Lavisse: The spade had a weight of 890g.
31 J. Kraus: The spade blade tips had to bend towards the inside: Prussia October 1909, Bavaria March 1910.
32 J. Kraus: Spade carriers with two leather straps were introduced as from 1909: Prussia June1909, Bavaria March 1910, Saxony August 1909.
33 J. Kraus: page 360: Cavalry shovel carriers were identical in design, but the carrier was made a bit longer to prevent the sharp shovel corners damaging the equipment.
34 J. Kraus: Shovel carries were made from wood and leather for a short time in Bavaria.
35 J.-L. Larcade: Stormtroopers often shortened the pioneer spade.
36 Regular foot troops also received the pioneer spade: December 1914.
37 Les coupe-fil Allemands 1914-1918, Eric Siegel.
38 Field Equipment of the European Foot Soldier, 1900-1914.
39 Le Havresac Allemand , Eric Siegel.
40 Le Havresac Allemand , Eric Siegel.
41 Eric Siegel: the lack of sufficient numbers of backpacks to equip the troops required the use of both civilian acquired backpacks and issue models.
42 An excellent overview of the different types of ersatz pouches was described by *Eric Siegel* in *Militaria Magazine* 201.
43 J. Kraus: The *'Trageriemen für Patronentaschen'* was dark brown for *Jäger-zu-Pferde* and *Stabsordonnanzen.*
44 Field Equipment of the European Foot Soldier, p. 128.
45 P. Pietsch, page 113: K.V. 7.4.1911.
46 J. Kraus: Trials with a new metal tent peg: March 1910.
47 P. Pietsch, page 114: 14.1.1910.
48 J. Kraus: Three types of canteens were issued in 1916: Prussia March 1916, Bavaria April 1916.
49 J. Kraus: Eliminate the tinned inside finish of the canteen: Prussia February 1917, Bavaria June 1917.
50 J. Kraus: The canteen was supplied with field-grey matt lack paint: Prussia and Saxony November 1914.
51 J. Kraus: The canteen was made from sheet metal "*Weissblech*": Prussia and Bavaria October 1914.
52 J. Kraus: The canteen was changed to double tin *'Stahlblech'* with a field-grey outside finish: Prussia June 1915, Bavaria 1.7.1915.
53 Eric Siegel, Militaria Magazine 219.
54 P. Pietsch, page 115.
55 Eric Siegel, Militaria Magazine 219.
56 J. Kraus: A new water bottle made from field-grey painted tinned sheet metal was adopted in 1915: Prussia June 1915, Bavaria July 1915, Saxony August 1915.
57 J. Kraus: Glass bottles were issued as of October 1917in Prussia, Bavaria and Saxony.
58 Eric Siegel, Militaria Magazine 219.
59 Eric Siegel, Militaria Magazine 221.

Chapter Three

Optical Instruments, Lights, and Compasses

Binoculars
Several manufacturers of field binoculars existed in Germany since the 19th century, like *M. Hensoldt & Sohne*, *Zeiss Jena* and *C.P. Goertz*. In 1895, *Zeiss Jena* made the models D.F. 95 and O.D.F. 95, the latter being one if the first official military prism glasses in Germany.[1]

The *Goerz*-company "*Optische Anstalt C.P.Goerz*"[2] was raised in 1886 in Berlin and was an important manufacturer of optical instrument, photo cameras, telescopes, etc. They managed to obtain several contracts with the German army for the supply of binoculars. One of the binoculars contracted to the army was the *Galileisches Fernrohr C.91*[3], introduced in 1891. It fulfilled all the requirements of the Weapons Testing Commission (*KgL. Gewehr-Prüfungskommission*).

Goerz was the sole supplier between 1903 and 1908 of prism binoculars (*Prismen-Doppelfernrohren*) for the entire Prussian infantry. During that time, 23.000 *Trieder-Binocles* (*Doppelfernrohr* 03) were delivered. *Goerz* started to make the *Goerz-Prismengläser* based on a design of *Zeiss*, which were officially introduced in 1908[4] as service binoculars (*Dienstglas 08*) by the *KgL*. Prussian War Ministry. The new binoculars replaced the *Goerz C.91 Fernrohre*. The army requested the development of a *Galileischen Fernrohr*, which *Goerz* successfully designed. This new model, designated "*Fernglass 08*", was introduced officially in 1909[5] for all group leaders (*Gruppenführer*) of the infantry.

Goerz Fernglass C91. Goerz Festschrift 1886-1911.

Goerz Dienstglass 08. Goerz Festschrift 1886-1911.

Goerz Fernglass 08. Goerz Festschrift 1886-1911.

A brown leather case for a *Goerz Doppelfernrohr 03* binocular. The pouch is marked *"C.P.Goerz A.P. Berlin"*. The name of the owner is written on the outside of the box. It belonged to *"Vizefeldwebel W.K. Essem..."* of the 3rd Machine gun company (*3. M.G.K. III*). *Courtesy of BT.*

Rear view.

Instruction sheet found in an ersatz leather and treated canvas case for the *Doppelfernrohr 03*. This case is marked to a sergeant in the 2nd. M.G.K. of the 30th L.I.R. *Courtesy of Brian Ludwig.*

A 6x24 *Dienstglas* produced by the firm *M. Hensoldt & Sohne Wetzlar.* The model looks identical to the *Goerz Fernglass 08*. It carries the serial number *D.F. N 2914*. The letters *"D.F."* stand for *Doppelfernrohr* (double telescope). *Courtesy of BT.*

Detail of manufacturer markings.

A pair of *Fernglas 08* with their original paper cloth neck strap and ersatz wood case. *Courtesy of Brian Ludwig.*

A *Fernglas 08* with original leather neck strap, lens cover, and paper cloth and fiberboard case. *Courtesy of Brian Ludwig.*

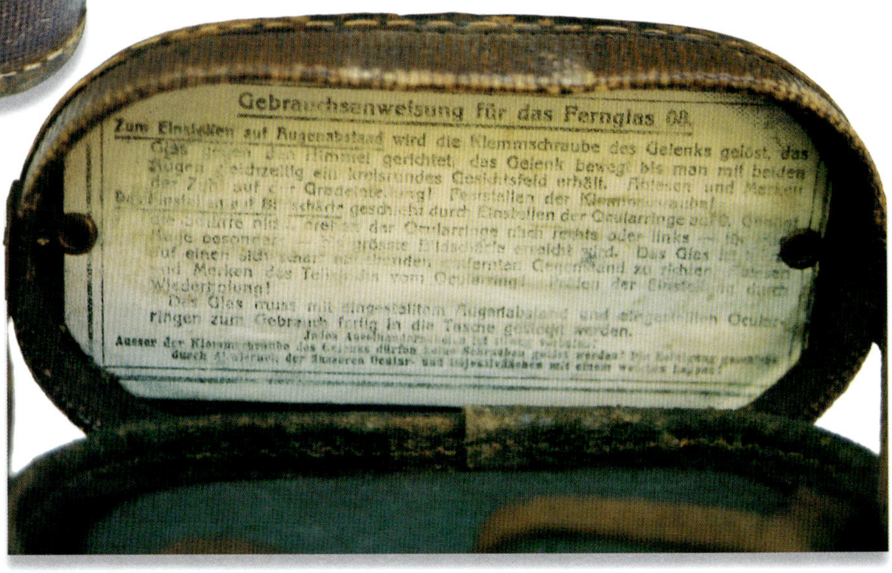

Instruction sheet for the *Fernglas 08*.

Fernglas 08

Leather *Fernglas 08* case with felt inner lining and a button tab for attaching the case to an overcoat button. *Courtesy of Brian Ludwig.*

Officers often obtained private purchase binoculars and cases. The brown case had a leather strap so it can be worn around the neck or across the shoulder. A leather loop at the rear allowed the case to be worn on the belt as well. *Courtesy of BT.*

High-quality officer's private purchase binoculars manufactured by *C.P. Goerz*. The case and binoculars are marked "*Wagner, Arty. 48*". *Courtesy of Brian Ludwig.*

Trench Periscopes

Trench warfare conditions made it difficult to observe the movements of the enemy and static positions across no-mans land. It was extremely dangerous for the soldiers to look over the trench, as snipers and enemy fire were a constant threat. Therefore, different types of trench periscopes were issued to the troops. Some models were made by front line troops using wood and mirrors, so the enemy line could be observed without raising the head above the trench. The bayonet was put through a clip on the back and then raised above the parapet. Other hand-held designs used two mirrors set in an angle in each end, so the observer could look into one end and see through the other, at a greater height. One of the following examples looks like a U-boat periscope, made by *Hensoldt-Wetzlar* in 1918.

Trench periscope and metal carrying container. The 61.8" (157cm) long periscope was manufactured by *Hensoldt-Wetzal* in 1918. It carries serial number 15719 and is marked *"V 1918 Periskoop-Hensoldt W A C H T". Courtesy of BT.*

V. 1918.
Periskop-
Hensoldt

Hensoldt-
Wetzlar
No.15719

Trench periscope made by *Goerz, Berlin. Royal Army and Military History Museum, Brussels.*

Wood box periscope mounted on standard *Goerz* tripod. The field-gray painted scope has no markings. Overall length (without tripod) is approximately 34" (87cm). *Courtesy of Brian Ludwig.*

Trench periscope with removable rubber eyepiece manufactured by *Emil Busch, Rathenow.* Overall length with handle is approximately 24" (44cm). *Courtesy of Brian Ludwig.*

Field-gray painted tin box periscope with spring mounting attachment. Overall length is approximately 16" (41cm). *Courtesy of Brian Ludwig.*

Trench periscope with removable handle and original canvas-covered steel carrying case. The case has several small shrapnel holes and clearly saw extensive field use. The periscope has two eyepieces, one for 15 and another for 10-power magnification. The scope is marked *Hensoldt & Sohne, Wetzlar, Halbscheren-Fernrohr No. 598, Vergr. 10X & 15 X.* With handle attached, the scope is approximately 24" (61cm) in overall height. *Courtesy of Brian Ludwig.*

Manufacturer markings.

Private-purchase periscope binoculars with original velvet-line black leather case and clip-on sun shades. Manufactured by *Carl Zeiss, Jena*. Flat field-gray painted with folding handle. Approximately 14" (36cm) overall length. *Courtesy of Brian Ludwig.*

Private-purchase periscope binoculars with original velvet-lined black leather case. Manufactured by *Carl Zeiss, Jena*, marked *DRP* and *Relief-Fernrohr, Vergr.8.* Marks are hand-engraved and not stamped. Approximately 8" (20cm) overall length. *Courtesy of Brian Ludwig.*

A trench section with a wooden improvised periscope .*Courtesy of Faris Siwadi.*

Flashlights (*Taschenlampe*)

Most probably, all flashlights were private-purchase pieces. However, they must have been fairly popular items considering how many different varieties exist and how often they appear in period photos. Although most of the flashlights had a rectangular shape, other types existed as well, like the round *Magnet-Lampe*. Usually, they were attached to one of the buttons of the tunic with a metal hook or a small leather strap having a buttonhole.

Flashlight marked *Petrix. Courtesy of BT.*

Pertrix No 647. *Courtesy of Eric Siegel.*

Pertrix No 658. *Courtesy of Eric Siegel.*

Commercial pocket light. Courtesy of Eric Siegel.

Trench flashlight marked *Militaria*. Light field-gray paint with wire belt loops and field-gray fabric and leather button loops. Manufacturer marked *PSO/DRGM. Courtesy of Brian Ludwig.*

Detail of "*Militaria*" marking.

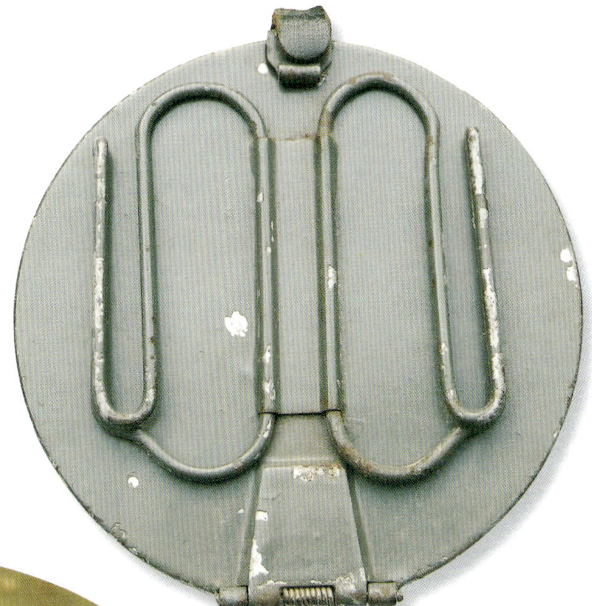

Perlux rear view.

Folding *Perlux* trench lantern. When opened, the light bulb reflects on a concave mirror. The backside has folding wire belt hooks and handle loops. *Courtesy of Brian Ludwig.*

Perlux in open position.

Hassia brand trench flashlight in dark field-gray with a single leather button look and protective lens cover. *Courtesy of Brian Ludwig.*

Typical field-gray painted trench flashlight. This version has field-gray and leather button tabs. *Courtesy of Brian Ludwig.*

Trench flashlight in field-gray and black paint with wire button loop on rear, marked *DRGM. Courtesy of Brian Ludwig.*

Magnetlampe. This is a nice example of a *Magnet-Lampe*. Interestingly, the light still has its original instruction sheet. An interior generator is triggered by pulling a chain; this provides light only while the chain is being pulled repeatedly and allows for temporary illumination. It is still in full working order, but makes an awful noise when in operation. One wonders if this was also the case when the lights were newly delivered. *Courtesy of Faris Siwadi.*

"*Tarnkapp*" flashlight in open position with leather button tabs and a folding cover for protecting the glass lens and dimming the intensity of the light to avoid detection at night. Both DRGM (*Deutsches Reich Gebrauchmuster*) and DRP (*Deutsches Reich Patent*) marks are found on WWI period items. *Courtesy of Faris Siwadi.*

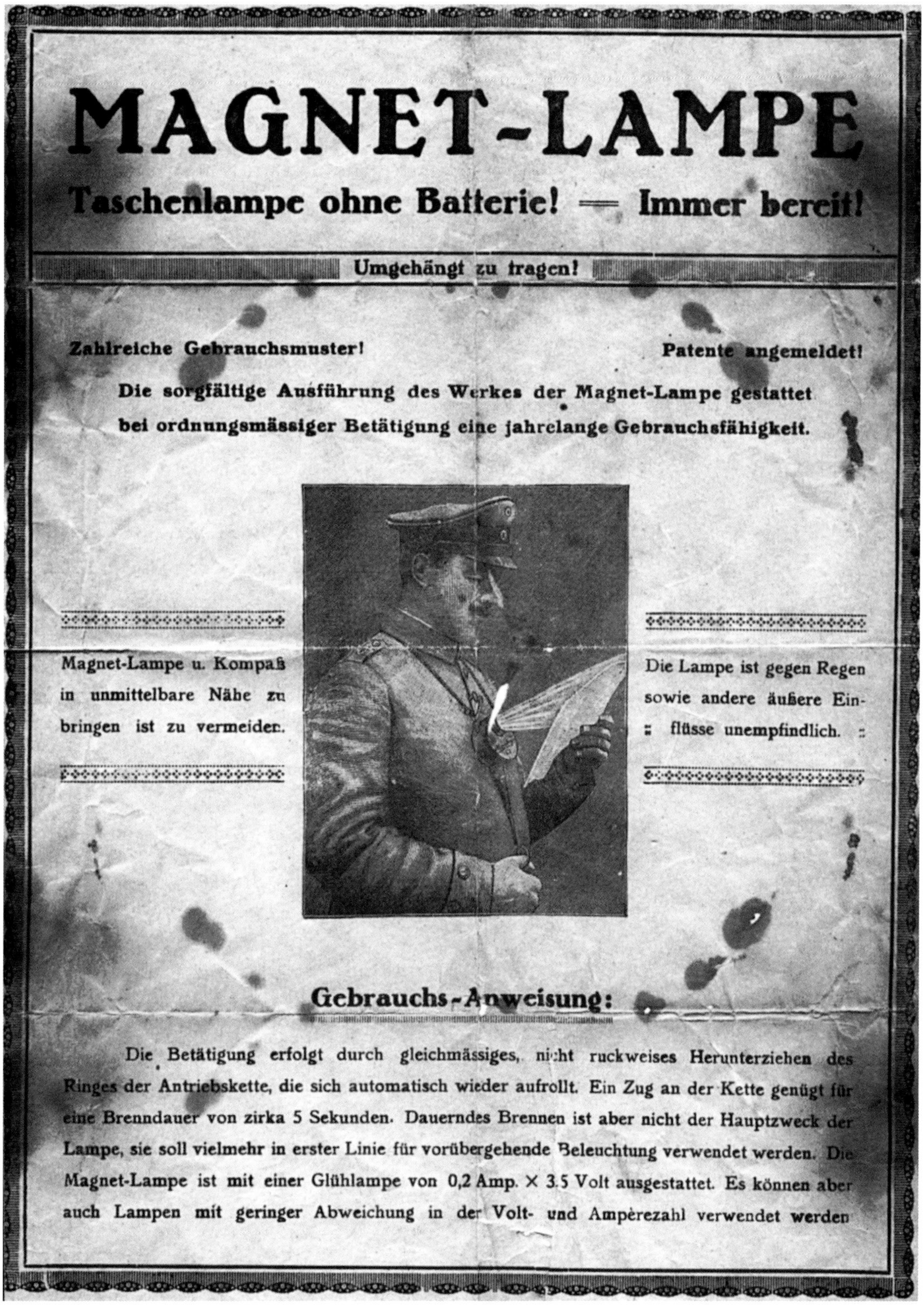

MAGNET-LAMPE

Taschenlampe ohne Batterie! == Immer bereit!

Umgehängt zu tragen!

Zahlreiche Gebrauchsmuster! Patente angemeldet!

Die sorgfältige Ausführung des Werkes der Magnet-Lampe gestattet bei ordnungsmässiger Betätigung eine jahrelange Gebrauchsfähigkeit.

Magnet-Lampe u. Kompaß in unmittelbare Nähe zu bringen ist zu vermeiden.

Die Lampe ist gegen Regen sowie andere äußere Einflüsse unempfindlich.

Gebrauchs-Anweisung:

Die Betätigung erfolgt durch gleichmässiges, nicht ruckweises Herunterziehen des Ringes der Antriebskette, die sich automatisch wieder aufrollt. Ein Zug an der Kette genügt für eine Brenndauer von zirka 5 Sekunden. Dauerndes Brennen ist aber nicht der Hauptzweck der Lampe, sie soll vielmehr in erster Linie für vorübergehende Beleuchtung verwendet werden. Die Magnet-Lampe ist mit einer Glühlampe von 0,2 Amp. × 3.5 Volt ausgestattet. Es können aber auch Lampen mit geringer Abweichung in der Volt- und Ampèrezahl verwendet werden

Instruction sheet for the Magnet-Lampe, which translates as follows:
Flashlight without a battery == Works always
Worn around the neck
Many ways to use — Patent requested
The excellent design and construction of the Magnet-Lampe will ensure a long life time when used properly.
It is not advisable to bring the flashlights near a compass.
The flashlight is resistant to rain and other outside conditions.
Instruction to use:
The light is operated by slowly dragging the ring - which is attached to the pull string - downwards. The pull string will automatically be retracted.
The flashlights will burn for about five seconds every time the cord is pulled. A constant light is not the purpose of this *Magnet-Lampe*. It should be more used for short periods of light, when in the first line. The *Magnet-Lampe* contains a light bulb of 0.2A x 3.5V. It is possible to use bulbs with a slight deviation in Ampere or Voltage. *Courtesy of Faris Siwadi.*

Torches, Lanterns and Gas Lamps

The German army used several devices for providing some illumination during the night. These were the efficient flare pistols (for more information, see the chapter on communication devices), lanterns, torches and lamps. Torches (*Dauerbrandfackeln*) burned for two to three hours and were intended to assist with night work in first line positions or to illuminate obstacles in front of the lines. For this role, torches were equipped with a tinplate cover (*Weißblech)* on the back, so that only the front was illuminated. Another type of torch existed as well, called *Leuchtfackeln*, which were mainly intended for illuminating obstacles around fortified positions.

Trench lanterns (*Laufgrabenlaternen*) were issued to provide light in trenches, communication trenches and infantry positions. Colored glass in either green or red could be inserted in front of the light to help reduce the possibility of the light being seen by the enemy.

Electrical and gas lamps (*Leuchtgaslampen*) were used to illuminate work stations in positions further to the rear. Some provided enough light to illuminate an area with a diameter of 100 meters.

An electrical lamp made by *Bosh (Projector Bosh). Royal Army and Military History Museum, Brussels.*

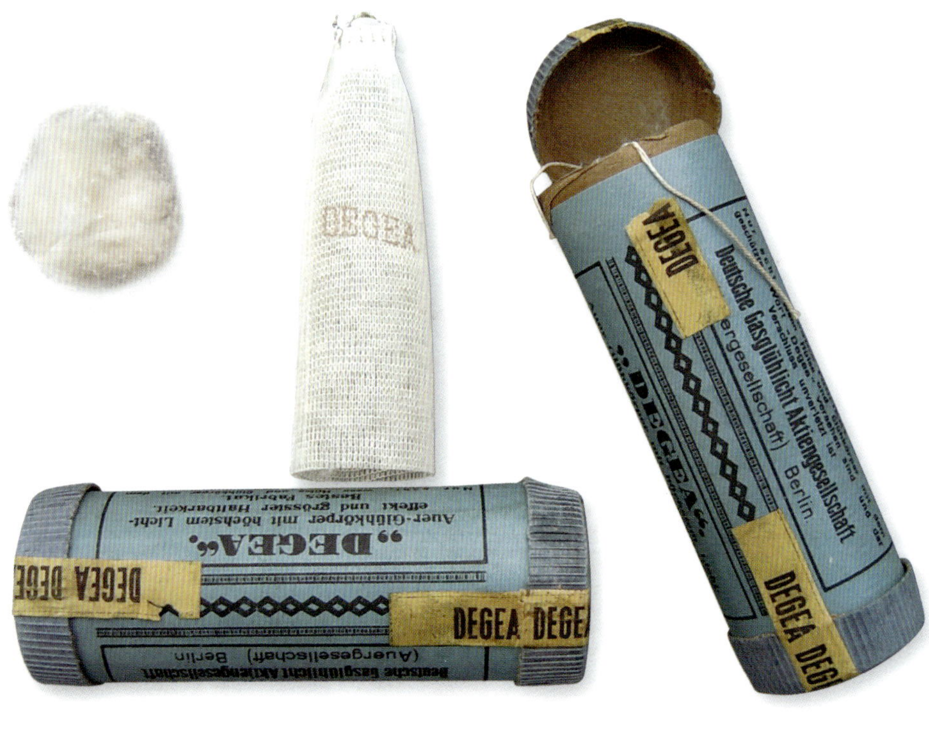

Lamp with original packaging. These were probably used in the garrison rooms and later at the Front. *Courtesy of Sven Kuczyk.*

Lantern PB17. *Courtesy of Eric Siegel.*

Lantern. *Courtesy of Eric Siegel.*

Blendlaterne 07.12 manufactured by *Bing. Courtesy of Eric Siegel.*

Floodlights (*Scheinwerfer*)

Floodlights were divided into heavy (*Schweres Gerät*), light (*Leichtes Gerät*) and mobile (*Tragbares Gerät*) devices. A heavy device could only be transported by road and was used primarily in attacks against fortresses, while the lighter device was transported on a special wagon and served with front line troops. An Army corps had direct control over the allocation of the floodlights, while the heavy apparatus was controlled by the sector commander (*Abschnittkommandeuren*). Mobile devices were also used by front line troops and for engagements against fortresses. All floodlights could be used for both attack and defense. The effectiveness depended on the terrain and the weather, but normally the following ranges could be achieved:

heavy floodlight	3 km
light floodlight	2 km
mobile floodlight	600 to 1200 m

The heavy floodlight could be lifted to a height of 10 meters to enable it to emit it's light beam above any nearby obstacles like trees or hedges, while the light device could be lifted to a height of 6 meters. The light beam (*Lichtkegel*) had a diameter of 40 meters over a distance of 1000 meters for the heavy and light apparatus, and a diameter of 15 meter over a distance of 500 meters for a mobile device. *Scheinwerfer* units performed the following duties:

Signaling up to a range of 100 km.
Blinding the enemy or enemy floodlights.
Providing direction for troops when crossing terrain.
Providing direction for artillery fire.

Ideally, two floodlights operated together, to increase the illumination capabilities, or one light could hold a certain position, while the other light searched for a target. An officer (*Scheinwerferoffizier*) was responsible for the correct technical operation of the floodlight.

The German firm *Kärting & Mathiesen* in *Leipzig* had been manufacturing floodlights since 1909. These devices (*Reinkohlenscheinwerfer*) operated on the principle that a lighting arc occurs between two spikes of charred wood (carbon electrodes or *Kohleneleklroden*) when they were connected to a high current supply. The device had to maintain a constant distance between both ends of the positive and negative electrodes when the arc was burning. The light generated had a very high intensity and the light beam was projected using a mirror reflector, creating a yellowish-light. The coal electrodes were held in place by a clamp and when in use burnt fairly quickly, having to be replaced regularly, a tricky task when the device was so hot. Coal electrodes had an approximate diameter of 1.4" (3.8cm) for 150 amperes. The positive and negative electrodes were supplied in tin cans and were of different lengths as can be seen in the photograph. The electrodes are dated 1914 and marked Ges. Geschützt (patent protection).

A new generation of *Beck*-floodlights, named after their inventor Heinrich Beck, were manufactured by the firm *Opt. Anstalt C.P. Goerz AG* and which had a diameter of 110 cm. The Beck system had been invented in 1912 and was in use onboard ships in

Far Left: Rare sealed can with ten pair of coal electrodes for floodlights, supplied by *Siemens-Schuckert*, found near *Metz*, France. Cans exist as well without a label, but with printed text. Left: Electrodes came in many different sizes and cans. *Both Courtesy of BT.*

Close up of one of the coals with a 1914 manufacturing date and marked *Ges. Geschützt* (patent protection) at the other side. *Courtesy of BT.*

the US Navy, but saw service in Germany only in the last year of the war. Beck floodlights had alcohol vapour cooled rotating electrodes and was about four to six times more powerful than the older lamps. The constant cooling prevented premature combustion and caused the current to emit from only the limited front tip of the electrode, creating a white light of extremely high intensity. The negative electrode had a combustion rate of 2" (5cm) to 2.4"(6cm) per hour, while the positive carbon electrode burned at a rate of 7.8" (20cm) to 9.7" (25cm) per hour. However, a new electrode could be inserted into a hot floodlight in a matter of seconds. The Beck electrodes were smaller and had a diameter of 11 to 16 mm for 150 amperes. (Source: *Electrical World, July 25 1914, Search Lamp with Vapour-Cooled Electrodes*).

Compasses

Magnetic compasses are amongst the oldest instruments used for navigation on land and water, and can be used to take bearings and map orientation. Every direction can be expressed as an angle with respect to north (azimuth), and bearings are expressed as a number of degrees. By setting the angle on the compass and keeping the needle aligned, a person can continue to go in the right direction. In addition, maps can be aligned with the terrain, by rotating the map until the "north lines" on the map are aligned with the compass needle. The German Army made frequent use of privately purchased instruments or the *Bezard's* patent *Armeemodell 1910,* of which several versions exist.

Bezard's patent *Armeemodell 1910, Model I* compass with original carrying case and purchase box. The Armeemodell 1910 added radium marks (glow in the dark), and was designated the *Modell 1913. Courtesy of Brian Ludwig.*

Bezard's patent *Armeemodell 1910, Model II* compass with original carrying case. *Courtesy of Brian Ludwig.*

Bezard's patent *Armeemodell II. Courtesy of BT.*

Armee-Kompaß

Patent v. Bézard, Major in der k. k. Oesterr.-Ung. Armee.
D. R. P. Nr. 157 329 und Auslandspatente.

Gebrauchsanweisung.

Von allen bisher bekannten Kompaßkonstruktionen zeichnet sich der Bézard-Kompaß durch seine vielseitige Verwendbarkeit ebenso wie durch seine praktische, zweckentsprechende Form und Ausstattung aus. Das Instrument ist dem Militär ebenso wie dem Touristen und Forstmann wie überhaupt jedem, der in die Lage kommt, sich ohne fremde Hilfe in unbekannten Gegenden zurechtfinden zu müssen, ein unvergleichliches und nie versagendes Hilfsmittel. Bei Beachtung der Anleitung ist es vollständig unmöglich, sich mit diesem Kompaß zu verirren, und selbst in vollständigem Dunkel, im Nebel oder im Schneetreiben genügt ein Blick auf das in der Dunkelheit stark leuchtende Instrument, um sich zu überzeugen, welche Richtung einzuhalten ist, um das Ziel zu erreichen. Da die magnetische Abweichung behoben ist, so ist die angezeigte Richtung stets genau und hat man nicht nötig, diese Abweichung wie bei allen anderen Kompassen in Rechnung zu ziehen.

Richtige Haltung des Kompasses.

12. 715. 5000.

Instruction sheet for the *Model I and Model II Bezard Armee Compass. Courtesy of Brian Ludwig.*

Private-purchase surveying compass. Manufactured by *Voigtlander, Braunschweig. Voigtlander* also made sniper riflescopes during the war. *Courtesy of Brian Ludwig.*

Grey fabric and leather carrying case for the *Voigtlander* compass.

Notes
[1]Hans Seeger.
[2]Merged with ZEISS IKON AG in 1926.
[3]Fernrohr = Telescope.
[4]Goerz Festschrift 1886-1911, page 27: 24.11.08.
[5]Goerz Festschrift 1886-1911, page 258: 13.8.09.

Chapter Four

Armor

Breast Plate (*Grabenpanzer, Sappenpanzer*)

Delivered towards the end of 1916, the model 1916 *Grabenpanzer* was – depending on the size – a 20 lbs (9kg) to 33 lbs (15kg) construction made of four steel plates which protected the soldier against bullets and shrapnel. It could stop a bullet fired from a distance of 300 meters.[1] The upper plate was curved to fit over the shoulders. It was possible to wear the armor back to front when the abdomen and groin were already protected when standing against a trench. The four plates of the first pattern of body armor simply fixed to one another with hooks. Unfortunately, moving or walking around made a terrible noise, clearly a problem on the battlefield. To reduce the noise, the second generation of armor had six wool-felt pads fixed between the overlapping steel plates.

Many activities, including shooting, proved difficult when the armor was being worn. To solve some of these problems, several different types were made in 1918. An experimental version existed with a cut away right shoulder so that the rifle could be put against the shoulder when firing[2], while another design had additional belt hooks and an additional steel sheet attached to the right shoulder to support the but of the rifle. It is estimated that approximately 500,000 sets were produced, most of them of the model 1916 design.

The size of the breastplate is often stamped in black paint on the inside surface. This piece is marked with the number "2" to indicate its size. There are no other markings on this item although some examples bear the *Krupp* mark.

The following breastplate has both original paint and straps. Because of the weight of the plates and the fragile material, the straps have broken in three different places; a common condition with original straps. The exterior of the plate has dark spots of thicker 'paint'. This is anti-oxidant applied to the steel surface, before it was painted green. The *Grabenpanzers* were produced in three sizes: 1, 2 and 3. *Courtesy of BT.*

Adapted design with a sheet metal plate to be used when firing the rifle. Equipment support hooks (one is missing on this example) and a waist strap was added on this late war design. *Courtesy of Freddy Raepsaet.*

Detail of the additional steel sheet. In some cases it was covered with thick felt.

Equipment support hook.

Waist strap attachment detail.

This *Grabenpanzer* was hit by a bullet. *Courtesy of Freddy Raepsaet.*

Trench Shield
(Infanterieschild, Grabenschutzschild, Sturmschild)

Several solutions were sought to reduce the risk of injuries during trench raids or when seeking cover in more or less permanent trenches or dugouts. A remarkable invention was a small carriage with two wheels, armored at the front and along the side. The soldiers had to crawl inside the carriage when attacking the enemy line. More effective were the rectangular plate steel trench shields (*Grabenschutzschild*), also known as "sniper loops", which were more mobile and could be carried short distances. General *Hauffe* ordered the manufacture of these shields in 1914.

The model 1914 trench shield (*Sturmschild*) was a half oval shield with leather carrying straps and a circular opening. This shield had a height of 18.9" (48cm) and a length of 21.2" (54cm).[3] Its prime function was to protect the soldier during an assault. The model 1916 trench shield (*Infanterieschild*) was a rectangular shield of 29 lbs (13kg), with a length of 23.6 (60cm) and a height of 17.7" (45cm) to 19.7" (50cm). It contained a vertical slot through which the rifle barrel could be inserted, which could be closed with a sliding shutter mechanism. The shield was 6mm thick and could resist machine gun fire from a distance of 100 meters. It could be set in the ground at a slight angle using one or two steel poles. They were often set inside the trenches as well to create sniper's posts. Shields were painted field-grey or were sometimes camouflaged using three different colors. The firm *Krupp* in *Essen* manufactured a large number of these shields.[4] Another pattern existed as well, which was convex in shape with an opening for the rifle in either the center of the shield or slightly offset.

A nearly identical shield was produced around 1916-1917. Here, the vertical slot was replaced by a half oval opening, which could no longer be closed. The weight of the new shield increased to 51 lbs (23kg).[5] Apart from these three models, many other variations existed as well.

This shield was dug up in Flanders on the *Kemmelberg* (Kemmel Hill). The *Kemmelberg* near *Ypres* was strategically very important and was the scene of fierce fighting on April 25th 1918. After an intense bombardment, the 5th Infantry Regiment[6] and mountain units (*Alpenjägern*) stormed the *Kemmelberg*. The French Army was unable to repel this attack and the German advance almost reached *Ypres* (Hellfire Corner). The French lost over 12,000 troops during the battle. Today, on the south slope is a French Ossuary, where over 5,000 unknown French soldiers now rest in peace.

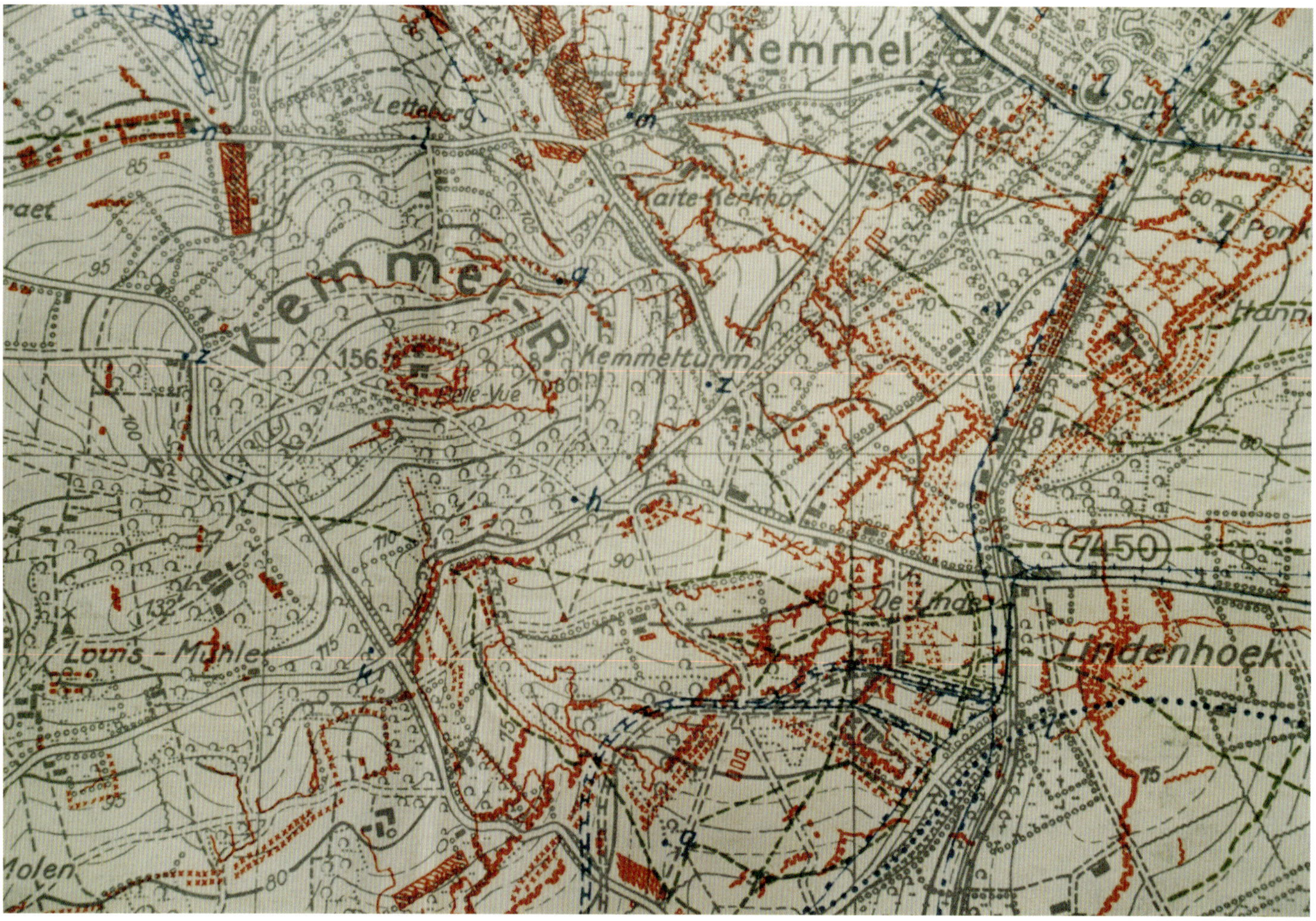

The *Kemmelberg* area, trench lines, and fortified positions on a German map of early 1918. *Author's collection.*

Opposite: A trench section reinforced with sand bags and shields.

Face Shield (*Schutzschild für Scharfschützen*)
Although only rarely used, snipers could use face shields (*Schutzschild*) to protect the face and eyes. These were small rectangular curved plates of approximately 13 lbs (6 kg)[7] and 0.58mm thick with two 1.78mm long and 0.76mm wide eye slits. The central part of the shield was curved to accommodate the face, while the outer edges were turned outwards. A small part was cut away into the lower right-hand side so that the rifle could be aimed more easily.

The facemask had leather straps to attach the shield firmly to the head. A surviving example, painted in field-grey can be seen in the Brussels museum. It is supposed that these shields were also painted in the 3-tone camouflage colors, like the steel helmets. The mask could resist standard rifle ammunition at very close range, but was helpless against armor-piercing rounds at 200 meters.

Notes
[1]Stephan Bull, page 84.
[2]Displayed at the Royal Army and Military History Museum, Brussels.
[3]Philippe Pierrejan, Militaria Magazine 209, page 18.
[4]Philippe Pierrejan, Krupp produced 280.000 shields.
[5]Stephan Bull, page 84.
[6]The 5th I.R. belonged to the 7. *Infanterie-Brigade, 4. Infanterie-Division, II. Bayerisches Armeekorps.*
[7]There were reports of similar shields weighing as much as 16.5 lbs (7.5kg).

Face shield displayed in *Royal Army and Military History Museum, Brussels.*

Chapter Five

Mine and Chemical Warfare

Mine and Chemical Warfare Respirators (*Selbstretter*)

An important evolution of the static trench warfare was the "*Minenkrieges*". Miners (pioneers) would dig tunnels from their own lines across "No Man's Land", so that mines could be laid and exploded beneath enemy positions. The explosion (*Minensprengung*) could destroy an entire section of a trench system, so their own troops could advance and exploit the benefit. A well as digging tunnels, pioneers had to detect any underground enemy activity. One method used to detect enemy miners was to fill a bucket with water and to install it in the floor of the trench. The water served to amplify faint sounds and vibrations and the pioneers would lower an ear into the water to listen for any noise that might indicate underground activity. Special devices were manufactured as well to detect sounds and noises, like the "*Horchgerät Waetzmann*", manufactured by *Siemens & Halske*. The mechanism was often carried in a model 1915 field telephone box.[1] Although mining operations were undertaken early on in the war, it wasn't until 1916 that regular specialized mining companies (*Pionier-Mineur-Kompanien*) were raised.[2] One of their roles was in performing counter-mining attacks. When an enemy tunnel was discovered, a new tunnel was dug near the enemy tunnel and a small charge detonated. Often, the same charges were used as employed in German submarines. U-boots carried charges, which could be used to either blow-up captured ships or to self-destruct the submarine whenever this was necessary.

All explosions produce a variety of gasses, like hydrogen, Carbon Monoxide (CO) and methane. Large quantities of CO could be fatal in a matter of seconds, while even 0.15% CO was dangerous between 45 minutes to two hours after initial release. Low concentrations could go unnoticed for hours, but lead to shortness

This is a *Kriegsmarine* marked counter-attack charge, one of several types used to destroy enemy tunnels. *Courtesy of Memorial Museum Passchendaele 1917.*

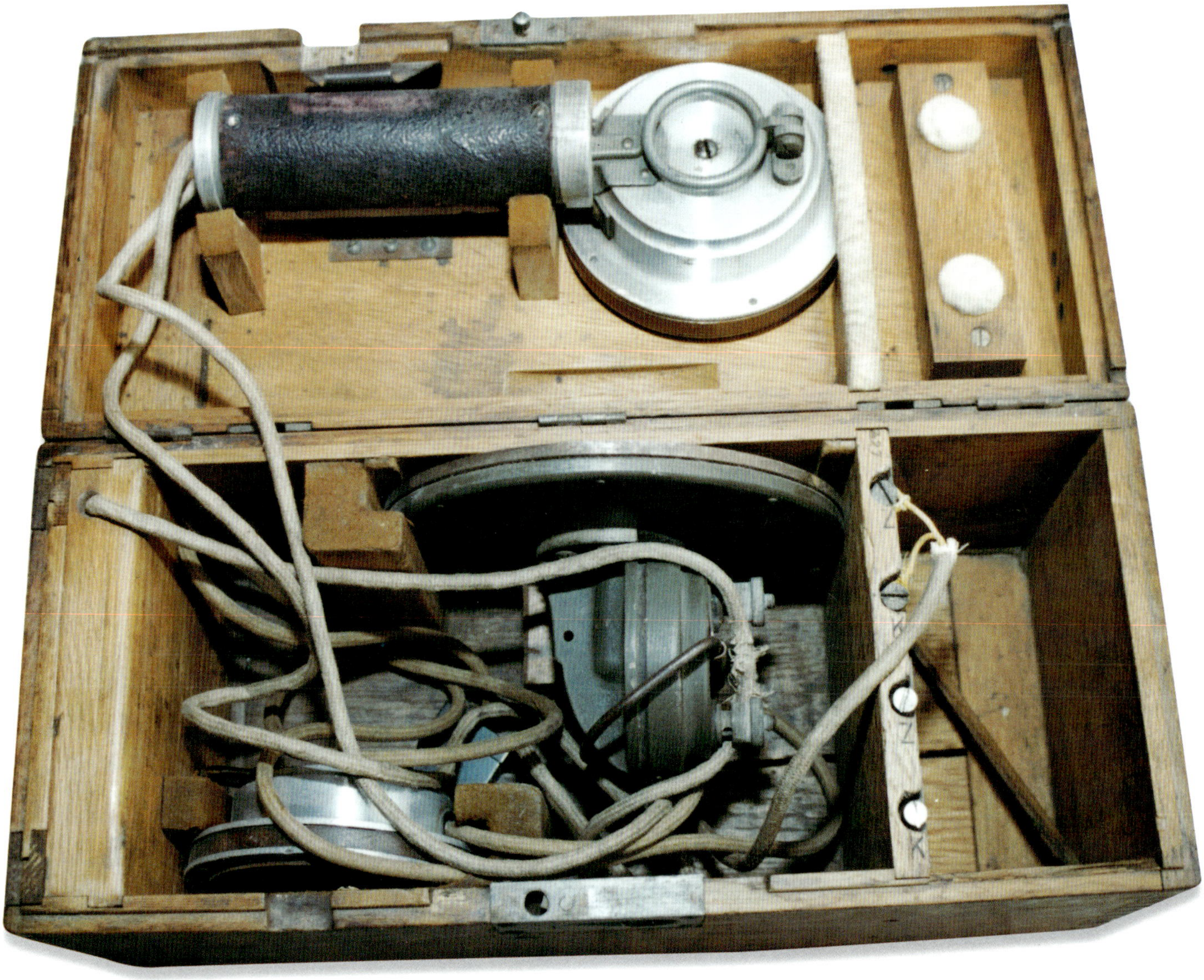

This device called "*Horchgerät Waetzmann*", was manufactured by *Siemens & Halske* and used to detect all sounds and noises, in particular, the sound of digging from enemy tunnellers. Only trained pioneer units used this device. *Courtesy of Memorial Museum Passchendaele 1917.*

A round disc was placed on the floor to capture the noise of underground activity.

of breath, giddiness, and confusion and finally loss of power in the limbs and unconsciousness. Infantry troops were warned for example not to enter the base of new craters until the CO was fully dispersed, but there was no escape route for these lethal gasses after underground explosions. The number of casualties caused by CO amongst miners far exceeded the number caused by explosions. Early in the war, breathing apparatus was used which consisted of a sealed helmet and a long hose, which supplied fresh air drawn in from ground level. These respirators were useful in the early stages of the war, when mine galleries were rather short and simple, but late war mines were long and complex with multiple shafts, listening posts and both offensive and defensive galleries sometimes up to 5 or 6 levels beneath the surface. Special hoseless respirators were required which supplied oxygen from cylinders, while the exhaled CO was absorbed through a filter containing caustic soda granules.

Pioneers responsible for the release of poison gas from cylinders were often equipped with these special respirators as well. The following chapters were written in close cooperation with *Arnaud Lejaille* and describe the *Draeger model 1910/11*, the *Draeger Tubben model 1914*, the *Modified Draeger Tubben model 1914*, the *Magirus Sauerstoffapparat model 1916* and the *Draeger HSS (Heeres Sauerstoff Schutzapparat)*.[3]

Manufacturer's identification plate.

Detail of a loudspeaker.

Draeger Model 1910/11

The *Draeger* model 1910/11 was originally developed for civilian mining purposes and consisted of a respirator bag, an oxygen bottle and a potash filter. It was only produced in very limited quantities.

Draeger model 1910/11. *Royal Army and Military History Museum, Brussels.*

Draeger Tubben Model 1914

This closed-circuit respirator (*Draeger Tubben* model 1914) was initially designed for attacking fortresses, but it was later issued to pioneers involved in mine and chemical warfare. The respirator (*Selbstretter*) weighted 9.9 lbs (4.5kg) and offered protection for approximately 45 minutes during rest or 20 minutes when working.[4] Compressed oxygen – stored in a bottle – flowed into a large breathing bag by manually opening an oxygen valve (see diagram, part U) for a short period of time. This time depended of the contents of the oxygen bottle. For a new bottle, still under high pressure, the time was much less than nearly empty bottles. During inhalation the oxygen went from the airbag, through a filter (*Atmungs-Patrone* or *Kalipatrone*) and via a tube into the mouth. This tube ended in a rubberized mouthpiece, which had to be inserted completely in the mouth and the soldier had to bite firmly on it. When exhaling, the CO (*Kohlensäure*) and condensation were absorbed by the filter and oxygen went back into the airbag. When the individual released too much oxygen from the bottle in the breathing bag, it became almost impossible to breathe out and some oxygen needed to be released from the bag, thus shortening the effective useful time of the respirator. The respirator was issued without eye protection, but when working in atmospheres were eye irritants were present, special goggles (*Rauchschutzbrille*) were worn. The *Draeger Tubben* devices were distributed across the different companies in the following quantities[5]:

Infantry company: 3
Pioneer company: 25
Pioneer mining company: 6
Medical services company: 20

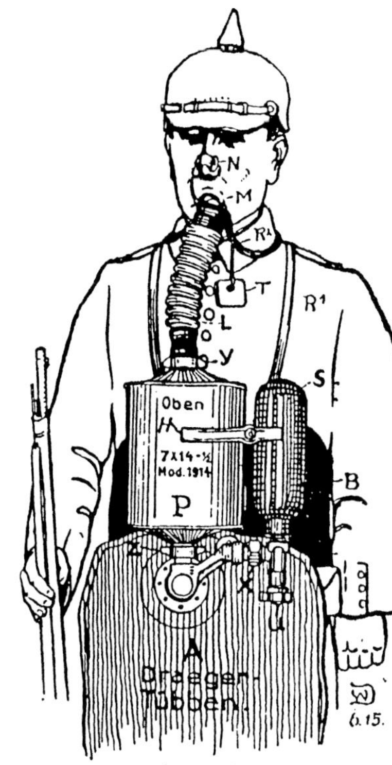

Selbstretter Dräger-Tübben, Heeres-B-Type.

Zeichen: N = Nasenklammer; M = Mundstück; T = Verschlußstöpsel für Mundstück; R¹ = Nackenriemen; R² = Halsschlinge am Atmungsschlauch; L = Atmungsschlauch; H = Halteschelle für Kalipatrone und Sauerstoffcylinder; P = Kalipatrone; Y, Z = Muttern der Anschlüsse für Kalipatrone; S = Sauerstoffcylinder; X = Anschlußmutter; U = Verschlußventil des Sauerstoffcylinders; A = Atmungssack; B = Schutzdecke.

Selbstretter Draeger Tubben. N=nose clip (*Nasenklammer*), T=mouthpiece closing peg, R1=neck strap, R2=neck strap for breathing tube (*Atmungsschlauch*),L= breathing tube, H=lock for filter (*Kalipatrone*) and oxygen bottle (*Sauerstoffzylinder*), P=filter, Z=filter bolt, S=oxygen bottle, X=connection bolt, U=Oxygen ventil, A=breathing bag. *Reproduced from Dräger-Tubben manual, Drägerwerk, Lubeck, 1915.*

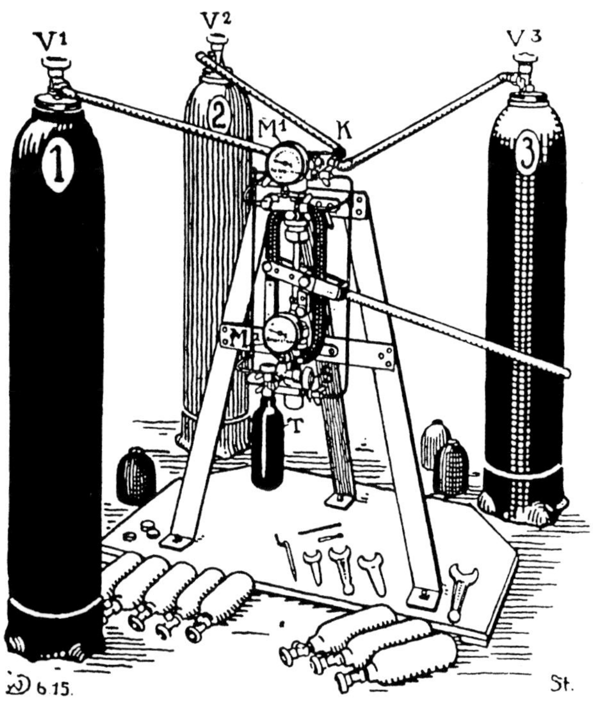

Bild 18.

Zeichen: 1, 2, 3 = Sauerstoff-Vorratscylinder; V¹, V², V³ = Verschlußventile der Vorratscylinder; K = Anschlußstück der Verbindungsrohre: M¹ = Kontroll-Finimeter für den Füllungsdruck der Vorratscylinder; M² = Kontroll-Finimeter für den Füllungsdruck des zu füllenden Arbeitscylinders; T = zu füllender Arbeitscylinder.

Refilling station for *Dräger* oxygen bottles. *Reproduced from Dräger-Tubben manual, Drägerwerk, Lubeck, 1915.*

A contemporary *Draeger* manual contained an interesting warning message. During operation, the filter became warm and eventually so hot, that it could not be touched with bare hands. The fact that the filter became warm and hot proved that the device was working correctly, as absorbing the exhaled CO_2 caused the increase in temperature. A filter, which would not become warm, was defective, and if the filter turned cold again, it was completely used. It was evident, that the individual would inhale warm air after a while. The manual also noted the fact that clothing or other respirator components would not be damaged due to the hot filter. It was recommended to keep some spare respirators nearby to help soldiers who suffered from gas poisoning, because they had lost the mouthpiece, or bullets or shrapnel damaged the oxygen bottle or air bag.

Empty oxygen bottles were refilled in a mobile workplace (*Umfüllstation*). This workplace was composed out of a high pressure pump (150 Atm), four large oxygen supply cylinders, one manometer to measure the pressure in the supply oxygen bottles and the *Draeger* bottle to be filled and several small work tools.[6]

The *Draeger Tubben* model 1914 in action. The right hand person wears a *DMAG* knife with *Troddel. Courtesy of Alberto Flórez.*

Selbstretter Draeger-Tubben in an original transportation box. *Courtesy of Memorial Museum Passchendaele 1917.*

Carrying harness.

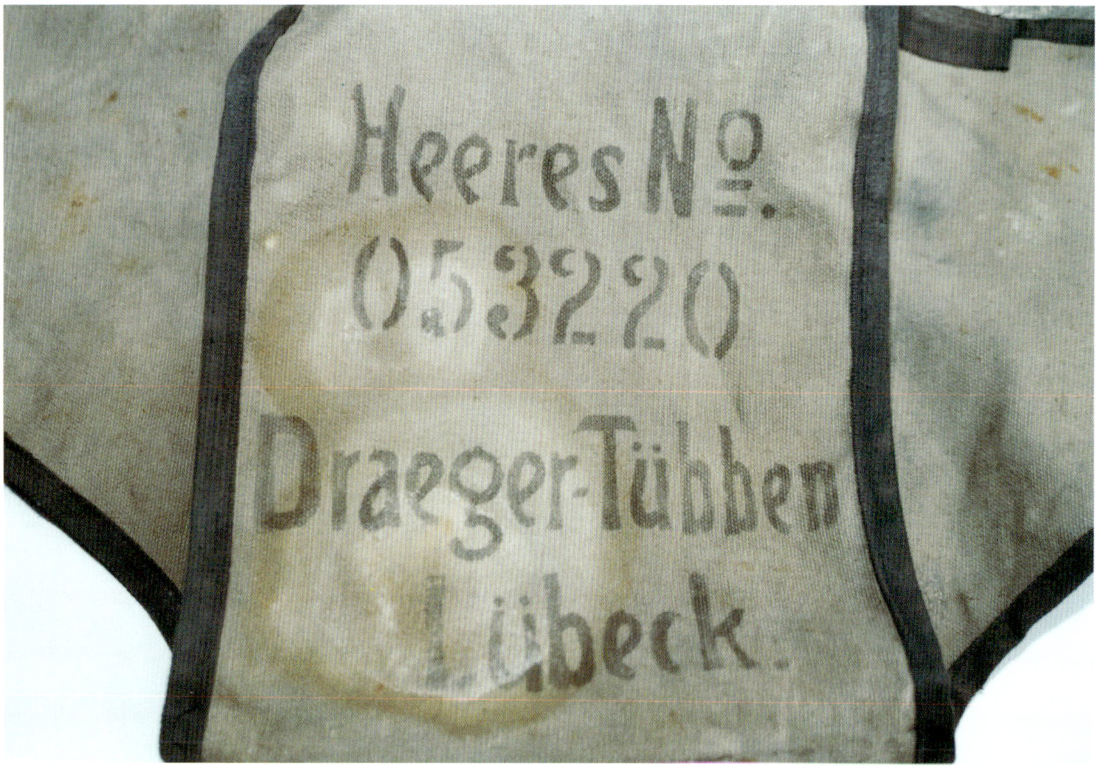

Manufacturer details and possible serial number.

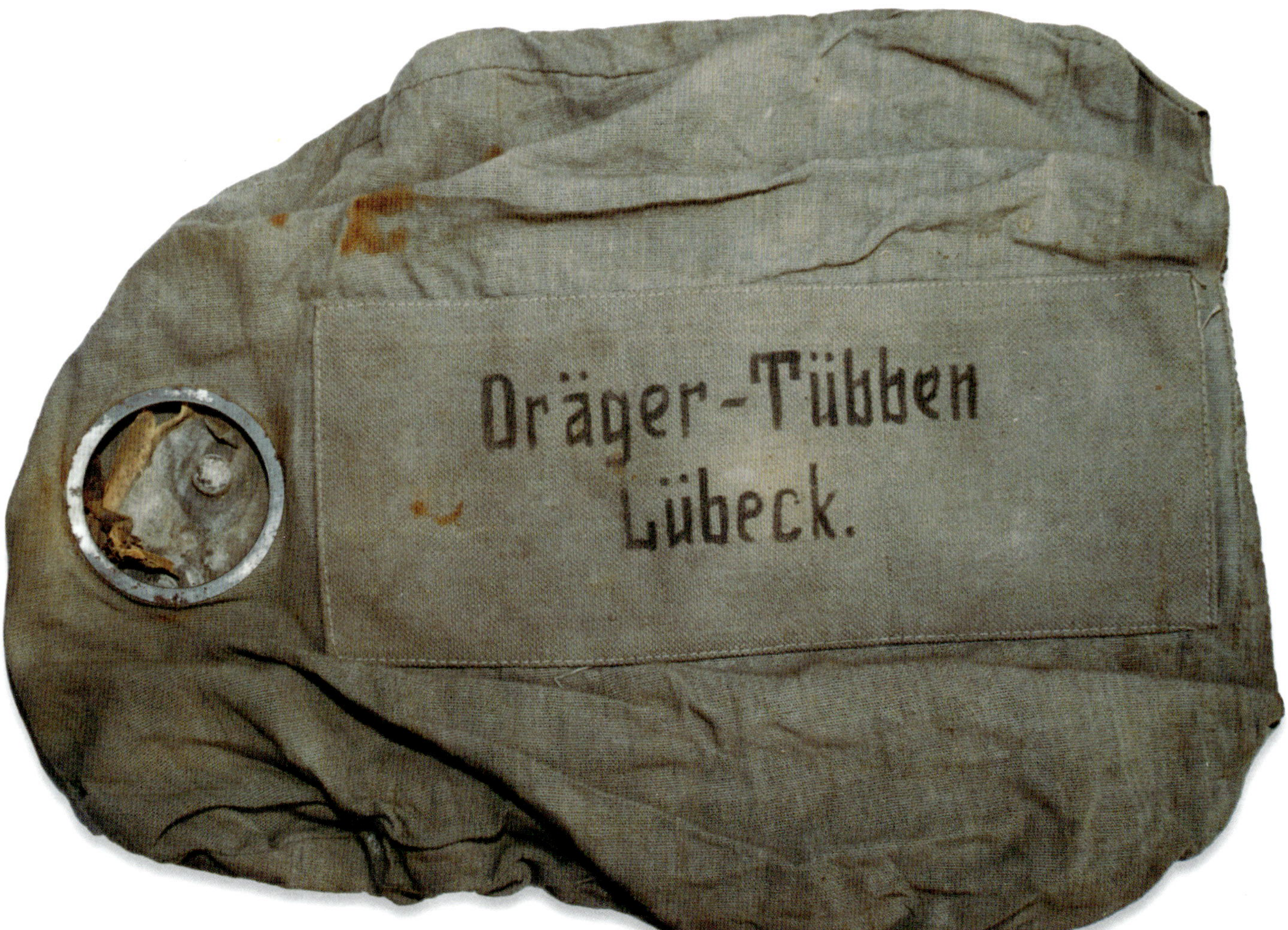

Air bag.

Filter, tube and mouthpiece.

Oxygen bottle.

Modified *Draeger Tubben* Model 1914

On May 31st 1918 the French "*Services Chimiques*" described the "Modified *Draeger Tubben* model 1914", although it is possible that this device was used prior to this date. The modified *Draeger* was using the same oxygen bottle as the model 1914 *Draeger*, with a capacity of 400cm^3, but it had several valves so that the wearer could inhale directly from the air bag and exhale through the filter. It was also easier to install and replace the filter, without the need for a tool as it could be unscrewed by hand. The pipes, which went to the air bag, were attached in the same way as on the *Draeger* model 1914 and the bag could easily be removed and replaced. Instead of being mounted underneath the device, the bag was now positioned at the rear. A new mouthpiece appeared in 1918, which allowed for use of either the mask or the oral nozzle.

***Magirus Sauerstoffapparat für Pioniere*, Model 1916**

With the *Magirus Sauerstoffapparat für Pioniere*, model 1916, the oxygen supply was carried on the back using special replaceable cartridges (*Patrone*). Each cartridge provided a guaranteed protection for 60 minutes. According to the instruction label of the *Patrone*, new cartridges had to be ordered from the firm *C.D.Magirus A.G.* in *Ulm a.D.*, because other types of cartridges were not compatible with the respirator. The large facemask had two rectangular lenses, which could be opened individually. Two tubes connected the mask with the oxygen supply.

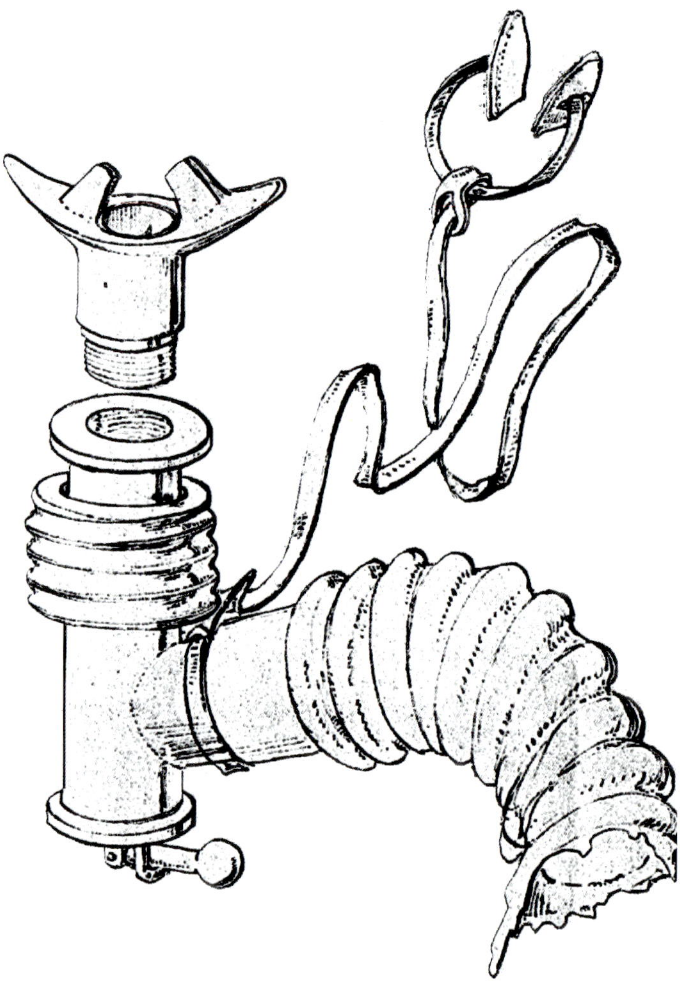

The *Modified Draeger Tubben model 1914* had several valves so that the wearer could inhale directly from the air bag and exhale through the filter. *Courtesy of Arnaud Lejaille.*

Magirus Sauerstoffapparat Patrone. Royal Army and Military History Museum, Brussels.

Magirus Sauerstoffapparat for pioneers model 1916. *Royal Army and Military History Museum, Brussels.*

Draeger HSS (Heeres Sauerstoff Schutzapparat)

The *Draeger Heeres Sauerstoff Schutzapparat* or HSC was a closed circuit respirator. It was an improved version of the *Draeger Tubben* model 1914 and a direct copy of the *Draeger* devices used in mines before 1910. The respirator could function for three hours during rest or one hour when working and was described by the French "*Services Chimiques*" in November 1916. It was also used on board Zeppelins.

To increase the comfort of the mask, the inhaled oxygen traveled from the air bag, passing through a valve, into the lungs, instead of passing through the soda filter cartridge. The volume of the soda cartridge and oxygen bottle was increased to allow for longer usage in contaminated environments. The entire set had a weight of 15.4 lbs (7kg) and was carried at the side. When the device was in operation, the oxygen bottle was open and when a button was pressed, the bag was filled with oxygen. Its mouthpiece was made larger and the flexible tube had an angle of 90 degrees. Like all German closed-circuit respirators, a manometer was available to verify the pressure.

Heeres Sauerstoff Schutzapparat. Royal Army and Military History Museum, Brussels.

L.A.S.A. model 1916 : Atem Schutz Apparat

The *L.A.S.A.* saw limited use, probably with flame-thrower pioneers. Not much information is known about this device.

Atem Schutz Apparat model 1916. Royal Army and Military History Museum, Brussels.

Side view of the *L.A.S.A.* The respirator cylinder is worn at the left. A tube connects the facemask with the cylinder. Another tube comes out of the cylinder, goes around the body and ends in a white metal horn. *Royal Army and Military History Museum, Brussels.*

Close up of the respirator canister. *Royal Army and Military History Museum, Brussels.*

Close up of the mask tube. *Royal Army and Military History Museum, Brussels.*

Gas Mask Protection

Gas attacks were either launched with gas grenades containing a liquid filling fired from artillery or mortars (*Minenwerfer*). Gas could also be released from cylinders, often using pipes laid as close as possible to the enemy, or launched with gas projectors (*Gaswerfer*). The *Gaswerfer* consisted of a steel tube of approximately 40" (102cm) in length. Sometimes as many as 1000 projectors were set side by side on wooden frames and all fired at the same time using an electrical ignition charge. The 66 lb bombs contained either a liquid or solid filling. During the war, two new pioneer regiments were raised who specialized in the offensive use of gas clouds and gas projectors, the 35th and 36th Pioneer Regiments, each consisting of two battalions with 3 companies and a park company. Each company handled approximately 6000 gas cylinders and 1000 gas projectors.[7]

Gasses were either lethal like phosgene, chlorine and diphosgene or were irritants. The purpose of the latter was aimed to create confusion and panic, to incapacitate the troops, by causing the eyes to water, blistering, sneezing, inflammation of the nose and throat, etc. although breathing large concentrations could be fatal as well. Apart from the two categories above, mustard gas (also called 'yellow cross' or *Yperite*) took a special deathly place. Mustard gas (*Dichlorethylsuplhide)* was actually a liquid and used for the first time in 1917. This chemical would not only attack the respiratory system, but also all exposed parts of the skin, resulting in severe injuries. A gas mask alone would never be able to provide 100% protection. At least six types of artillery shells were in use during 1917 with different contents, which were 'Green cross', 'Green cross 1', 'Green cross 2', 'Blue cross', 'Yellow cross' and 'Yellow cross 2' which was filled with mustard gas. These shells were usually brought to the artillery battery just before the attack started.

Gas artillery shell chemical agent bursting bottle: Sometimes issued in slightly different sizes depending on the caliber of the shell. The bottle was made from translucent green mold-pressed glass, had a glass cap and contained an egg white to a brown yellow fluid (Diphenyl-chlorarsine gas – an irritant of eyes, nose and chest introduced in 1917 and which smelt like shoe polish). The bottles were loaded into shells marked with a blue cross and for example fired with 7.7 cm calibre guns. When the projectile exploded, the glass bottle was shattered and the fluid vaporized. *Author's early collection.*

Gas signal horn with British capture tag. Manufactured from brass and galvanized sheet steel it was made by *Deutsche Signalinstrumenten Fabriken, Mark Neukirchen. Courtesy of Brian Ludwig.*

The severe threat of chemical warfare and resulting injuries demanded proper protection for the troops. The first real protection was introduced in 1915 and improvements continued until the end of the war. These were:

1915: Impregnated mouth pad, introduced on April 22nd, 1915
1915: Face masks
1915: Gummimaske - type 1 Gasschutzmaske 1915 or Linienmaske
1915: Gummimakse - type 2 Bandmaske
1916: Gummimaske - type 3 Rahmenmask
1917: Gummimaske - type 4
1917: Ledermaske (Lederschutzmaske, Gasmaske 17)
1918: Gasmaske 18

Impregnated Mouth Pad (bandages), introduced for the *Ypres* poison gas attack of April 22nd 1915.

The German army launched the first gas attack on the Eastern front on January 3rd, 1915 and later on the Western front on April 22nd, 1915 at the village of *Langemarck* near *Ypres*. In order to protect their own troops, who followed the greenish-brown toxic cloud of chlorine gas, the first primitive protection was provided by means of small rectangular 3.5" (9cm) by 5.5" (14cm) impregnated mouth pads, of which 20,000 were produced locally in Ghent, Belgium. These were little more than gauze bandages with ties, filled with cotton and moistened with a solution of *Hyposulfite*, which absorbed the chlorine, carried in a bottle and reapplied when necessary. The bandages were worn in 4" (10cm) by 5.9" (15cm) cloth waterproof rubberized pouches, which were mostly worn on the left shoulder.[8] Separate goggles were worn with this type of mask.

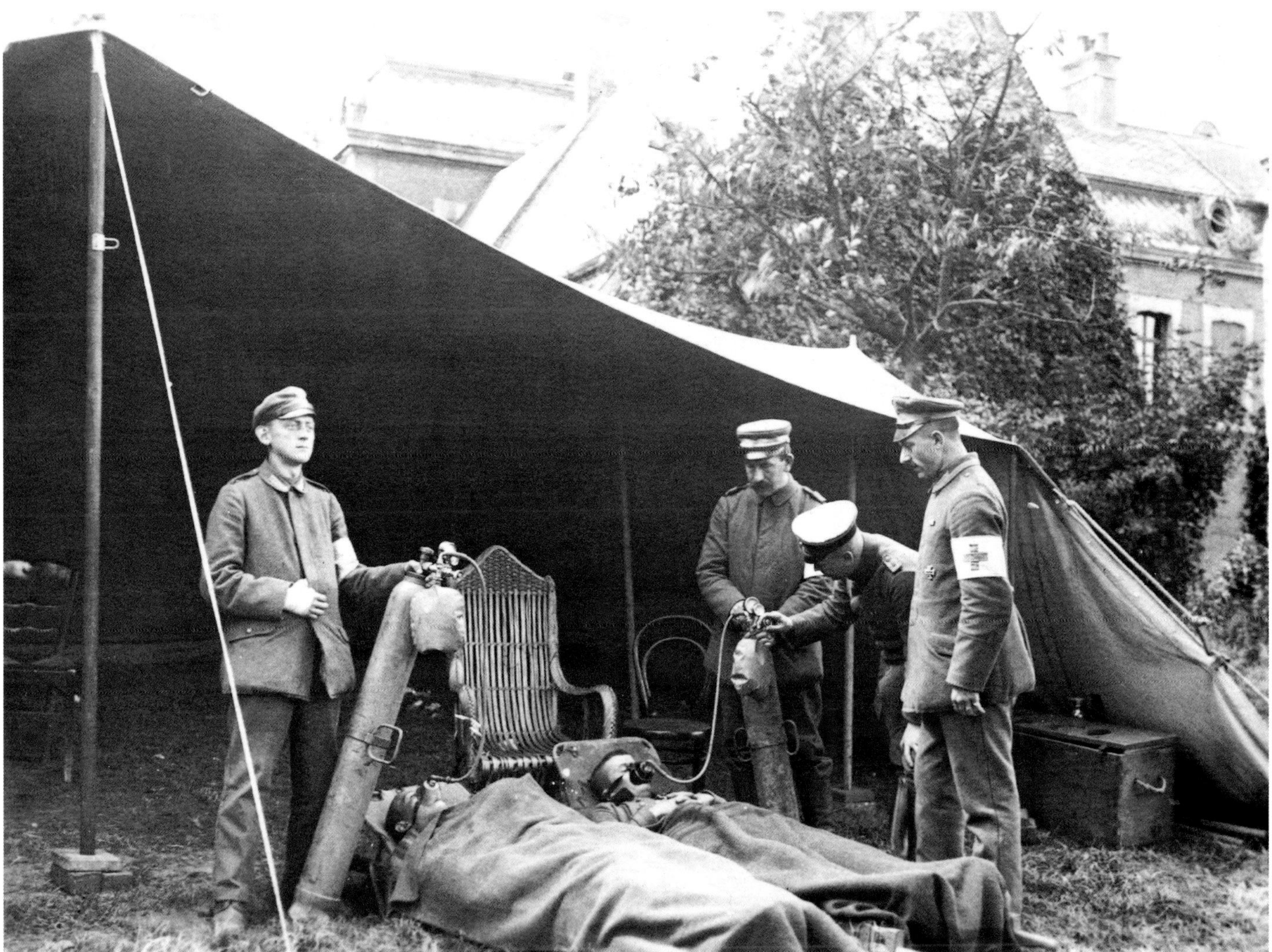

Poison gas victims receive initial oxygen treatment behind the front line. *Courtesy of BT.*

This is a group from the 74th *Landwehr* Regiment, 9th Co. 3rd Bn with the first type gas tampon masks, stored in cloth waterproof rubberized pouches. The photo is dated August 1915. *Courtesy of Faris Siwadi*

Fabric goggles for use with the early tampon gas mask and their 1915-dated case with straps for attachment to tunic buttons and shoulder straps. *Courtesy of Brian Ludwig.*

Goggles case.

Gas mask tampon as issued in 1915. It provided very limited protection. *Courtesy of Stephen Chambers.*

Gas mask tampon. The pouch is a rather unusual model not often seen. *Courtesy of Stephen Chambers.*

Improved Mouth Pad

At least three different types of mouth pads were introduced in 1915, each better performing than the previous model. The new mask covered the mouth and nose. A neutralizing liquid was carried in a separate glass bottle, and applied before use. Because some space existed between the mask and the nose and mouth, the entire impregnated surface was used to filter the air. The respirator only provided protection against small concentrations of chlorine.

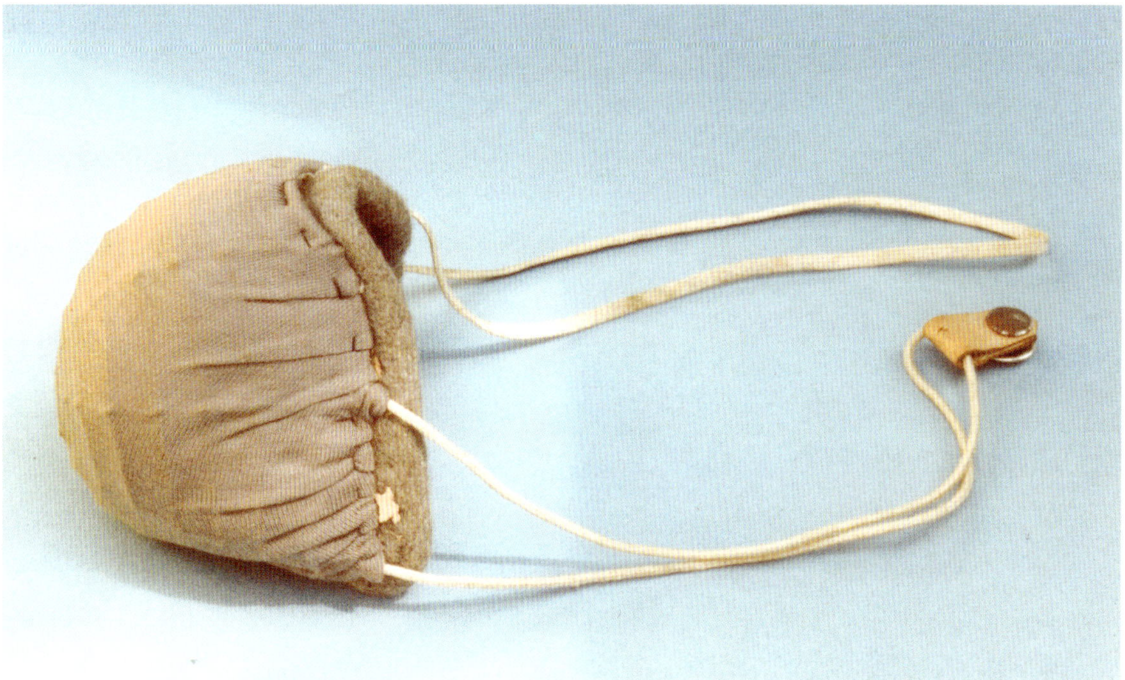

Courtesy of Arnaud Lejaille.

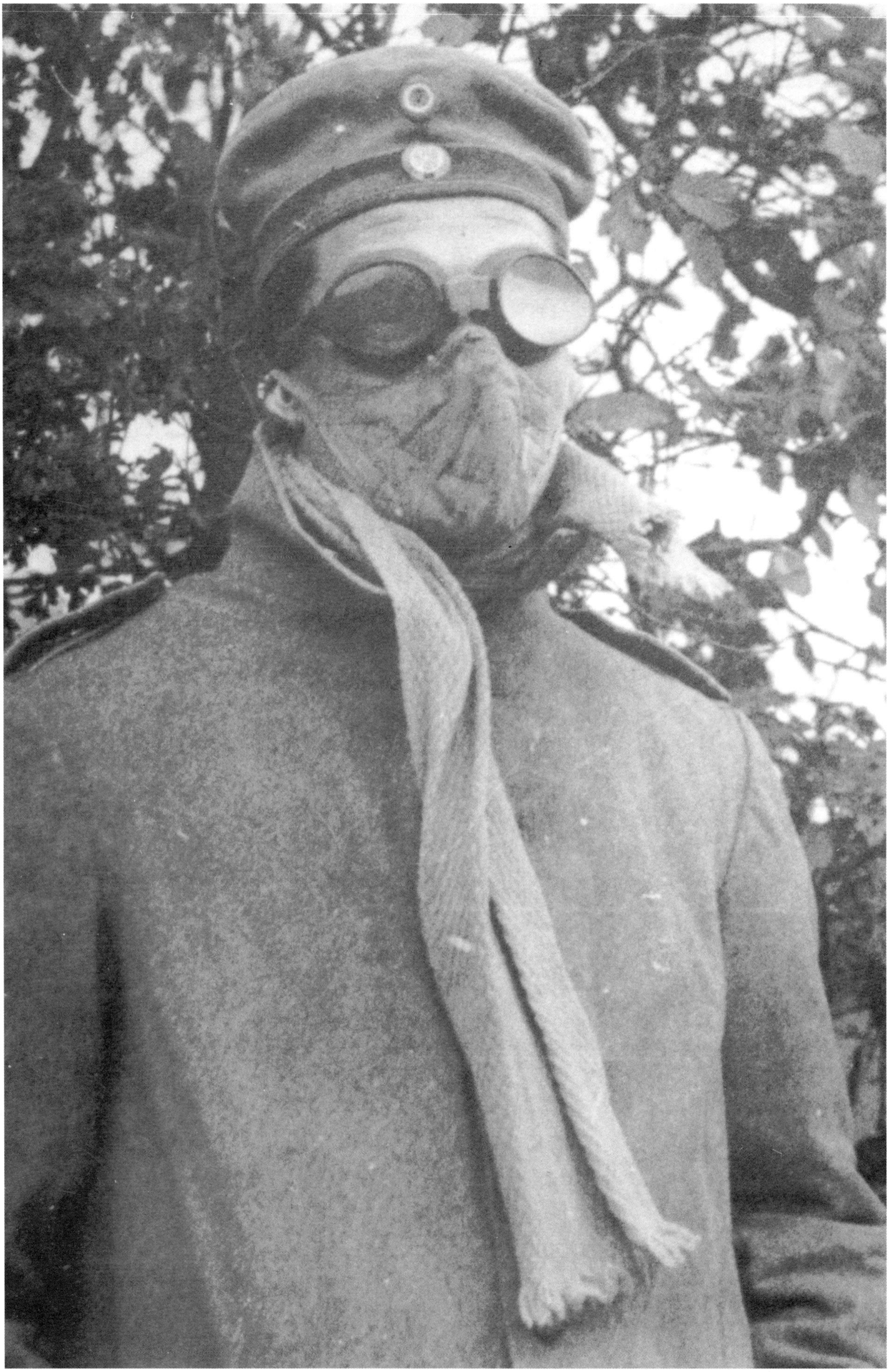

Soldier wearing an impregnated mouth pad. *Courtesy of Arnaud Lejaille.*

Gummimaske (Gasschutzmaske 1915, Linienmaske, Bandmaske, Rahmenmaske)

The *Gummimaske* was introduced during 1915. These respirators had a rubberized fabric face piece and a detachable filter. They were developed to protect the soldiers against the deadly chlorine gas and tearing agents such as *xylyl bromide*. The masks were not able to filter out the more deathly phosgene.

The mask was wide enough to allow the lenses to be cleaned with a finger when it was being worn. The two lenses were not reinforced with spiders – which were metal webbing frames that reinforced the lenses as seen on the later *Lederschutzmaske*. They were made from acetyl-cellulose, had a metal band around them and were fixed into the body of the mask. Breathing was possible only through the filter of the mask, which meant that no breath-outlet valve as on some of the allied masks was present.

The head harness was made of two elastic straps – each fixed to the front and back of masks body. A long 35.4" (90cm) strap was attached to the mask so that it could be worn around the neck in alert situations. The mask was manufactured in three different sizes, usually marked with the number 1, 2 or 3 on the outside surface. These masks were a real innovation at the time and the first complete protection with a mask body, goggles and a filter, which cleared the air through a chemical process. The first filters used in 1915 were the "*Einschichteneinsatz Modell 21/8*". Mask and filter protected against high concentrations of chlorine, but failed to protect against phosgene and mustard gas, which went directly through the rubberized material the mask was made of. Three changes were proposed to improve the *Gummimaske* until it was replaced by the leather gas mask in 1917. A first improvement in 1915 (*Type 2 - Bandmaske*) was very similar to the initial model, but it had an improved head harness and was better sealed against toxic gasses. The filter was modified so it could be swapped with a spare one during a gas attack.

A third Y-strap was added during 1916 and an improved filter (*Dreischichteneinsatz 1916 Modell 11/11*) appeared, which protected against phosgene as well. These filters were divided internally in three compartments and carried the markings 11-11 or 11-11-S. They lasted for 20 to 30 minutes before they had to be replaced. The *Gummimaske* was changed for the third time in 1916 (*Type 3 - Rahmenmaske 1916*), when the outside band around the mask was modified and made stronger. The bottom plate used to insert the filter was now much smaller. In addition, the mask was made smaller as well, so it fit the head more tightly and the air inside the mask reduced in volume. During 1917, cloth covered springs replaced the elastic straps (*Type 4*). Better performing filters appeared in 1917 and 1918.

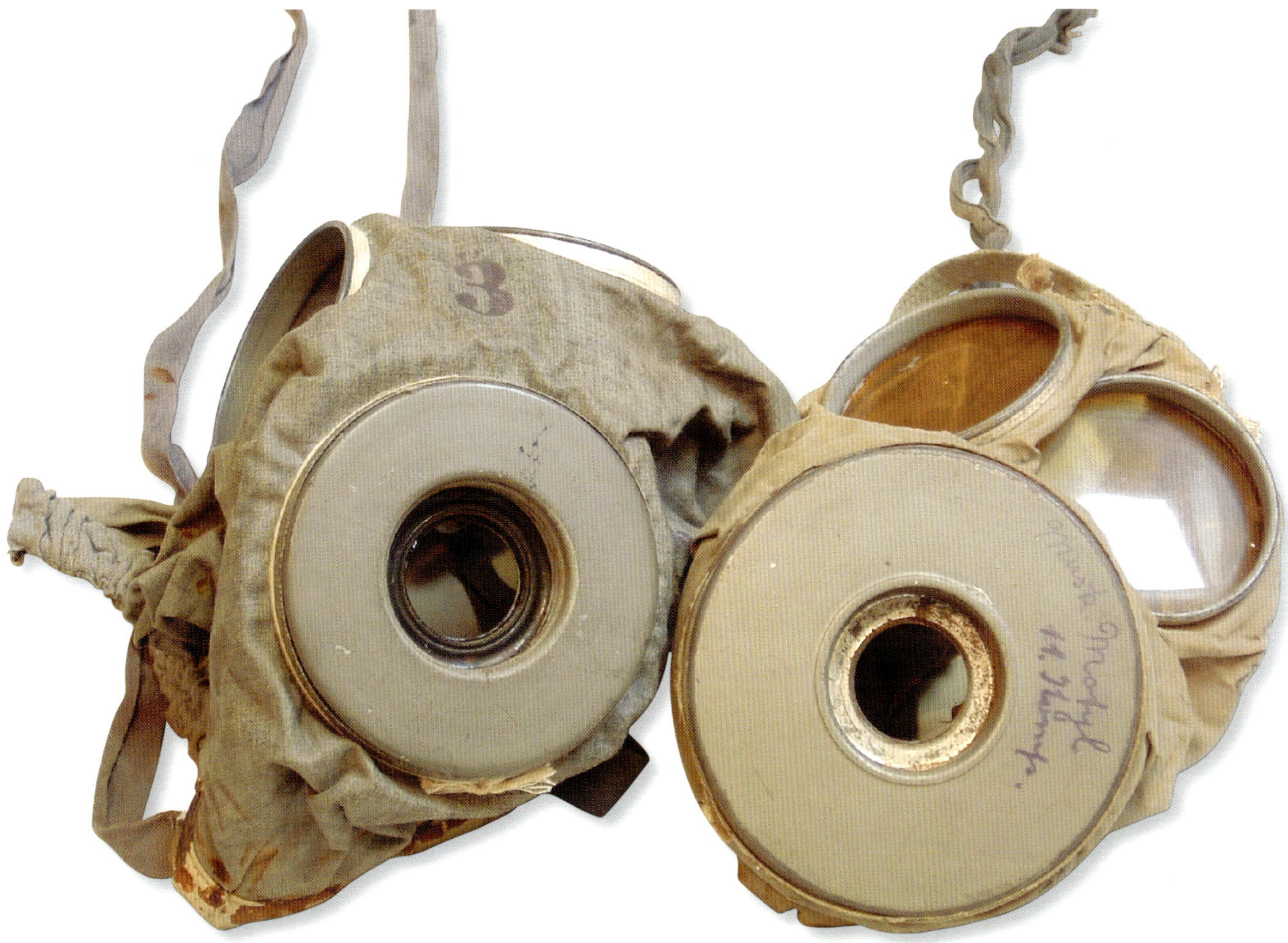

Two different masks with a different filter attachment base plate. The type 3 masks had a smaller diameter base plate. *Courtesy of Arnaud Lejaille.*

Gas mask drill with the *Gummimaske* at the Eastern Front.

An impressive photograph of a group of soldiers wearing the *Gummimaske*-type 1. They also wear gas protective hoods. *Courtesy of Faris Siwadi.*

This is a type 3 - "*Rahmenmaske 1916*". There were different mask sizes in use. A number on the front of the gas mask indicates the size, "2" in this case. The mask has the following markings on the outside: "*Draeger C.R. 138 2.17*". The small strap to fix the box to a tunic button can be seen on the photograph. The mask has the typical spring type Y- straps to fix the respirator on the head. Springs were introduced in 1917. *Courtesy of BT.*

Gas Mask Bag (*Segeltuchtasche*)

Initially, the mask was supplied without a bag or metal can and was stored away in the bread bag or in cans fabricated in the field.[9] Later in 1915, special bags were distributed for the *Gummimaske.* These grey cloth bags (*Segeltuchtasche 15)* had three compartments. The mask was stored in a tin can and put inside the canvas bag. A spare filter was stored in a smaller can and positioned next to the gasmask can and the third compartment contained another filter as well. The canvas bag had two canvas belt loops at the back and was worn at the hip. Both ends of the bag are stamped in black ink with the number 1, 2 or 3, corresponding to the three sizes of gas masks. During a gas attack, it proved very time consuming to open the bag and the cans for the mask and the filter, assemble the two parts together and then put the mask on the head. Therefore, larger cans (*Bereitschaftsbuchse neuen Munster*[10]) were issued as of 1916. These cans were larger in design and could contain the pre-assembled mask and filter canister. The mask and filter canister were protected by the can and stored away in a new pattern of canvas bag (*Segeltuchtasche 16*).

This bag was nearly the same as its predecessor, but had two instead of three compartments: One compartment contained the can and the second compartment a smaller can with a spare filter

Segeltuchtasche containing a size 2 filter, next to a marine bread bag and late war water bottle. The smaller compartment can be found on either the right or more generally at the left side of the bag. Most bags had two canvas belt loops or sometimes two "D" rings at the rear for attaching a bread bag strap as a sling.[12] *Courtesy of Domein Raversijde -Ostend.*

Lacquered tinned steel canister for the spare gas mask filter. The canister has a corrugated cardboard liner and the un-used filter retains its paper seal and a lacquered screw cap. *Courtesy of Brian Ludwig.*

Members of the 149th Infantry Regiment commemorate around a picture of a fallen comrade during March 1916. The soldier on the right wears a *Segeltuchtasche. Courtesy of Stephen Chambers.*

canister (*Ersatzeinsatz*). Existing three compartment bags were sometimes modified by cutting away one of the compartments, so the larger can, could be stored in these bags as well. The *Segeltuchtasche 16* was made a bit longer in 1917 to accommodate the 0.8" (2cm) larger can of the new leather gas mask. All sorts of canvas materials were used to construct the bags, going from thin to a thick stiff canvas. The color of the cloth was a shade of grey, but examples have been observed in a reddish color, similar to, but darker than the red/brown of the earlier shelter half and bread bag materials.[11]

Stofftasche für Atemeinsatz 1917

Later in the war, enlisted men carried an extra respirator cartridge in a small cloth bag, attached on the belt. "The spare filter canister compartment of the bag was meant to carry the filter in its original issue tin can. This lacquered tin can was cardboard lined and sealed with adhesive tape. The spare filter was factory sealed to keep out dirt and moisture. There was a tin screw cap on the mask end and a brown paper seal with a metal pull-tab on the other end."[13]

The filter canister above still contains a small metal cover to close the cartridge. A carbon plate is covering the large filter. The metal ring and cardboard contain the letters: "RF". The filter is of the 11-C-11 type and dated May, 5th 1918 followed by XIX. *Courtesy of BT.*

Leather Gas Mask Model 1917 (*Gasmaske 17*)

Due to material shortages and the poor protection of the *Gummimaske* against certain substances like phosgene, a new mask with a different design was introduced in June 1917.[14] It was made from inexpensive brown leather with black oilcloth edging and acetate eye lenses with metal "spider" reinforcements. The leather was made from dog skin or other animals that did not have sweat glands, i.e. without pores in the leather that gas could seep through. The leather was also impregnated with oil to prevent the gas from penetrating the mask.[15] (it was called *'Ledermaske 17'*, *'Lederschutzmaske'* or *'Gasmaske 17'*). Even after the introduction of the new mask, the *Gummimaske* remained in service. The new leather gasmask was less ergonomically than the *Gummimaske*. The lenses were set at an angle to the eyes, which made aiming the rifle more difficult. The mask also had an unpleasant odour.[16]

Apart from the material (leather), the new mask was designed differently compared with its predecessor.[17] The internal space of the mask was reduced, which made breathing much easier. When wearing the *Gummimaske*, the German soldier could clear the lenses by using one or more fingers inserted between the mask and his face. This was not possible any longer with the model 1917 mask. The two lenses were made from two separate layers. One layer – on the outside – was fixed onto the mask, using acetyl-cellulose, while the other one was removable and fixed with gelatin and cellulose on the inside of the mask. For reducing the weight of the filter on the mask-body, a small strap was fixed to the head harness, running from the filter over the nose to the main straps.

Leather Gas Mask Model 1918 (*Gasmaske 18*)

The leather mask was improved in 1918. A couple of months before the end of the war[18], the *Gasmaske 18* were introduced. Very similar to the model 1917, it had several improvements. The best way to recognize this model is because of the lack of the 'spider' behind the lenses. The mask had two improved head straps running horizontally around the rear of the head.[19]

This is a "*Gasmaske 17*" with an 11-C-11 filter canister. The mask is marked "*A.G.11 8*" and the name of the owner is written onto the mask: "*Lüdwig Becks*". Height: 6.7" (17cm), diameter: 4.7" (12cm). This filter is marked: "*326*" (in red numbers) and "*B.13. Marz 18 11-C-11*". *Courtesy of BT.*

Close up of the inside of a *Ledermaske* (*Gasmaske 17*) with the typical spider reinforcement in front of the lenses. The spiders were removed on the improved *Gasmaske 18*.

Gas Mask Cans (*Bereitschaftsbüchsen*)

Initially, cans fabricated in the field were made from tin ration cans and other scrap containers and were worn on the chest suspended by a string around the neck. It is surmised by *Dr. Fuchs* in his 1930 article for *Zeitschrift fur Heereskunde*, that these makeshift carriers were the prototypes for the official gas mask carrying cans.[20]

This photograph shows an example of one of these early field-fabricated cans. It was made from two cans, the lower portion being the shipping can that the filter canister came in. This can was attached to the larger upper section, which held the cloth portion of the mask. *Courtesy of Arnaud Lejaille.*

Early gas mask can. *Courtesy of Eric Siegel.*

This soldier wears a simplified model 1915 *Waffenrock* and is holding a British grenade. A bread bag is slung around his shoulder. Of interest is the early pattern gas mask can. *Courtesy of Stephen Chambers.*

Part of a trench section with a Trench mortar in action. An early gas mask in its can at the ready. *Courtesy of Stephen Chambers.*

The soldier is the middle wears an early fabric gas mask can used to store the *Gummimaske*, while the soldier at the far right is already equipped with a large gas mask bag. *Courtesy of Stephen Chambers.*

Two different metal cans were issued for either the *Gummimaske* in 1915 or the *Ledermaske* in 1917. The most obvious difference between the two patterns is the height. The can for the 1917/1918 *Lederschutzmaske* (*Bereitschaftsbüchsen*) was 0.8" (2cm) higher than the can for the 1915 *Gummimaske* (*Bereitschaftsbuchse neuen Munster*). In addition, the 1917 can contained a small compartment in the lid for a spare set of lenses and contained an instruction sheet at the bottom explaining how to use the gas mask. Apart from metal, ersatz materials were used as well in the production of gas mask cans. The author has seen a model 1917 pattern can with a wooden field-grey painted body and a metal lid. It's design and appearance was almost identical to the metal version.

The gas mask can for the1917/1918 *Lederschutzmaske* was 0.8" (2cm) higher than the can for the 1915 *Gummimaske*. The latter had a height of 5.9" (15cm) and a diameter of 14.5" (1.5cm), while the 1917 model used for the *Lederschützmaske* was 6.7" (17cm) in height. Left is a model 1917 can and right a model 1915 can. The "*Bereitschaftsbuchse neuen Munster*" model 1915 can was introduced for the *Gummimaske*. The black paint at the inside and the white markings are typical for this type of can. The crossed metal bars in the lid, kept the mask firmly in place. Often, one can find the name of the owner in white paint on the exterior of the can. *Courtesy of Arnaud Lejaille.*

Period photograph of the adapted MG gas mask can in use. *Courtesy of Sven Kuczyk.*

The gas mask can with long straps proved to be very cumbersome for Machine Gun units and existing cans were modified. They were made a bit shorter and could be attached to the belt. This example has a height of 4.6" (12cm). *Courtesy of Sven Kuczyk.*

Instruction sheet for the *Bereitschaftsbüchsen* found inside the model 1917 can. *"Verify if the filter is properly screwed into the mask and if the lenses are secured. Hang the mask with filter around the neck. Take the mask straps with both hands and put the chin deep into the mask. Pull the straps over and behind the head, as far as possible". Courtesy of BT.*

Two sets of spare lenses carried inside the lid of the model 1917 can.

Ersatz gas mask can with a wooden body. *Courtesy of Eric Siegel.*

Drivers or Pilot's Gas Mask (*R.Z. Mundstück*)

A simple gas mask (*R.Z. Mundstück*) was introduced for vehicle drivers and pilots. The mask allowed for better all round vision, but was also used to protect soldiers with head wounds and who could not wear the normal *Gummimaske* or *Ledermaske*. It consisted of a normal gas mask filter canister screwed into a flexible 2.8" (7cm) long tube, which had a diameter of 1.6" (4cm). At the end of the tube were a mouthpiece and a small clip to put over the nose so one could only inhale through the mouthpiece. This mouthpiece was closed with a wooden peg when the mask was stored in the gas mask can, which had different dimensions to the normal gas mask cans issued in 1915 and 1917. It was higher (9.6" - 24.5cm) with a smaller diameter (4" - 10cm) and worn around the neck with a canvas strap and attached to a tunic button with a small strap. Goggles were worn in conjunction with the mask. The *R.Z. Mundstück* on the following photograph is dated 26.4.1917 on the mouthpiece and still has the original wooden peg attached to the tube with a small piece of string. An adjustable canvas strap is attached to the tube, so the mask could be slung around the neck.

Can for the driver's gas mask. *Courtesy of BT.*

A small flexible tube is connected with a normal gas mask filter.

Goggles for use with the driver's gas mask. Manufacturer unknown, although the metal adjusting clip is marked with the *Siemens & Halske* logo. *Siemens & Halske* also made 08/15 machine guns and communications equipment. *Courtesy of Brian Ludwig.*

Brown ersatz vulcanized fiber and leather belt carrying case for the driver's gas mask goggles. Manufactured by *A. Ditmar*, Berlin. *Courtesy of Brian Ludwig.*

Gas Mask for Persons with Head Wounds
(*Gasschutzhaube für kopfverletzte*)

The *Gasschutzhaube für kopfverletzte* was issued during the last year of the war and replaced the *R.Z. Mundstück* to protect soldiers with head wounds during a gas attack. The body of the mask was made from leather, the same material as used for the leather gas mask issued in 1917. The lenses are the same as for the leather gas mask, but padded on the interior with a double protective layer, which rested against the eye-sockets to prevent new or extended injuries by using the mask. The inside of the mask contains a metal cylindrical piece with small holes. It prevented the opening of the filter from becoming obstructed so the wounded soldier would be able to breathe properly. A piece of grey flannel was attached to the inside rear of the mask to avoid irritation of the neck area where a strap adjusted the mask to the head. The filter plate is slightly smaller in diameter to those of the leather gas mask. The respirator was usually carried in a field-grey painted rectangular metal box, marked in large letters "*Gasschutzhaube für kopfverletzte*" and a red cross.

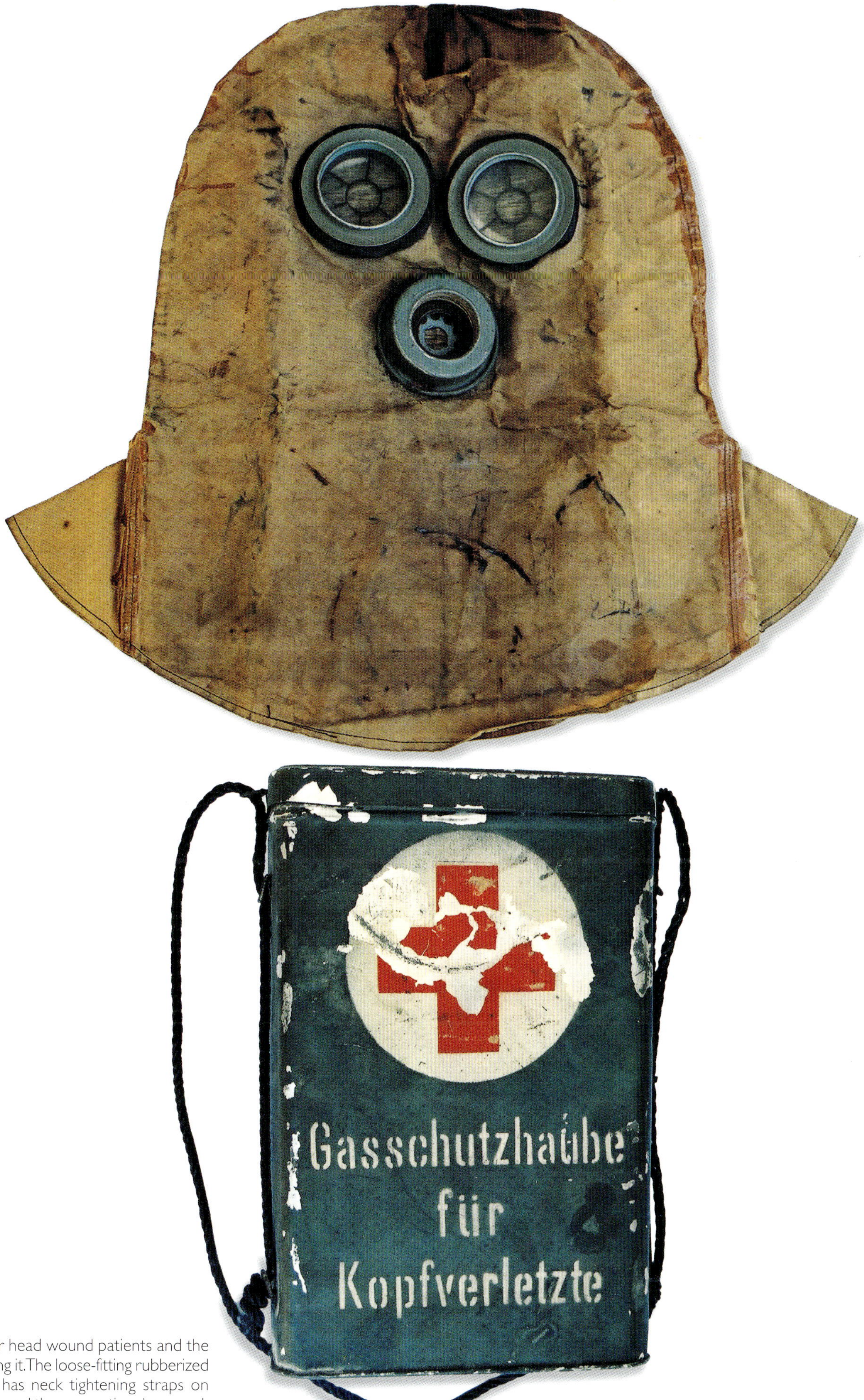

Gas mask for head wound patients and the box containing it. The loose-fitting rubberized fabric hood has neck tightening straps on the rear and used the conventional gas mask filter. *Courtesy of Brian Ludwig.*

Gas Mask Filters

In April 1915, the German chemist *Fritz Haber* requested several private companies to start developing a device to protect the individual soldiers against poison gas. The *Kaiser Wilhelm Institut* improved the chemical substances in the filter before it was being used. A replaceable filter had a major advantage. The capabilities of the mask could be adapted quickly by just improving the content and quality of the filters, without changing the mask body itself. During the war, several types of filters were thus developed. (source: *Arnauld Lejaille*)

Single Layer Filter (September to October 1915)

The first filter was made of a metal truncated canister with a diameter of 4" (10cm) at the top and 3.5" (9cm) at the bottom. The total height was 1.7" (4.3cm). The canister was filled with a filtering composition, separated at the bottom with a metallic wire netting and held in the canister by gauze and a disc fixed into a notch. The chemicals used had a weight of 180 gram and composed of 30% small fragments of porous pumice surrounded by 10.7% very fine charcoal, moistened with hyposulphite and soda carbonate. These filters only protected against chlorine and did not protect the wearer against phosgene and tear gas. These filters were probably issued during September 1915.

The French Army used several types of gas masks. The successful M2 gas mask provided similar protection compared with the *Gummimaske* and was issued from 1916 to 1918. However, because the mask had no removable filter, it was not possible to continuously improve its capabilities as the war progressed. *Courtesy of BT.*

Single Layer Model 1915 (*Einschichteneinsatz Modell 21/8*)

The next generation of filters followed quickly, as described by a French report of October 29th 1915.[21] The new filter required a change in the design of the mask body. The circular bottom plate of the facial mask now had a diameter of 4" (10cm) with a female screw thread in the middle for the filter canister. This system allowed the filter to be changed whilst under attack, and to keep the respirator in position whilst sealing the filter opening with a hand. The new filter was made of a truncated metal canister with a diameter of 37.4" (9.5cm) at the top and 3.1" (8cm) at the bottom. The total height was now 2" (5cm). The upper part had a screw with a diameter of 1.6" (4cm). The bottom part was closed with metallic gauze, which was protected with an iron grill held into position with crossed tin plates (see photograph). The content of the filter was changed as well. The hyposulphite and soda carbonate were replaced with 21% carbonate of potash. This mixture ensured an average protection against chlorine, but was still vulnerable to phosgene and tear particles.

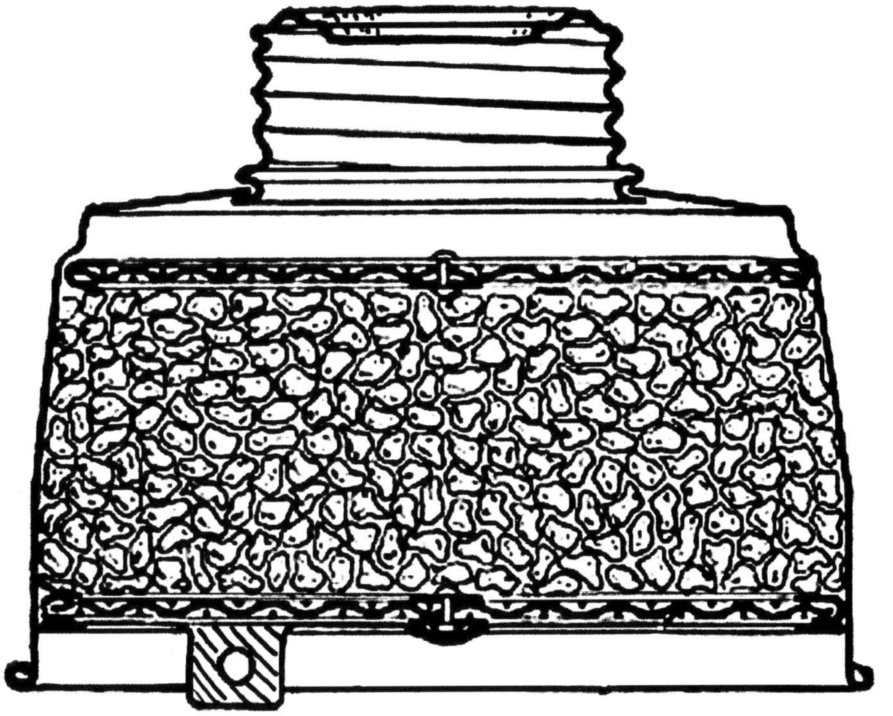

Single layer model 1915 (*Einschichteneinsatz Modell 21/8*) filter. *Courtesy of Arnaud Lejaille.*

Triple Layer Model 11-11 - Type 1 (*Dreischichteneinsatz*)

The initial filters provided only very limited protection. In addition, several new developments allowed for the creation of better performing filters by the end of November 1915. A new filter was constructed, containing three layers of different chemical products. Each layer was separated using thin metallic gauze and one or two sheets of muslin. At the bottom, the metallic gauze was replaced with a perforated tin plate. The first compartment (at the top) contained approximately 26 gram of pumice treated with *Utropine* (hexamethylene tÉtramine) in an attempt to neutralize phosgene. The second compartment in the middle contained 125-grams of fragments of granulated charcoal. This layer assured the neutralization of tear particles.

Finally, the last compartment at the bottom was filled with approximately 85 gram of pumice covered with a light coating of coal powder. Everything is soaked with carbonate of potash. The filters were adopted as of January 1916.

Triple layer model 11/11 - Type 1 (*Dreischichteneinsatz*). *Courtesy of Arnaud Lejaille.*

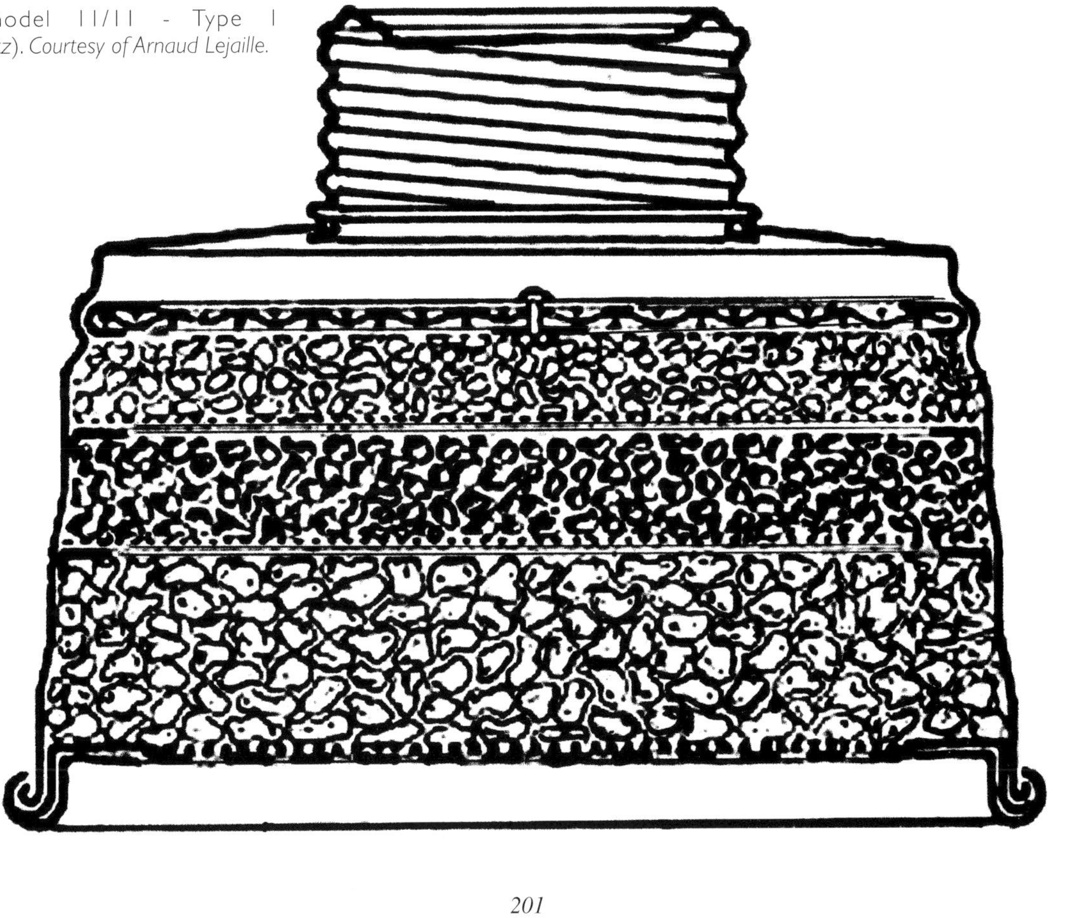

Above: Triple layer model 11/11 - Type 1 (*Dreischichteneinsatz*). Right: The metal grill was replaced with a perforated tin plate. *Courtesy of Arnaud Lejaille.*

Triple Layer Model 11-11 - Type 2 (*Dreischichteneinsatz*)
In December 1916, a new type of filter was made which could contain another 10 gram of chemical gas neutralizers. Moving the small grill to the top part of the filter, 0.2" (5mm) higher, achieved this. The construction of the filter body changed only slightly (see picture). The charcoal parts were much finer to reduce the resistance of the air going through the filter.

Some filters have a white letter "V", a "C" or a white cross. These are dated between February 1917 and April 1917. The meaning of these markings is still unknown. These filters have

Left: Some of the markings usually found on the filters: "11-11-S", date, manufactured identification stamped into the metal: "*9 AGD*". *Courtesy of Arnaud Lejaille.*

These photographs clearly show the minor differences between the two types of 11-11 filters. Left the 11-11 type 1, and right type 2. Markings observed on a type 2 11-11 filter are "*A3, B7*" followed by "*11-11*", ink marking "*Geprüft*" (after 05/17 ?), a date, a red and a black number indicated the lab number and the number of the series. *Courtesy of Arnaud Lejaille.*

red-brown painted shiny metallic gauzes between the different layers of the filter. From this time onwards, the filters always carry the following markings[22]:

The number of the laboratory in black ink.
The manufacturer, i.e.
AGFA, Bierdet, WO-B, Kahlbaum, GJB, B.
The date of manufacture.
The type of filter (*11-11, 11-C-11*).
A red number (meaning unknown).

Triple Layer Model 11-C-11 - 1917 (*Dreischichteneinsatz*)
The 11-C-11 appeared in May 1917, although some of the 11-11 Type 2 filters can have dates after May 1917 as well, so that it is assumed that old stocks of the 11-11 were used after the introduction of the 11-C-11 filters. The new filters were marked 11-C-11 in black ink. The exterior of the 11-C-11 was identical with the 11-11, but the content was changed by increasing the weight of the charcoal and to lower at the same time the amount of pumice, to provide better protection against tear gas and to reduce the resistance of the air passing through the filter.

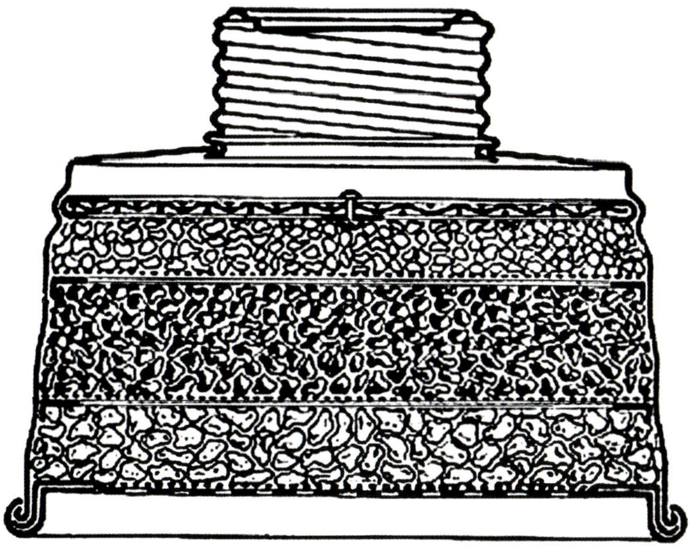

Triple layer model 11/C/11 – 1917 (*Dreischichteneinsatz*). *Courtesy of Arnaud Lejaille.*

Markings on a 11/C/11 filter. *Courtesy of Arnaud Lejaille.*

Markings on a 11/C/11 filter. *Courtesy of Arnaud Lejaille.*

Double Layer Model 1918 (*Sonntagseinsatzes*)

The model 1918 filters appeared during July 1918. They contained just two layers instead of three. The bottom layer of carbonate of potash was replaced with active coal. Zinc was also added to the composition.

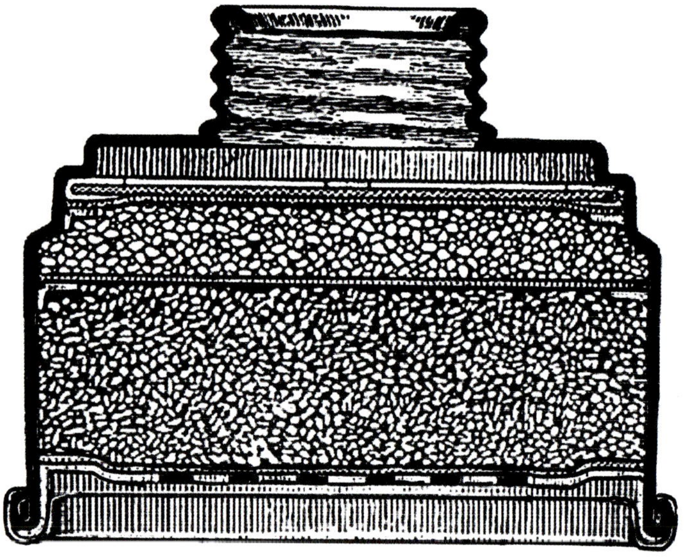

Double layer model 1918 (*Sonntagseinsatzes*). *Courtesy of Arnaud Lejaille.*

Double layer model 1918 (*Sonntagseinsatzes*). *Courtesy of Arnaud Lejaille.*

Filter Quality Control Machine (*Atemwiderstand Feldprüfer*)

The quality of the filters could be verified with a special machine introduced on October 25th, 1916. It was basically a wooden box with a lid opened by a hinge. The two sides each had an opening to insert the filter to be verified at one end and a standard filter, which worked correctly, at the other end. Two of these correctly working standard filters were supplied with each box and marked with a diagonal yellow arrow. In order to compare the pressure of the filter to be tested, a manometer operating with water was placed between the test filter and the standard filter. A pump forced air through the filters and the tester would look in which direction the water of the manometer went.

Filter quality control machine *(Atemwiderstand Feldprüfer). Royal Army and Military History Museum, Brussels.*

A period photograph with the filter quality control machine. *Courtesy of Arnaud Lejaille.*

Notes

[1] Correspondence with Eric Siegel.
[2] The German Army Handbook, 1918. p. 99.
[3] I would like to thank *Arnaud Lejaille* for writing these chapters.
[4] Source: *Arnaud Lejaille.*
[5] Based on a German document, translated by the French "*Services Chimiques Français*" in 1917.
[6] *Feld-Anweisung R Dräger-Tubben.*
[7] The German Army Handboek, p. 98
[8] Les masques à gaz allemandes, Yves Mouchet.
[9] J. Kraus, p. 356: the mask was supplied without a bag or metal can and was stored away in the bread bag or in fabricated cans in the field.
[10] J. Kraus: *Bereitschaftsbuchse neuen Munster* were issued in 1916.
[11] Correspondence with Chip Minx.
[12] Correspondence with Chip Minx.
[13] Correspondence with Chip Minx.
[14] Yes Mouchet, Militaria Magazine 220.
[15] Stephen Bull, page 87.
[16] Stephen Bull.
[17] See also "*La guerre des gaz 1915-1918*".
[18] J. Kraus, p 358: *Gasmaske* 18 was introduced: 29.9.1918.
[19] Yes Mouchet, Militaria Magazine 220.
[20] Chip Minx,
Kaiserzeit, Vol. XI, Number One, 1983, pp. 16-19.
[21] Report G.102 of Mr. Kling.
[22] According the "*Commission de Protection des Services Chimiques français*".

Chapter Six

Communication Equipment

Introduction

It is crucial that military commanders are well informed and can make good tactical and strategic decisions. It is therefore essential that messages and reports can be quickly and easily communicated between army formations, commanders and subordinates, even under difficult situations. Until the end of the 18th Century, communication relied on messengers on foot or on horses, but other means of communication emerged, like semaphores or message flags on ships. During the 19th Century, more advanced communication techniques were developed and railroads, telegraphs and radio signals started to be used. By the outbreak of the First World War, the German army had an impressive inventory of means to communicate messages or signals between troop formations. These were[1]:

Message pigeons *(Brieftaube, Meldebrieftauben)*
Message dogs *(Meldehunde, Kurierhunde)*
Optical signals *(Lichtsignale, Blinkgeräte, Winkzeichen* and *Fliegersichtzeigen)*
Smoke signal cartridges
Telephone *(Fernsprecher)*
Telegraph *(Telegraf)*
Wireless radio communication
Message grenade fired with a rocket launcher *(Nachrichtengeschosse)*
Light grenade *(Leuchtsignale)*
Acoustic signals *(Schallsignale* like *Signalhorn, Signalpfeife* and *Sirene)*
Human transportation of message (*Meldeläufer, Meldereiter, Meldefahrer, Meldekraftfahrer, Meldeflieger*)

In 1914, eight telegraph battalions *(Telegraphen-Bataillon)* and eight fortresses telegraph companies (*Festungs-Fernsprech-Kompanie*) existed. Three schools were used to train personnel. The telegraph troops wore a shako instead of a spiked helmet. In July 1917, a major reorganization was undertaken and the telegraph battalions were regrouped and renamed into *Nachrichtentruppen.* In addition, each infantry and artillery unit had its own communications (signaling) detachment, composed of lamp

Pigeon gas protection box. *Courtesy of Eric Siegel.*

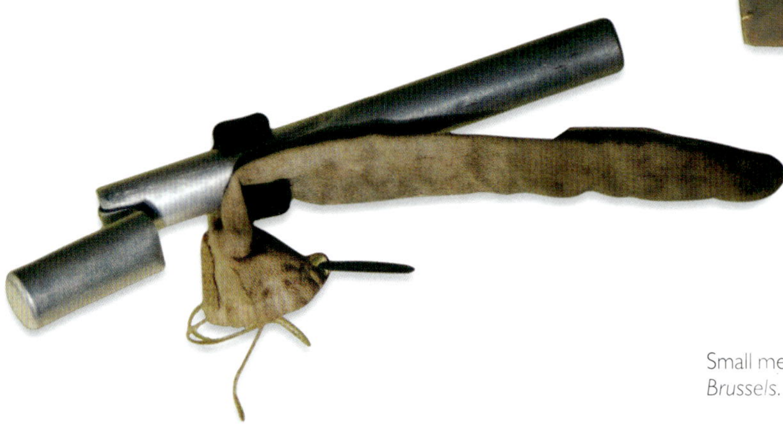

Small message container for pigeons. *Royal Army and Military History Museum, Brussels.*

signaling (*Blinkertruppen*) and telephone (*Fernsprechtruppe*) sections:

Telegraphen-Bataillon Nr.1 (Army Corps Garde)
Telegraphen-Bataillon Nr.2 (Army Corps III)
Telegraphen-Bataillon Nr.3 (Army Corps IX)
Telegraphen-Bataillon Nr.4 (Army Corps XIV)
Telegraphen-Bataillon Nr.5 (Army Corps XVII)
Telegraphen-Bataillon Nr.6 (Army Corps X)
Kgl. Sächs. Telegraphen-Bataillon Nr.7 (Army Corps XII)
Telegraphen-Bataillon Nr.8
Festungs-Fernsprech-Kompanie Nr.1
Festungs-Fernsprech-Kompanie Nr.2
Festungs-Fernsprech-Kompanie Nr.3
Festungs-Fernsprech-Kompanie Nr.4
Festungs-Fernsprech-Kompanie Nr.5
Festungs-Fernsprech-Kompanie Nr.6
Kgl. Sächs. Festungs-Fernsprech-Kompanie Nr.7
Festungs-Fernsprech-Kompanie Nr.8
Kriegstelegraphenschule
Funkerschule
Kavallerieschule-Telegraphenschule

Message Pigeons (*Brieftaube, Meldebrieftauben*)
War pigeons could transport a message over a distance of 800km. Messages were attached to the bird's collar in a waterproof container, in a roll attached to the back of the pigeon or fastened at the foot. They were especially useful on board ships or seaplanes, but also saw action in Europe, being deployed from the front line and returning back to movable pigeon lofts or houses that had been transformed and which served as the home base. Cavalrymen could transport pigeons using special pouches.[2] Two pigeons were thus carried on the chest and two at the back. According to an Internet source[3], many captured pigeons moved to the US after 1918. The most famous one was named the "*Kaiser*", a very intelligent bird born in 1917. He was trained for special missions and captured during the battle of the *Meuse* in 1918. He died at the age of 32.[4] It was reported that pigeons were often dyed in a distinctive army color to be easily recognized.[5]

Message Dogs (*Meldehunde, Kurierhunde*)
Dogs were used during the First World War by telecommunication and medical troops. They carried messages, drawings of enemy positions and orders between the troop formations using a message carrier harness or a message transportation tin cylinder around the neck (6" long and 1 1/2" in diameter). Using specialized carriers, it was possible to even transport message pigeons (*Brieftauben*) or to extend field cables to a distance of 500 meters.[6]

Message dogs could also perform missions at night, which was an advantage compared with pigeons. In addition, dogs could be trained in about a week to transport messages from one location to another, while pigeons needed at least a month to get familiar with a certain area.

Smoke Signal Cartridges
Smoke cartridges containing messages were dropped out of airplanes above friendly infantry positions. The smoke served to pinpoint the exact location of the cartridge, which could easily be found and collected by soldiers. The cartridge contained a message, drawing or report.

Flare Pistols (*Leuchtpistole*)[7]
Flares served a number of purposes during the war, for example illuminating the battlefield at night to assist the artillery in locating enemy targets. To accomplish this, the two soldiers responsible for operating the flare pistols (*Leuchtpistolenschützen*) had to work in close co-operation with the artillery observation officers (*Feuerleitenden Offizier*) and were usually positioned either side of the officer. Flare pistols also served as a method of communication to signal the commencement of artillery bombardments or infantry assaults. Various flare colors (yellow, white, green, and red) and star patterns (one, two, or three stars)

Flare pistol manufactured in German occupied *Lille*, Belgium. Crudely machined and fit parts attest to its late-war manufacture. *Courtesy of Brian Ludwig.*

"Kommandeur de Lille" details.
Courtesy of Brian Ludwig.

"Kommandeur de Lille" 1st type.
Courtesy of Eric Siegel.

"Kommandeur de Lille" 2nd type.
Courtesy of Eric Siegel.

could indicate an advance, retreat or other combat activities. Although mortar, *Granatenwerfer*, artillery and the *Signalwerfer* could deliver flares, smaller versions were commonly launched using pistols.

All Imperial German flare pistols used 26.5mm brass or cardboard cased flares (*Leuchtmunition*) made by a wide variety of military and private sector manufacturers. *Deutsche Waffen und Munition* and *Fabrik Bischweiler* were two of the more well known makers and the *Artillerie Werkstatt* in various cities made many of these flares. Brass cases sometimes had grooved or knurled bases so identification of flare colors or star patterns could be made by touch alone at night. Although *Granatenwerfer* or *Signalwerfer* could launch parachute flares, flares used with pistols consisted only of the more conventional colored star pattern varieties. A flare pistol cartridge (*Leuchtpatrone*) had a range of about 200 meters and illuminated an area with a diameter of 100 meters for 8 to 10 seconds. Even bad weather conditions or heavy rain would not reduce the efficiency of the cartridge significantly.

The flare pistol most frequently encountered today and seen in period photos is the "*Hebel*" model of 1894 with its distinctive barrel breaking level located underneath and forward of the trigger guard. The *Hebel* pistol is made entirely of blued steel with the exception of the wood slab grips. Typically, these are profusely marked with Imperial acceptance stamps, maker's names, and serial numbers which often appear on virtually every piece, including screw heads and interior parts.

The rugged *Hebel* pistol replaced the earlier *Druckknopf* pattern designed with a spur trigger and button-style barrel breaking mechanism mounted on the frame. The fine machining and somewhat delicate features of this pistol may have led to the development of the *Hebel* in later years. The *Druckknopf*, as was the *Hebel* pattern was made in steel but at least one example with a brass frame is known to exist.

As the war progressed, rough workmanship and expediency

Early pattern flare pistol with brass frame and spur trigger. Although complete with matching serial numbers, the brass trigger guard was a later addition designed to prevent accidental discharge. *Courtesy of Brian Ludwig.*

became the norm with much German field gear and flare pistols were no exception. The "*Kommandanteur Lille*" (referring to the mark stamped in the wood grip) pistol was manufactured under contract in the German-occupied Belgian city of *Lille*. Of late war manufacture, this extremely simple and crude pistol has rough finished slab grips, cast steel parts, and a minimum of machining. The barrel opens on a pivot and it is cocked by pulling out the knob at the breech.

Although several patterns of naval flare pistols were utilized on ships and U-boats, the all-bronze example here appears to have seen fairly extensive use in the trenches. Once it became clear that the German fleet was going to be bottled up in harbor for the duration of the war, heavy guns and a variety of gear was stripped from the vessels, including flare pistols. The author has seen a double-barrel U-boat version of this pistol marked to the 62nd Infantry Regiment.

Ersatz flare launcher for the standard 26.5mm cartridge. A strong flick of the wrist closes the breech and simultaneously strikes the flare primer against the built-in firing pin. *Courtesy of Brian Ludwig.*

This soldier of the 147th Infantry Regiment wears a grey overcoat with collar patches bearing a NCO stripe. He is equipped with a flashlight, binoculars and a *Hebel* flare pistol. *Courtesy of Stephen Chambers.*

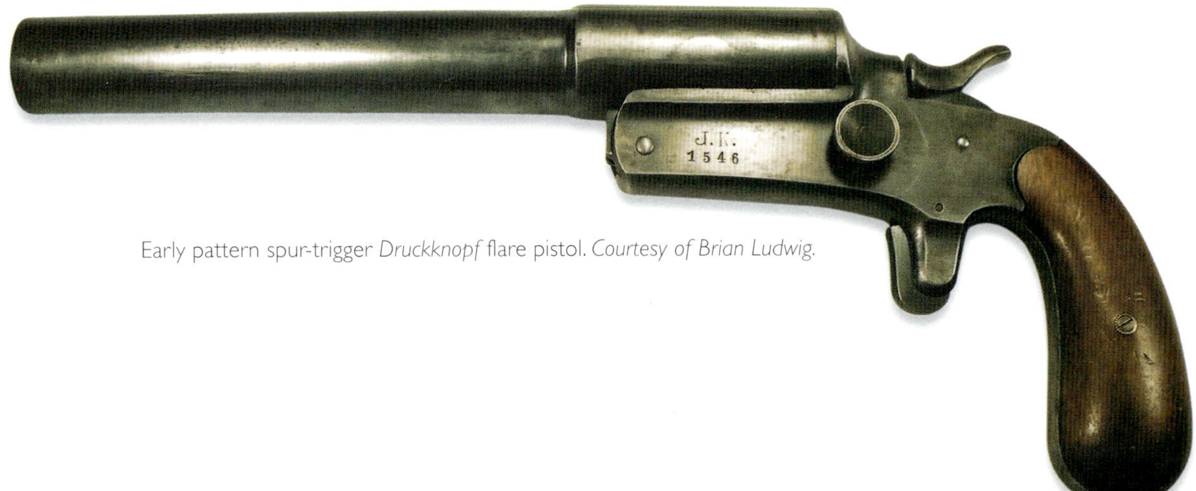

Early pattern spur-trigger *Druckknopf* flare pistol. *Courtesy of Brian Ludwig.*

On the brass *Druckknopf* flare pistol, the risks of an exposed spur trigger were apparently realized before this pistol was manufactured and a trigger guard was added. On this pistol, the trigger guard serial number matches the number of the gun, indicating it was factory installed and not added at a later date. *Courtesy of Brian Ludwig.*

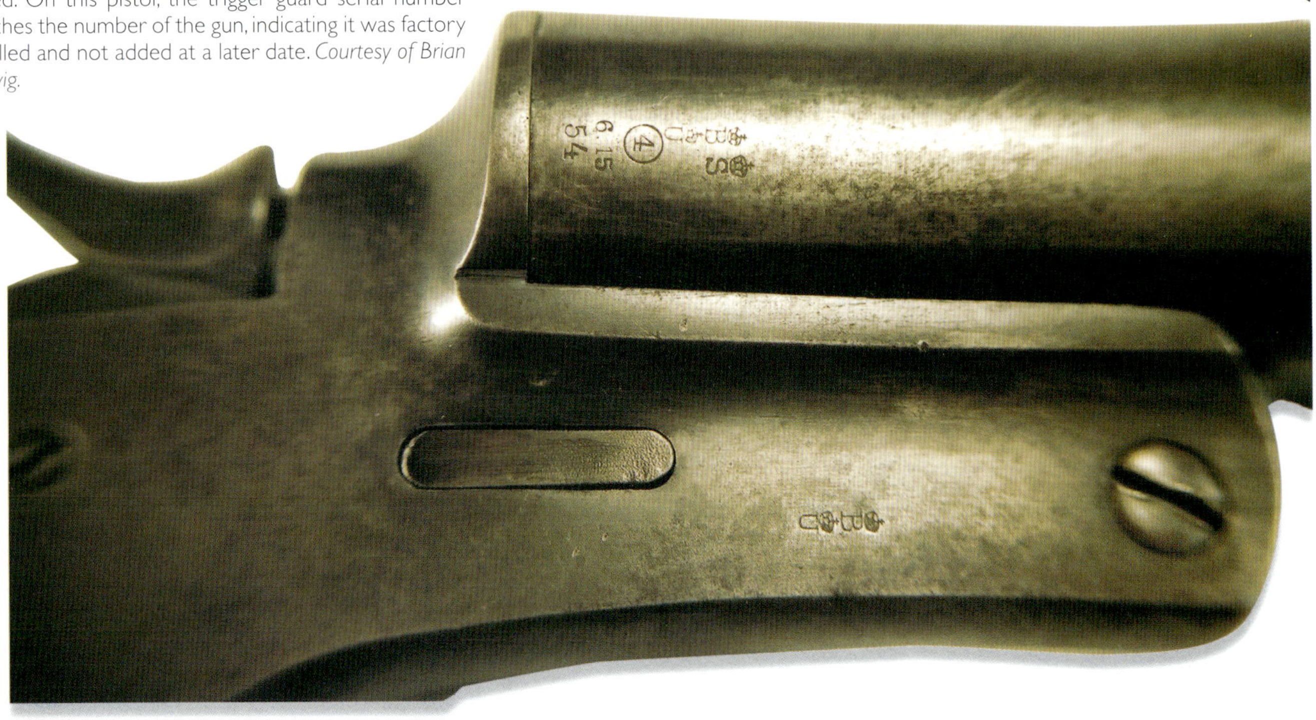

Model 1895 "*Hebel*" flare pistol manufactured in Germany by *Tesco* but with possible Austrian issue marks. *Courtesy of Brian Ludwig.*

TESCO.

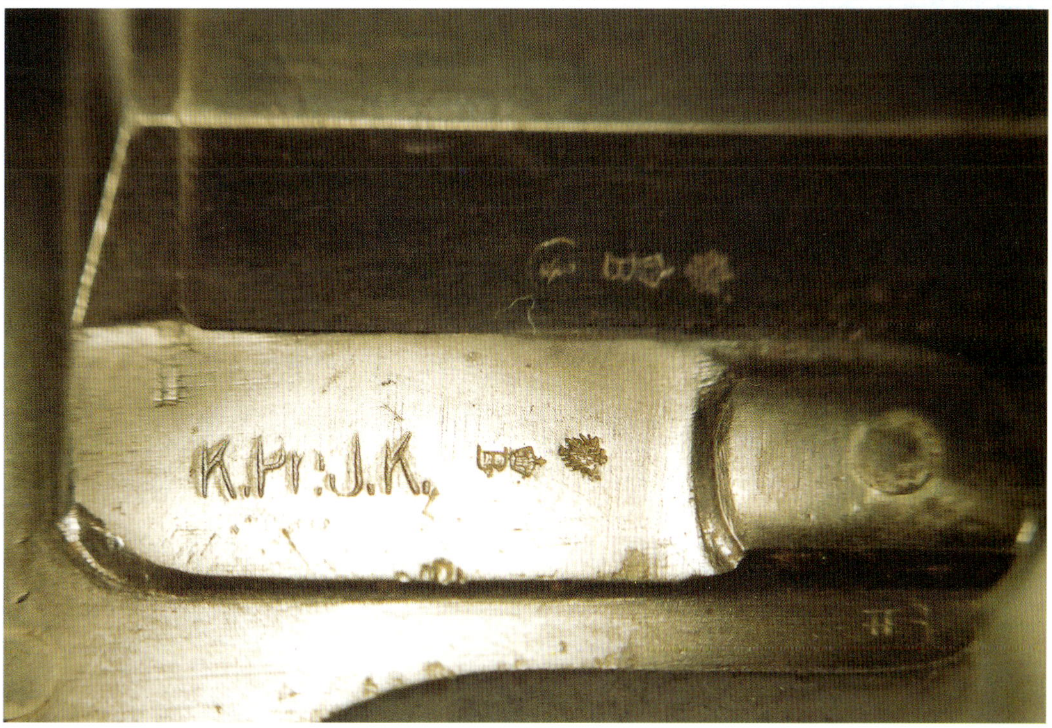

Hebel markings.

Copper marine flare pistol and cartridges. *Courtesy of Domein Raversijde -Ostend.*

Since the German naval fleet was confined to port for much of the war, many pieces of equipment were stripped from the ships and sent inland for the land war. A bronze flare pistol can be seen hanging on a bunker wall, above the officer's left shoulder, to the right of a bunch of trench knives. *Courtesy of Brian Ludwig.*

Date and unit markings.

Brass naval flare pistol marked to the *Werft zu Kiel* (Kiel dockyards) and dated 1914. This pistol was removed from naval use and transferred to a land unit. It is marked "O" on the back strap for *Hauptquartier-Armee* (Main Headquarters Army) or *Oberkommando einer Armee* (High Command of the Army). *Courtesy of Brian Ludwig.*

A small pouch was looped around the belt and contained five flare pistol cartridges. *Royal Army and Military History Museum, Brussels.*

Various 26.5mm flare cartridge cases. Left - brass, *Artillerie Werkstatt* group marked, 102mm overall length. Middle - brass, *Deutsche Waffen und Munitions* and ordnance marked, 82mm overall length. Right - cardboard and brass case, *WM Fabrik Bischweiler*, 79mm overall length. *Courtesy of Brian Ludwig.*

Optical Signals *(Lichtsignalgeräte, Blinkgeräte, Winkzeichen)*
A wide range of instruments were used to communicate with light signals. *Heliographs* reflected the sunlight using mirrors. These devices were useful in sunny deserts or in tropical locations, but only had limited use on the European front. A heliograph signaler had a dangerous job as well as he was exposed to sniper fire, especially when transmitting towards the frontline. All optical signals required a direct line of sight and were thus of very limited use during the conflict.

Semaphore flag signals (*Winkerflaggen*) were only used to a limited extent. During excellent weather conditions, flags signaling in Morse could be observed from a distance of 3 km with the naked eye or 5 km with binoculars, but visibility soon diminished when the weather was bad or when it became dark. Trained soldiers could transmit 12 words a minute, but the speed of transmission had to be adapted depending on visibility. An average of ten words in five minutes could be realized. A soldier trained to transmit flag

Goerz Heliograph. *Goerz Festschrift.*

signals (*Winkzeichen*) wore special insignia made of two crossed flags on the right upper sleeve. One NCO and two soldiers formed a flag signal section (*Winkertrupp*). All officers and NCOs were obliged to understand flag signals, including 6 soldiers per company and all musicians. The semaphore flags were in three colors, white, yellow and blue. Abbreviations were often used to indicate messages, which occurred frequently. These included among others:

a v	. - ...-	"*Vorgehen*" ("advance")
g v	- - . ...-	"*Eigenes Geschützfeuer weiter vor verlegen*" ("own gun fire should aim further")
h l	.... .-..	"*Halt*"("Stop")
m u	- - .. -	"*Munition erforderlich*" ("ammunition required", when this signal was send to second line positions)
m u	- - .. -	"*Munition kommt*" ("ammunition on its way", when this signal was send towards first line troops)

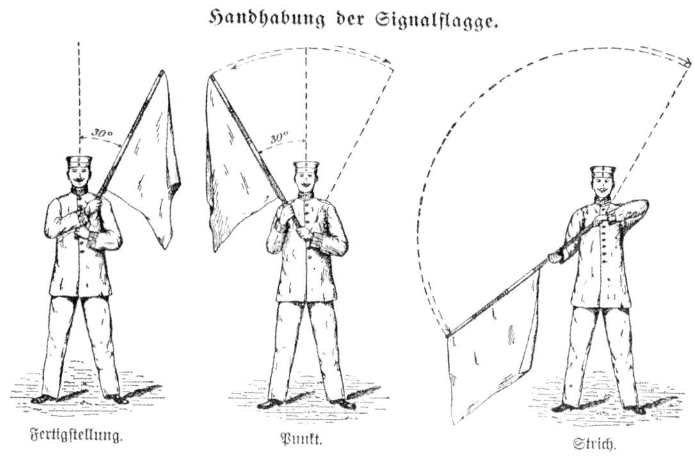

Use of signal flags for transmitting Morse signals. The first person is ready to start emitting a signal, the second person signals a 'dot' and the last soldier a 'dash'. *Reproduced from "Der Einjährige Freiwillige der Infanterie, Berlin 1916".*

The heliograph relied on direct sunlight and had a limited use and thus electrical and gas operating lamps (*Karbidlampen* or *Azetylensauerstofflampen*) were developed which could transmit Morse signals with short flashes (*Blinken*) of light. *Karbidlampen* were carbide signal lamps, manufactured for example by *KARL ZEISS* in Jena.[8] These lamps produced a gas using water and carbide. Carbide is made of limestone after burning it with coke in a specific process. When water is added an exothermic reaction starts, which produces acetylene gas, which burns very hot. Depending on the weather conditions, these signals had an impressive range of 50 km during the day and 100 km during the night.[9] Around 60 to 80 words could be transmitted in half an hour between two stations.[10]

Morse-Signalzeichen und Abkürzungen

für

Einübung und Gebrauch der Signalflaggen

zusammengestellt von

Schubert,

Major beim Stabe des Pionier-Bataillons von Rauch.

3. vervollständigte Auflage.

Josef Graveur's Verlag (G. Neumann.) Neisse.

Small postcard size 1914 semaphore signals instruction book, *"Morse-Signalzeichen und Abkürzungen für Einübung der Signalflaggen".*

Lampe 17 trench signal lamp with carrying case and instructions. The case lid retains the original paper label instructions and case contents and has space for the lamp, a spare battery, and three light bulbs. The lamp has one red lens, one green, and one white, each accompanied by individual blackout covers. The lamp and case are painted dark field-gray. Manufactured by *Elektromechanische Industrie, G.m.b.H.* Berlin. *Courtesy of Brian Ludwig.*

Elektromechanische Industrie
G.m.b.H. Berlin.

The box, light, and instruction sheet.

Open projector *Karl Zeiss*, a carbide signal lamp. *Courtesy of Eric Siegel.*

Closed lamp.

The electrical lamp *Blinkgerät* 1916, made by *Carl Zeiss* was used to transmit signals. The lamp was mounted on a wooden tripod. The blinker operated by means of two easy to transport wooden boxes, which were carried on horseback or on a bicycle. The first box was a dry battery, while the second one contained a hand driven generator, a voltage meter, a compartment to store the flash lamp and a compartment to store small metal boxes containing spare bulbs in various colors, like green or red. A small rectangular box with a push button was connected to the lamp and battery box and used to transmit flashes of light. The flash devices were issued in three sizes, large, medium and small with a range of 6.600, 3.300 and 900 yards.[11] *Courtesy Brian Ludwig.*

Complete *Lichtblinkgerät* unit manufactured by *Karl Zeiss*. The set includes a standard *Goerz* tripod, the generator/component storage case, generator handle, electric trigger, spare green and red bulbs, and an insert holding a pair of pliers, a screwdriver and a tin containing electrical tape. The backside of the case also has a shoulder-strap arrangement for field transport. The small spotting scopes were frequently removed from the mirror unit and turned into private-purchase, non-military monoculars after the war. These are, however, frequently interpreted as wartime pieces. *Courtesy of Brian Ludwig.*

Manufacturer's mark and serial number.
Courtesy of Domein Raversijde -Ostend.

Battery box, front view. *Courtesy of Domein Raversijde -Ostend.*

Manual generator box. A handle would be inserted into the rod, front view. *Courtesy of Domein Raversijde -Ostend.*

Courtesy of Brain Ludwig.

Battery box, rear view. The leather straps are missing. *Courtesy of Domein Raversijde -Ostend.*

Close-up of the voltage meter and the rectangular box with push button to operate the flashlight. *Courtesy of Domein Raversijde -Ostend.*

A *Lichtblinkgerät* being used in the field in 1917. *Courtesy of Brian Ludwig.*

A 1917 dated photograph showing men of a signals unit. Note the covered light and the glass panel, which can be closed if necessary. *Courtesy of John B. Price.*

An electrical light on a tripod in operation.

Telephone (*Fernsprecher*)

Telephone (*Fernsprecher*) equipment used by the German Army can be categorized as "field telephones" (*Feldfernsprecher*) and "army field telephones" (*Armeefernsprechgerät*). While the telegraph units were using a fairly heavy "field telephone" (*Feldfernsprecher*) in 2nd, 3rd line positions or headquarters, each infantry or *Jäger* regiment had a number of units equipped with a lighter "army field telephone" (*Armeefernsprechgerät*), which was introduced in 1905.[12] According to the "*German Army Handbook*", during the war, each battalion had a telephone unit (*Fernsprech-Abteilung*) consisting of four company squads (*Trupp*) of 3 soldiers, led by one NCO. This unit had four army field telephones and 13,000 yards of cable. Special backpacks were used to carry this equipment. Several telephone types, which saw service during the war, will be discussed, starting with the "army field telephones" plus batteries, followed by the "field telephones".

Dienstunterricht
für
Telegraphentruppen.
Kriegsausgabe
mit Anlage: Neue Uniformen des preußischen Heeres.
Auf Veranlassung der
Königl. Inspektion der Feldtelegraphie
bearbeitet von
Hille
Major z. D. bei der Verkehrstechnischen Prüfungskommission.
Sechste
nach den neuesten Vorschriften umgearbeitete
Auflage.
1916.
Druck von Carl Küster.
Hannover
Baringstraße 7.
Zu beziehen von der Buchdruckerei oder vom Geschäftszimmer der Verkehrstechnischen Prüfungskommission, Berlin-Schöneberg, Siegfriedstraße 2.

Telegraph troop's manual. Dated 1916. *Courtesy of Brian Ludwig.*

An impressive telephone center built into a coastal battery fortification in Belgium, *Ostend. Courtesy of Domein Raversijde -Ostend.*

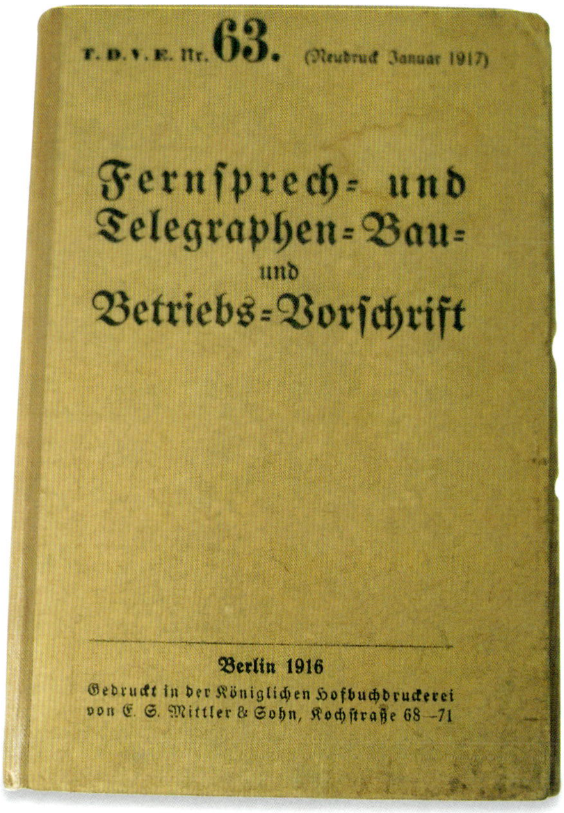

Telegraph troop's field manual, dated 1916. *Courtesy of Brian Ludwig.*

Stoneware beer stein presented to members of a Bavarian telegraph *Abteilung* for Christmas, 1917. *Courtesy of Brian Ludwig.*

Army Field Telephone
***Patrouillenapparat* Model 1894**

The first telephone introduced in 1894 was the *Patrouillenapparat*. It was adopted in 1899 by the *Telegrafen-Bataillons* when they were raised. It had a weight of 1.4 kg and together with its battery was worn on the belt. The shape was very similar to its successor, the *Armeefernsprechgerät*. The *Patrouillenapparat* was used on national territory and connected into the national telephone network (*Reichstelegrafie*).

Telephone Model 1905 (*Armeefernsprechgerät alter art*[13])

The model 1905 telephone had an aluminum cylindrical body. A lever was pressed to create a connection on the line, similar to a walky-talky, and a small white button was present to emit Morse signals. The lever needed to be pressed when transmitting Morse signals. The earpiece was made from either leather or wood and/or covered with felt. The felt kept the ear warm when using the telephone.

A cable with four wires ended in two plugs, two wires connected to each. Both plugs were made from Bakelite and were different in shape. The round plug was used to draw power from the battery and the square plug was used for transmitting signals and grounding the device. Each connector had two metal pins different in size, to prevent the plugs interchanging by accident. A special carrier made from metal and bound in leather was available to carry the telephone. The telephone could work using the battery model 1905 (*Armeesprechbatterie alter Art*).

Telephone Model 1913 (*Eiserner Armeefernsprecher*)

Very similar to the model just described, the 'iron telephone' was introduced in 1913 and was a more economical version made from an iron body and painted field-grey. Its weight was 1.2 kg and slightly lighter than the *Armeefernsprechgerät alter art*. The device operated in exactly the same way as its predecessor, apart from the lever which was replaced by a wooden or bakelite pen at the left side, which had to be moved 90 degrees to create a connection. The telephone could work with the special "field artillery battery", the "telephone battery model 1913" and the "telephone battery model 1916" (see later for a description of these batteries).

Model 1905 detachable telephone handset with blue felt ear cushion, aluminum, nickeled brass, and leather trim. Manufactured by *Mix & Genest*, Berlin. *Courtesy of Brian Ludwig.*

Model 1913 Army telephones were issued with small modifications as the war progressed. The early versions had a leather earpiece, which changed to wood during the war. *Courtesy of BT.*

The lever was made from wood or Bakelite. The Bakelite version is marked "*Zum sprechen und hören hochklappen*" (pull upwards to talk and hear). Both phones were made by *Zwietusch & Co.*

Special cases were developed for the "Army telephones", made from sheet metal and covered with leather. These cases were either carried inside the telegraph *Tornister* or with a strap around the neck. The combined weight of the telephone and case was approximately 2.2 kg. The carrier had a length of 14.7" (29cm) and a depth between 3.5" (9cm) and 4" (10cm). *Courtesy of BT.*

Black leather telephone handset carrying case. Marked with Imperial crown over *BN. Courtesy of Brian Ludwig.*

Field-gray painted metal telephone handset carrying case. Marked with Imperial crown over *BN. Courtesy of Brian Ludwig.*

Brown leather telephone handset carrying case with shoulder strap. Manufactured by *Karl F. Hartmann*, Berlin. *Courtesy of Brian Ludwig.*

Army Field Telephone Batteries

Telephone Battery Model 1905 (*Armeesprechbatterie alter Art*)

This was a fairly large wooden box with a length of 12.4" (31.5cm), a height of 5.9" (15cm) and a depth of 3.3" (8.5cm). It resembled the battery box used for the *Patrouillenapparat* from 1899. The battery box was intended to be used with the *Armeefernsprechgerät alter Art* and contained three individual rectangular batteries coupled in series. The outside featured two large connector plugs. It was carried using a leather handle fixed on top of the lid, or, alternatively could be carried around the shoulder using the bread bag strap. The bread bag strap buckles were inserted into two small iron clips on each side of the box.

Side view with connection for the telephone.

Battery model 1905 (*Armeesprechbatterie alter Art*) with model 1913 telephone (*Eiserner Armeefernsprecher*). The wooden telephone's earpiece is marked with the manufacturers name and location: *"E. Zwietusch & Co Charlottenburg 110621". Courtesy of BT.*

Alphabet.

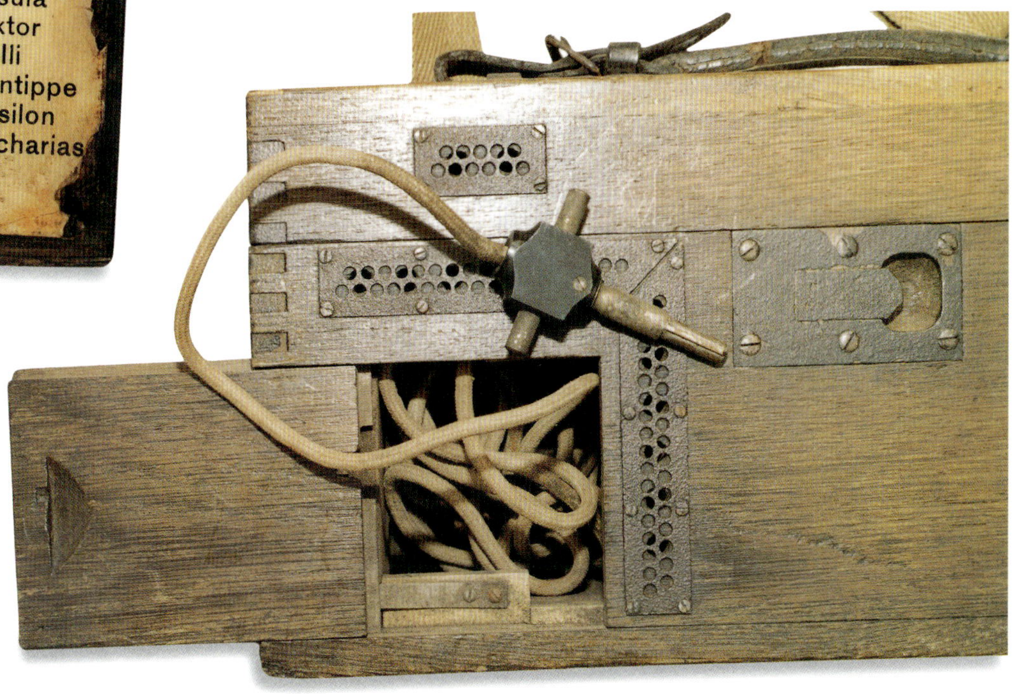

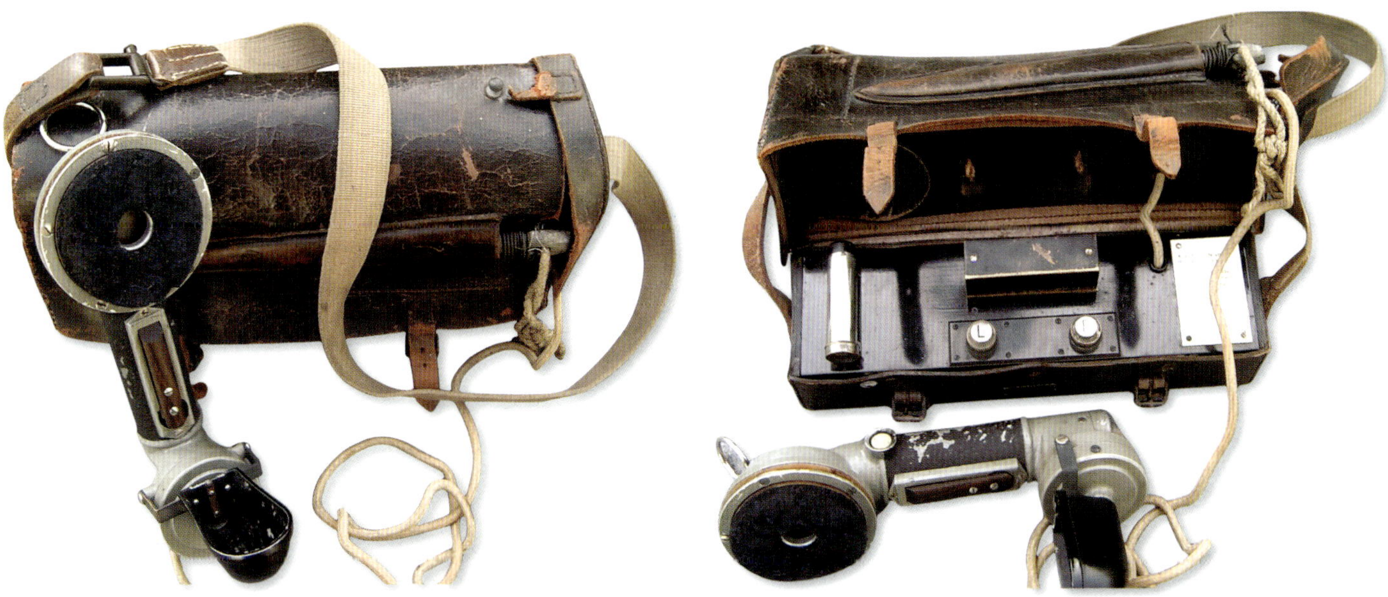

An early *Patrouillenapparat* carried around the belt in a leather pouch. *Courtesy of Sven Kuczyk.*

Telephone Battery for Field Artillery (*Sprechbatterie für Feldartillerie*)
Field artillery units were using a smaller version of the battery, called *'Sprechbatterie für Feldartillerie'*. Apart from the reduction in size and weight, it had three instead of two line connectors.

Telephone Battery for Foot Artillery (*Artillerie Lautsprecher*)
This telephone was only used by the foot artillery and not by the field artillery regiments. The device had the same functions as a classical field phone, but was equipped with a loudspeaker. Basically, it was an early type of intercom and enabled easy communication between an artillery observer and the artillery battery commander. The wooden box contained two large batteries, identical to the batteries found in the other field telephones, but larger in size. Siemens & Halske produced two types of Foot artillery telephones. The first experimental model had a separate box, which contained the batteries, and was only used for trials before the war. The second model had the batteries and telephone mechanism combined in one single box. The telephone was mounted on a wooden tripod.[14]

Telephone Battery Model 1913 (*Armeesprechbatterie neuer Art*)
The Field artillery battery box was further developed and in 1913 a new model was introduced for the Army. The *Armeesprechbatterie neuer Art* had a length of 8.5" (21.5cm), a height of 5.9" (15cm) and a depth of 3.3" (8.5cm). Its total weight including the three batteries was 2.6 kg and 1.2 kg without. Four large connectors can be seen on one side. Three were line connectors and the fourth one was the earth. Two connection plugs for the field telephone and a connector for other telephone units are present at the other side. The box was either carried inside a special backpack or in a black leather pouch attached to the belt.

Brown leather *Tornister* for the *Armeesprechbatterie Neuer Art*. It was manufactured by *Bruno Wiedermann*, Berlin 39 and is marked with the crown and "*BN*" mark seen on other carriers for telephone and telegrapher's gear. The remains of a paper tag indicate it was battlefield capture made by an American captain. *Courtesy of Brian Ludwig.*

Telephone battery for foot artillery (*Artillerie Lautsprecher*). *Courtesy of Eric Siegel.*

Telephone Battery Model 1916 (*Feldsprechbatterie 16*)

Introduced in 1916, the *Feldsprechbatterie* was almost identical to the previous model. It had only one line and one earth connector. Three batteries were stored inside the wooden box and connected to each other with wires. Each battery measured 2.3" (5.8cm) by 2.3" (5.8cm) with a height of 4.3" (11cm).

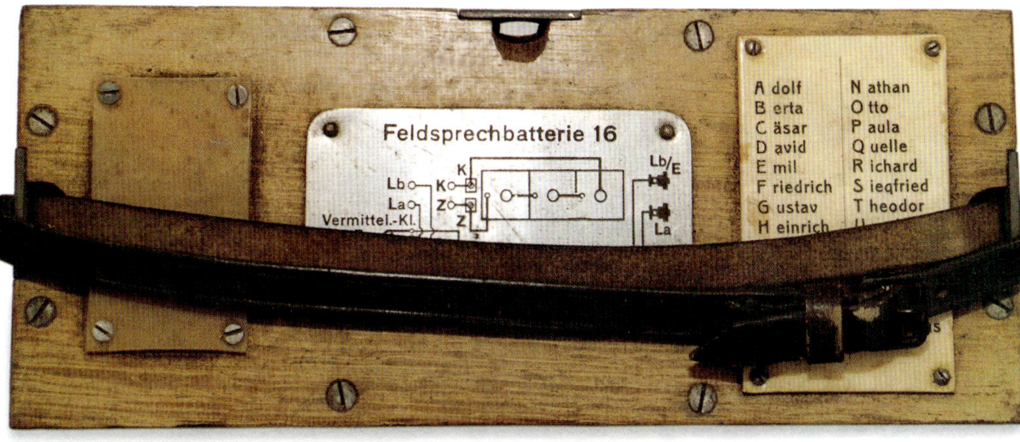

Top view with the alphabet and instructions of how to connect the battery.

Telephone battery model 1916 and field telephone model 1913. *Courtesy of BT.*

The battery box contained three batteries connected to each other.

This photograph shows the batteries in the wooden box.

Additional Army Field Telephone Box Model 1913 (*Zusatzkasten zum Armeefeldfernsprecher*)

The "field telephone model 1913" was not completely compatible with the similar army field telephones, which contained many additional functions. In order to solve this problem, an additional wooden box (*Zusatzkasten zum Armeefeldfernsprecher*) could be used to enhance the capabilities of the army field telephone. The box also contained a bell.

The "Additional army field telephone box" could be carried with a bread bag strap. *Courtesy of BT.*

Headphone (*Kopffernhörer*)
Additional headphones were introduced in 1905 (*Kopffernhörer alter Art*) together with the "Army field telephones". It was a large circular device with a diameter of 4" (10cm) and an aluminum body. The headphone was carried in a brown or black leather pouch, or a paper cloth or painted metal later in the war, which had a height of 5.1" (13cm) and a width of 4.7" (12cm). Interestingly enough, the headphone could also be used as a microphone. A new economic design appeared in 1913 (*Eiserner Kopffernhörer*).

Pre-war/early war telegrapher's headset with polished aluminum fittings and blue felt ear cushion. Manufactured by *Mix & Genest*. *Courtesy of Brian Ludwig.*

The headphones earpiece was initially covered with felt (as above), but later wartime versions had wooden or leather covers. This headphone is marked "*Karl Hartmann Berlin*". The headphone and case had a weight of 0.8 kg with a height of 5.1" (13cm) and a width of 4.7" (12cm). *Courtesy of BT.*

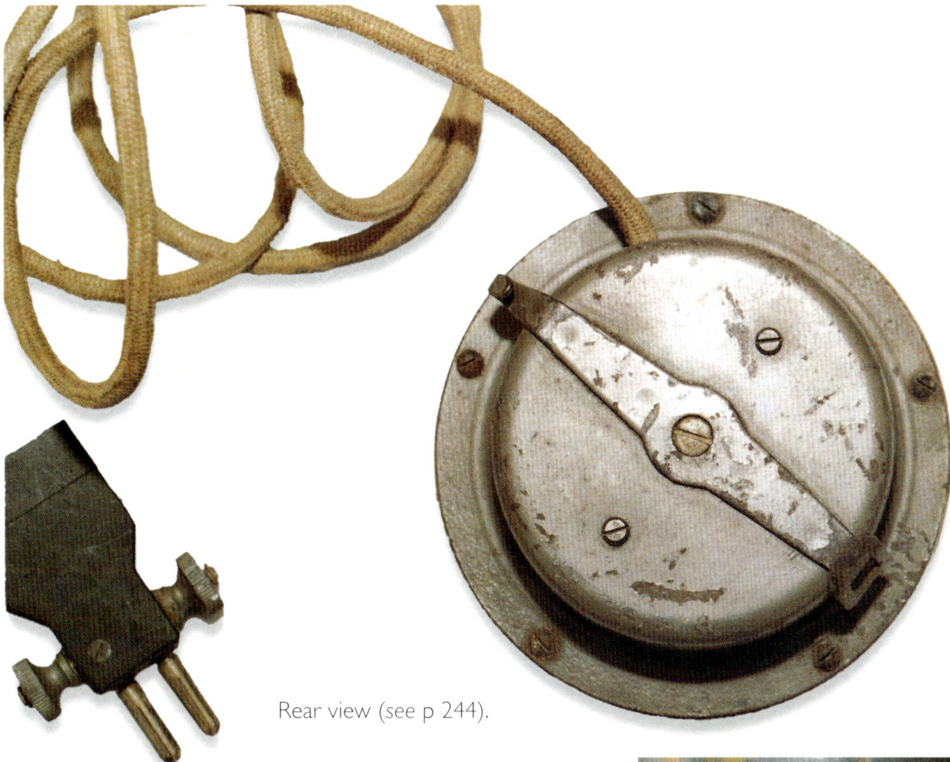

Rear view (*see* p 244).

Headphones with leather earpiece. *Courtesy of Domein Raversijde -Ostend.*

Kopffernhörer 1917. Courtesy of Eric Siegel.

Above: Black leather telegrapher's headset carrying case. Felt lined, manufactured by *Franz Cobau*, Berlin, 1916. *Courtesy of Brian Ludwig.*

Headphone pouch.

Ersatz steel carrier for the telegrapher's headset. *Courtesy of Brian Ludwig.*

Paper cloth telegrapher's headset carrying case made by *J.A. Stanienda*, 1918. *Courtesy of Brian Ludwig.*

Interior view of paper cloth carrying case showing the placement of the telegrapher's headset and the signal whistle (*Ruftrompete*). This device was used by inserting it into the earpiece of the phones and blown into to create a tone. It called up an answering station in cases where the buzzer (*Summer*) failed or when the earpiece (*Fernhörer*) was used as a sender. Two patterns existed, the *Ruftrompete* and the *Ruftrompete neuer Art*. The first pattern was cylindrical, made of nickeled brass with a hard rubber mouth end. The *Ruftrompete neuer Art* was made of horn or a horn-like material and was tapered toward the mouth end. It weighed 25g as opposed to the first model that weighed 65g. *Courtesy of Brian Ludwig.*

Telegrapher's *Ruftrompete* carried in the headset carrying case. *Courtesy of Brian Ludwig.*

Field Telephones (*Feldfernsprecher alter Art, Eiserner Feldfernsprecher, Feldfernsprecher 16 & 17*)

There existed at least four types of field telephones (*Feldfernsprecher*) used mainly by telegraph units and transportation troops (*Verkehrstruppen*) in more or less permanent positions. These were called *Feldfersprecher alter Art*, *Eiserne Feldfernsprecher*, *Feldfernsprecher 16* and *Feldfernsprecher 17*. All telephones could either communicate with the *Armeefernsprecher* devices already discussed or could be connected to the *Reich Telegraphen Verwaltung* (RTV). The weight of the wooden box and telephone was could be 9 kg depending the model. Cavalry regiments serving within cavalry divisions carried two army telephones on horseback, together with 15.300 yards of cable.[15]

The field telephone model 1905 (*Feldfernsprecher alter Art*) was introduced between 1905 and 1910, and had a toggle to switch between civilian and military networks, which operated differently. All metal parts were made of high quality brass. The box contained a battery and a telephone. The field telephone model 1915 (*Eiserner Feldfernsprecher*) was nearly identical to the 1905 model but all brass parts were replaced with grey painted metal. The telephones now operated with two separate cables (*Doppelader-Betrieb*) instead of one as seen on the previous model (one cable increased the risk of someone tapping the telephone conversation). As a result it had a total of three instead of two connection outlets at the side. The switch between the civilian and military network was made using the buzzer/Morse button instead of a switch. Not many of these telephone set were produced. It is assumed that most of them were manufactured from the middle of 1915 to early 1916. The box itself contained a telephone.

The field telephones model 1916 and 1917 (*Feldfernsprecher 16 and Feldfernsprecher 17*) no longer had the special earth connector as seen in previous versions. They were manufactured in larger quantities from the middle of 1916. The model 17 was available in two different sizes.

Field telephone model 1905 (*Feldfernsprecher alter Art*). *Author's early collection.*

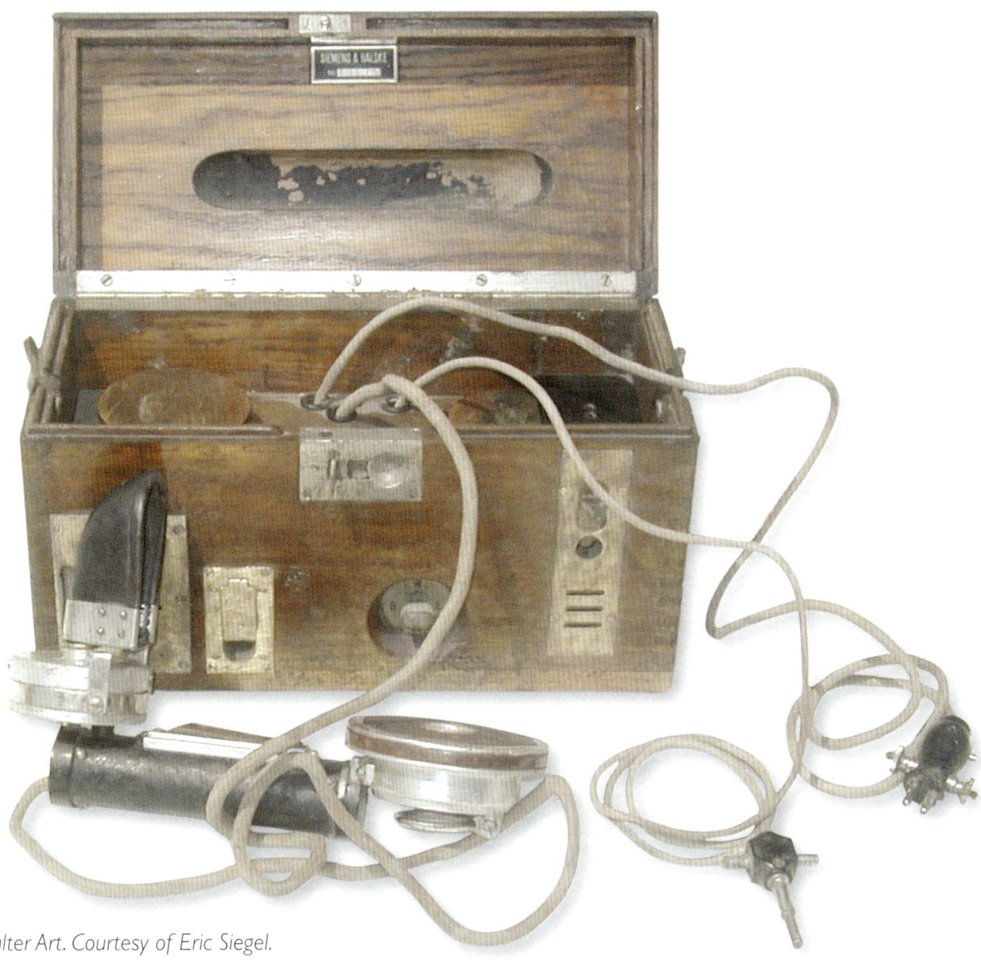

Feldfernsprecher alter Art. Courtesy of Eric Siegel.

This photograph was taken in France and shows most probably a field telephone model 1905 (*Feldfernsprecher alter Art*) with battery box. *Courtesy of Brian Ludwig.*

A *"Feldfernsprecher 16"* and a telephone can be seen at the right hand side. Note the difference in design compared with the *"Feldfernsprecher alter Art"*. *Courtesy of Faris Siwadi.*

Closed *Feldfernsprecher 16 Type B. Courtesy of Eric Siegel.*

Open *Feldfernsprecher 16 Type B. Courtesy of Eric Siegel.*

Feldfernsprecher 17. Courtesy of Eric Siegel.

Grosser Feldfernsprecher 17 with leather carrying strap and papercloth tool pouch. *Courtesy of Brian Ludwig.*

Telephone center with an impressive civilian type (government owned) table telephone (*Tischapparat OB 05*). These telephones were brought into military service and only used in permanent positions, headquarters, etc. *Courtesy of Faris Siwadi.*

A Belgian Army telephone station, shortly after the war, using an OB.10, a table telephone which stands on top of a small unidentified switch board. The soldier on the far left is *Albert Van Frachem*, the author's grandfather who served in the *Corps des troupes de transmission, Bataillon de télegraphistes, 2° Compagnie*.

Telephon central. *Courtesy of Sven Kuczyk.*

Type *O.B.05 Tischapparat* telephone. Black painted sheet metal case with polychrome emblem, black-painted wood case top and base, nickeled fittings and black bakelite hand piece handle, ear cushion and mouth piece. Braided dark green cord. Marked *O.B.05.K* and dated 5.8.16. Manufactured by *Keifer & Schmidt,* Berlin. *Courtesy of Brian Ludwig.*

Telegrapher's Special Equipment
Backpack (*Fernsprechtornister*) and Contents

Telephone cables were laid across the terrain and were either dug in (*Kabelleitungen*) or were installed on telegraph poles (*Blanke Leitungen*) depending on the terrain conditions. Telegraph units were using a special backpack, which was identical in size to the infantry model 1895 *Tornister*, but was deeper and had a weight of 2.2 kg. Two large compartments, one at the upper right and one at the lower left side and two small sections at the upper left and lower right were used to carry specific telephone equipment like wire drums (*Armeekabeltrommel*). Three soldiers formed a telegraph section (*Trupp*) and each carried one of these backpacks, but with different contents. A small leather tag sewn to the outer flap showed the content of the backpack with the numbers '1', '2' or '3'.

According a contemporary instruction book, a telegraph section with three soldiers was equipped as follows:

Number 1	Number 2	Number 3
Special telegraph belt buckle	Special telegraph belt buckle	Special telegraph belt buckle
Backpack "1"with contents	Backpack "2" with contents	Backpack "3" with contents
Overcoat and tent half	Overcoat and tent half	Overcoat and tent half
Tent poles inside the backpack	Tent poles inside the backpack	Tent poles inside the backpack
Mess kit attached to the backpack	Mess kit attached to the backpack	Mess kit attached to the backpack
Drahtgabelteil (left side pack)	*Drahtgabelteil* (left side pack)	*Drahtgabelteil* (left side pack)
Pouch with battery of the rear belt	Infantry shovel with bayonet	
Pouch with a telephone slung around the neck instead of the left ammo pouches	Pouch with headphone on the belt instead of the left ammo pouches	Map/dispatch case instead of the left ammo pouches
Bayonet without saw tooth edge	Bayonet without saw tooth edge	Bayonet with saw tooth edge

During longer marches, it was recommended that the map case was carried by 'number 1' and the pouch with telephone by 'number 3'. The left backpack strap of 'number 3' was not used and rolled up.

The wire drums contained 250 to 500 meters of cable, depending on the type and thickness. The drum had a diameter of 6.8" (17.5cm) and a net weight of 430g. Later patterns of drums could be dismantled to fit more easily into the telegrapher's backpack. Over the years, variety of cables were used, depending on the branch of service. Some of those in use were as follows:

Model 1888 cable
Model 1908 heavy cable for telegraph troops
Feldkabel model 1910 for artillery
Iron *Kavaleriedraht* without insulation for cavalry formations
Leichter Feldkabel 16 for infantry
Armeekabel 08 for infantry, in use from 1912
Armeekabel 15 for infantry
Artilleriekabel 12 for artillery, in use from 1912

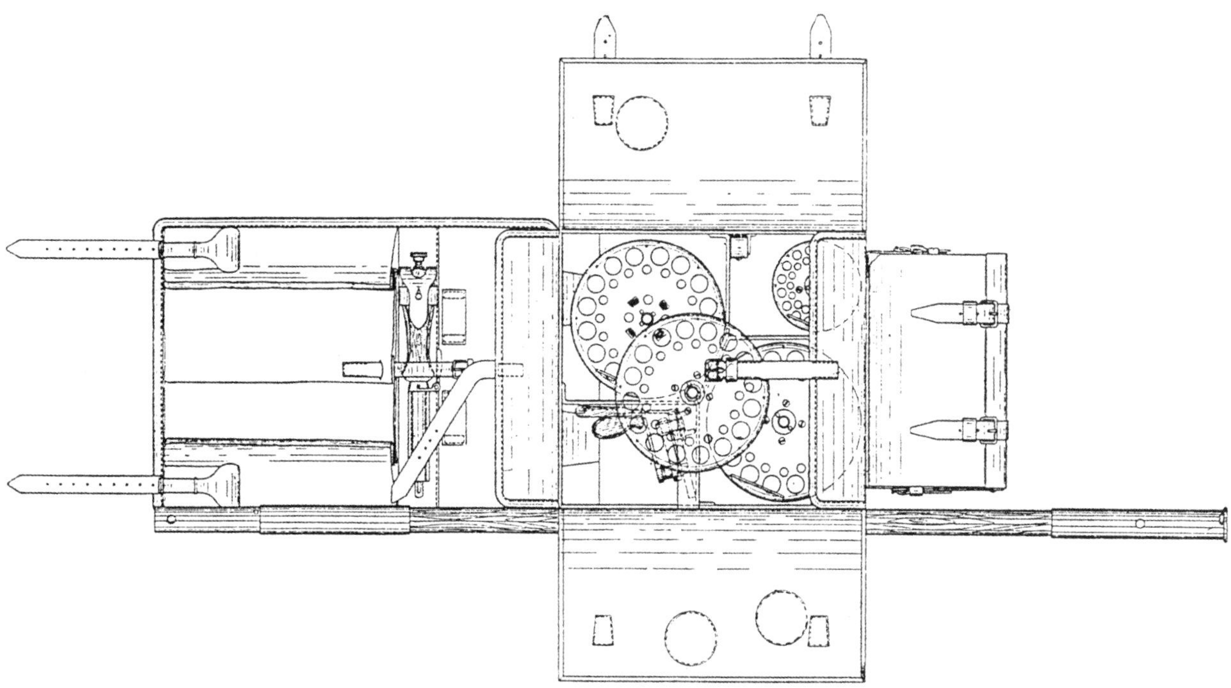

Telegrapher's *Fernsprechtornister* number 1. The telephone battery box stored in a black leather pouch could be attached to the backpack using two large rings on the bottom of the *Fernsprechtornister*. These rings were also present on backpack 3. The large compartments contained wire drums (*Armeekabel*), the lower right section a smaller drum for underground wire (*Erdleitungsdraht)* and nails, the upper left section contained amongst other items a large wheel with a wooden handle for the *Aufspuler* (a device used to wind up cable) and a screwdriver. A large disassembled wire drum was stored above the compartments. The flap of the backpack was used to store the *Abspuler* (a device used to roll out cable).

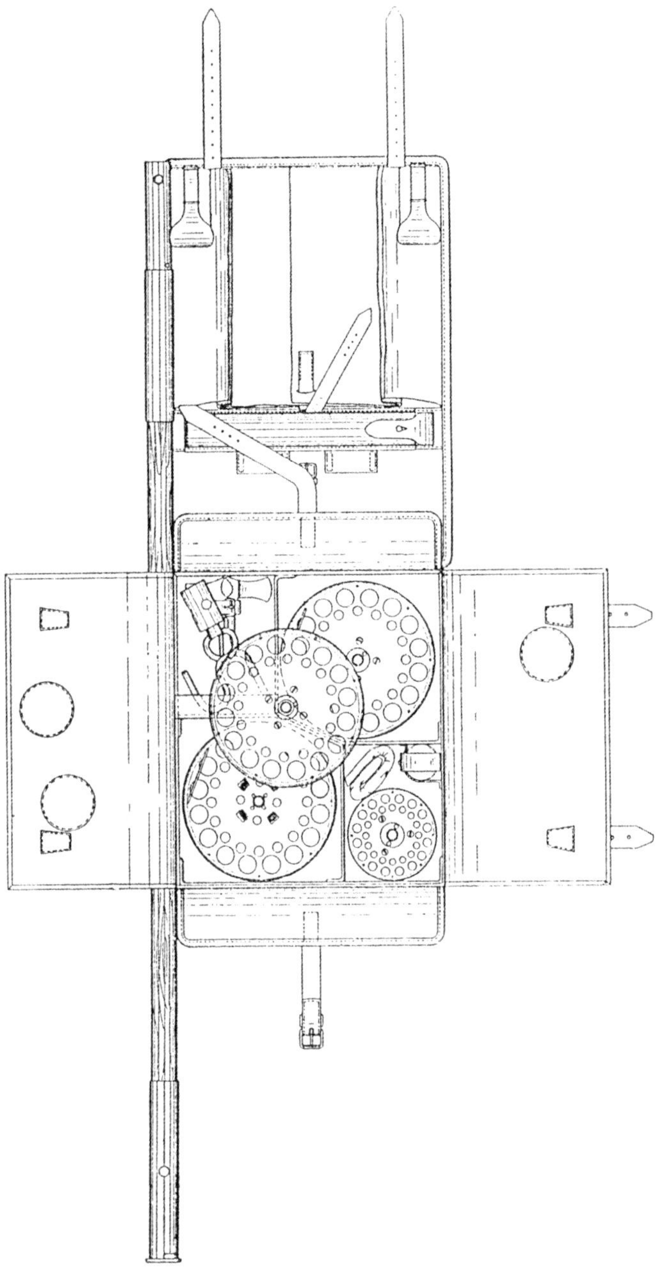

Telegrapher's *Fernsprechtornister* number 2. The large compartments contained wire drums (*Armeekabel*), the lower right section a wire-laying mitten (*Handschuh*) and nails, the upper left section the combination tool (*Werkzeug*) and the upper part of the cable fork (*Drahtgabelaufsatz*), which is discussed in the next chapter. A large disassembled wire drum was stored above the compartments. The flap of the backpack stored the handle for the cable fork.

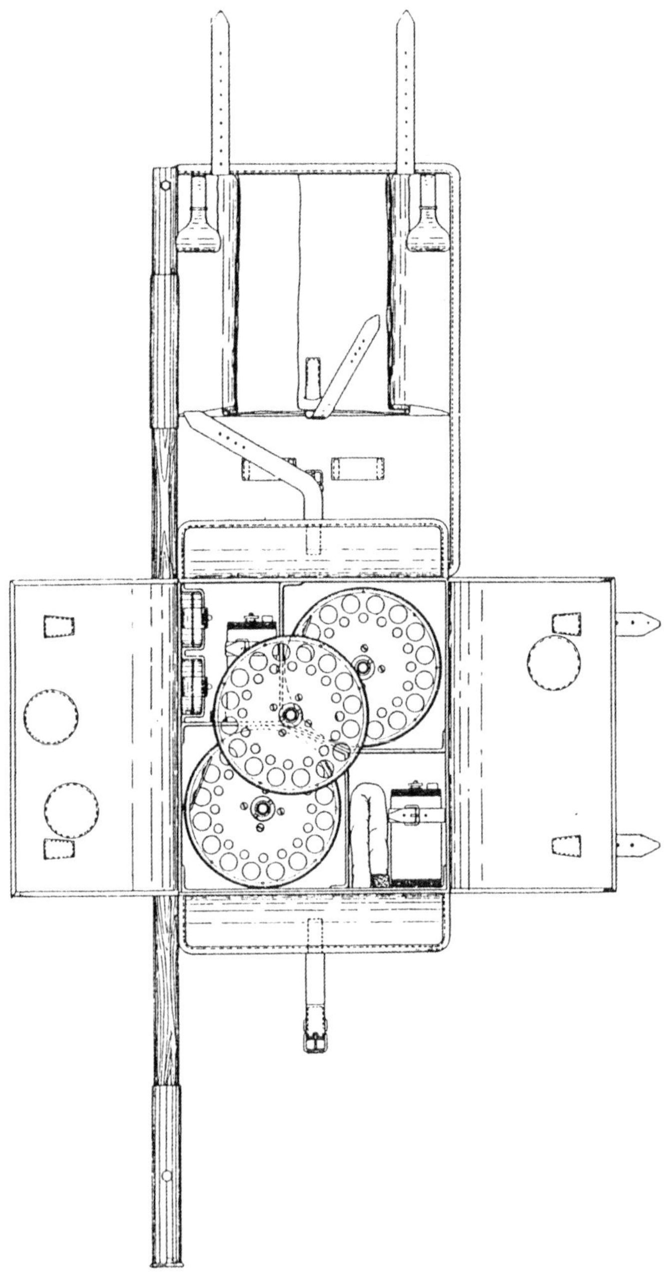

Telegrapher's *Fernsprechtornister* number 3. The large compartments contained wire drums (*Armeekabel*), the lower right section a wire-laying mitten (*Handschuh*) and a battery element, the upper left section a second battery element and two tin cans (*Blechschachteln*) with a spare microphone. A large disassembled wire drum was stored above the compartments. The internal backpack pouch contained the *Abspuler*.

Fernsprechtornister number 3. *Courtesy of Eric Siegel.*

Fernsprechtornister number 1. The leather tag with the number "1" is sewn onto the flap of the backpack. Drums and other tools specific for the number "1" *Tornister* are carried inside. *Royal Army and Military History Museum, Brussels.*

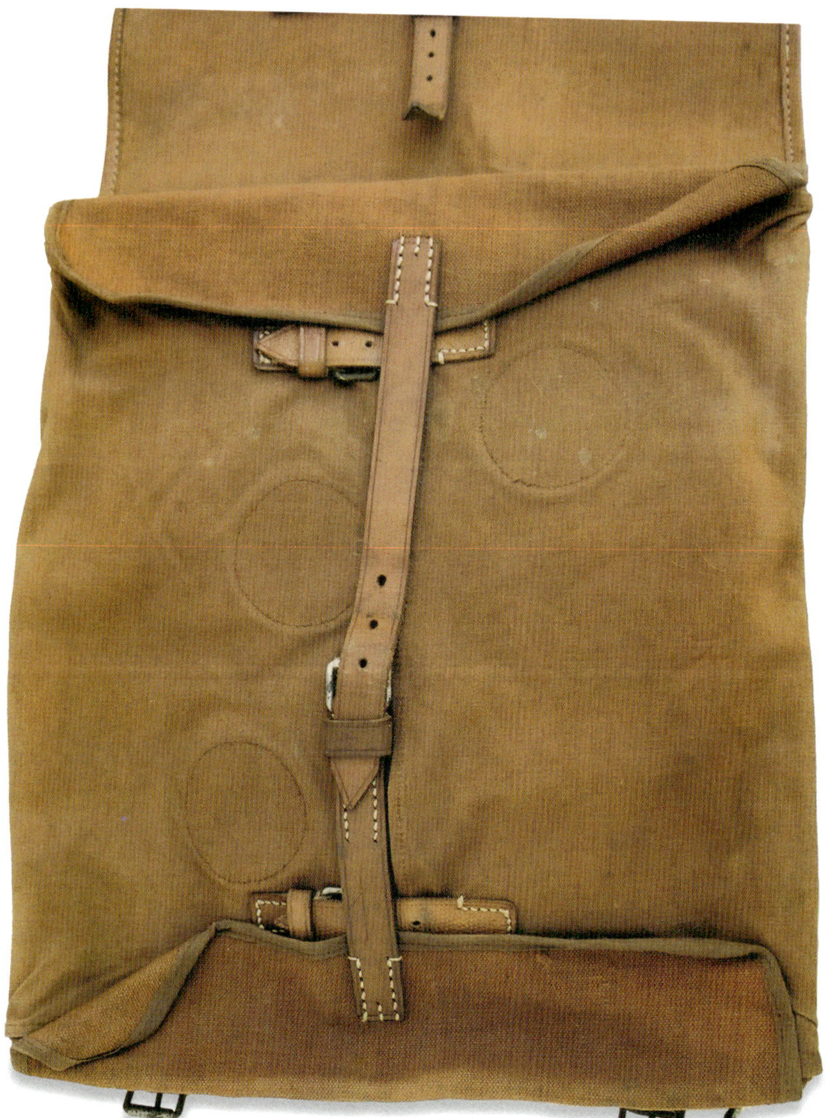

Early *Fernsprechtornister Nr. 2* in ocher canvas and pony hair. The ends of the pack closure straps contain crown markings typical of Bavarian manufacture. The exterior is almost identical to the standard infantry *Tornister* with the exception of an additional leather equipment loop on the left side. The interior of the pack is very different and the main body has reinforced flaps for containing three wire reels. A leather compartment is visible at the top of the interior flap. This particular pack has no military markings and appears to have never been issued. *Courtesy of Brian Ludwig.*

Small can with spare microphone stored inside *Fernsprechtornister 3. Courtesy of Domein Raversijde –Ostend.*

Left: Telegrapher's/electrician's wiring pliers/cutters marked "*Berlin*". No military marks are present although these do appear in period photos. *Courtesy of Brian Ludwig.*

Telegrapher's/electrician's wire pullers marked "*DRGM*" and possibly dated (19)17. Similar tools are used by electricians today. *Courtesy of Brian Ludwig.*

Military-issue telegrapher's combination tool (*Werkzeug*) with intertwined TMV maker's mark and stamped *Eigentum der Heeresverwaltung*. The 300g tool was a combination of a hammer, screwdriver, axe and wire cutter. They were copied extensively in later decades for civilian use and are readily available. Only those with the *Eigentum der Heeresverwaltung* mark were Imperial military issue. *Courtesy of Brian Ludwig.*

Issue telegrapher's pole climbing spikes with leather attachment straps. Galvanized steel and marked *DRGM* and size stamp (12). *Courtesy of Brian Ludwig.*

Telegrapher's wire-laying mitten (*Handschuh*) with leather reinforcing patch at the thumb. These items had a weight of 0,1 kg and could be worn on either the left or right hand. *Courtesy of Brian Ludwig.*

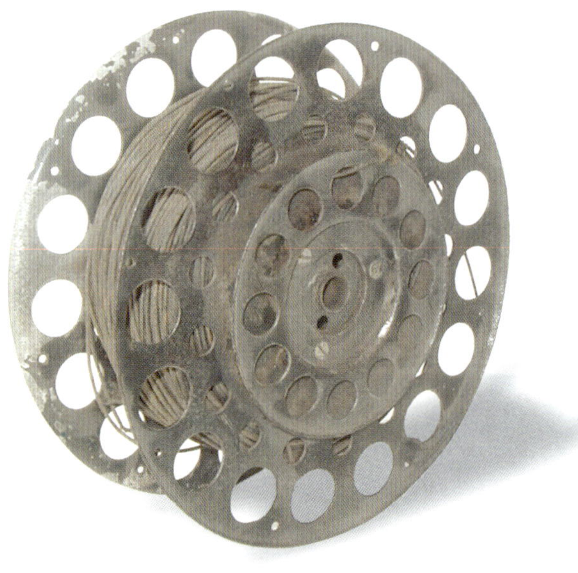

Kabeltrommel used by Field artillery. *Courtesy of Eric Siegel.*

Wire drum marked "*Simson & Co*". *Courtesy of Domein Raversijde -Ostend*

Armeekabeltrommel and *Erdleitungsdrahttrommel*. *Courtesy of Eric Siegel.*

This large cable drum was carried on the back. *Royal Army and Military History Museum, Brussels.*

Brown leather telegraph troops map/dispatch case (*Meldekartentasche*). Marked *Wilhelm Knoll, Stuttgart*, 1915. The case was worn by the number 3, and in which were stored 3 books, each containing 25 pages. Also carried in the case were 2 pencils, a folding lantern and 5 candles. One in every 12 cases instead contained a battery tester and just one candle.[12] *Courtesy of Brian Ludwig.*

The Cable "Fork" (*Drahtgabel*)[19]

A pole ending with a "fork" was used to attach or detach telegraph cables to trees or other high level positions. There were two models. The first one was made of two main components (*Zweiteilige Drahtgabel*) and the second one from multiple components (*Mehrteilige Drahtgabel*). The *Mehrteilige Drahtgabel* consisted of three pole sections (*Drahtgabelteil*), each carried at the left side on one of the three *Fernsprechtornisters*. The sections comprised of wooden poles with metal connecting devices on each end. Each section was 48" (122cm) long and they were connected to each other to achieve the height needed, up to 142" (366cm) (another source indicates a total height of 4.8m). The attachment was made by means of a socket bayonet fitting and held in place with a spring-catch. The connecting hole for the base pole was protected from getting fouled with dirt by adding a handle with a solid end (*Einsatzstück*). Regulations forbade the use of this apparatus without this piece being attached. The top piece or fork (*Drahtgabelaufsatz* or *Aufsatzstück*) had forward swept and rear swept hooks, which were used to lift the wire up to a resting place (tree branch) or to pull the wire down. The wire could be inserted between the hooks and when the pole was given a 180 degree turn, the wire would be trapped in a guide ring and therefore more easily controlled. When not in use, the top piece and the handle were stored in a compartment in *Fernsprechtornister* number '2'.

Artillery units were issued with the *Zweiteilige Drahtgabel* which was a two section pole. The apparatus consisted of only two wooden pole sections, each 1.4" (3,5cm) in circumference and with metal fittings on each end. The upper pole section was topped by the "fork", which was permanently attached. The top pole section attached to the bottom section by means of a socket bayonet fitting and was held in place by a spring-catch. The base of the lower pole section was fitted with a metal ring to keep the wood from splitting. The "fork" configuration was different from that of the *Mehrteilige Drahtgabel*, having additional useful tools.

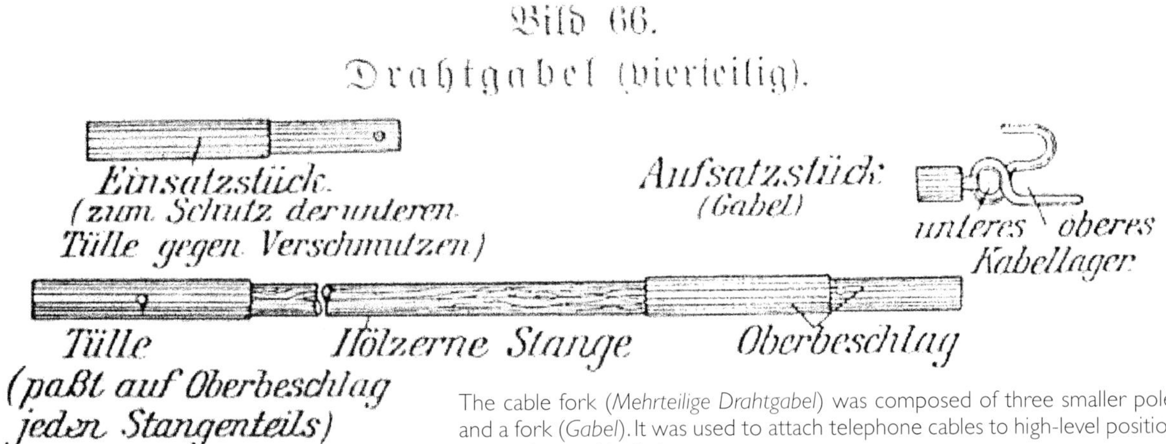

The cable fork (*Mehrteilige Drahtgabel*) was composed of three smaller poles, a handle (*Einsatzstück*) and a fork (*Gabel*). It was used to attach telephone cables to high-level positions. Artillery units received a two-piece cable fork.

A groups of telegraph troops posing with various pieces of equipment including their cable fork (*Drahtgabel*), wire reels, telephone handsets, and battery boxes. It is interesting to note that many of the men in this photo are wearing belt loops for attaching the *Feldfernsprech Tornister* without cartridge boxes. *Courtesy of Brian Ludwig.*

Aufspuler[19]

The *Aufspuler* was a piece of field equipment that was used to retrieve telephone wire. As the army moved back and forth across the battlefield, its communications network had to move with it. The *Aufspuler* was developed to make this process more efficient. The device consists of two parts, the winding apparatus and the special belt buckle. The winding apparatus was a "U" shaped metal frame with two "feet" at the open end that allowed it to be attached to corresponding slots on the buckle. A leather suspension strap ran from the extended end of the frame around the wearer's neck to assist in supporting the weight of the wire reel (*Kabeltrommel*).

When the spring-loaded pin on the left side of the frame was retracted, a wire reel was dropped in. The reel was held in place on the right side by matching a pair of pins on the turn-shaft to the

The *Aufspuler* was supported with a leather strap slung around the neck. *Courtesy of Chip Minx.*

corresponding holes in the reel. On the left side, the spring-loaded pin is released, thus securing the reel in place.

A crank handle with a cog wheel was attached on the outer right-hand side of the frame, with the cog teeth meshing with those of a smaller gear that turned the shaft. The cranking motion of this handle wound the wire reel. At the closed end of the frame there was a tension bar, which could lock or release a traversing spiral wire feed. This allowed the wire to be controlled as it was brought into the device and thus properly wound onto the wire reel.

The wire on *Aufspuler* could be used at any point by attaching a live wire to the frame or the belt buckle. The wearer had to be grounded with a piece of wire.

The *Aufspuler* and special buckle were eventually issued to many units other than the technical troops. The ever-expanding role of the telephone in wartime communications brought about the need to increase the army's capabilities. Telephone detachments were created within units, using existing personnel. This explains why the special buckle is seen being worn by soldiers from all branches.

When not in use, the parts of the *Aufspuler* were carried in the special telephone backpacks. The cogwheel crank handle was carried in a compartment of backpack Nr.1 and the frame was stored in a pouch on back (inside) of the pack flap of backpack Nr.3.

Cavalry *Aufspuler* mounted on a tube that slipped over the end of the lance. *Private collection.*

The lance mounted cavalry *Aufspuler. Private collection.*

Abspuler[19]

The *Abspuler* was a hand-held device, which was used along with a wire reel to feed out or retrieve telephone wire. It consisted of a wooden handle, through which passed a steel rod. A reel of telephone wire was slipped on to the rod and a pivoting clip at the rod's end kept the reel in place. The reel could spin freely on the rod. A reel brake, mounted near the handle, could adjust the speed of the wire's exit from the reel or could stop the reel if it became necessary to adjust incoming wire.

At the other end of the handle was a metal terminal used for attaching a live wire. This would allow the wire on the reel to be used to make a phone call without having to splice the two wires. The circuit would flow from the wire attached to the terminal, through the handle rod to the metal reel and its wire.

A crank handle accessory (*Kurbel*) could be attached to the wire reel by sliding it onto the rod and matching the pins on the crank's arm to the corresponding holes in the reel. The cranking motion of the handle would spin the reel, pulling the wire in. The Abspuler was carried in a leather pouch, attached under the back flap of telephone pack Nr 1.

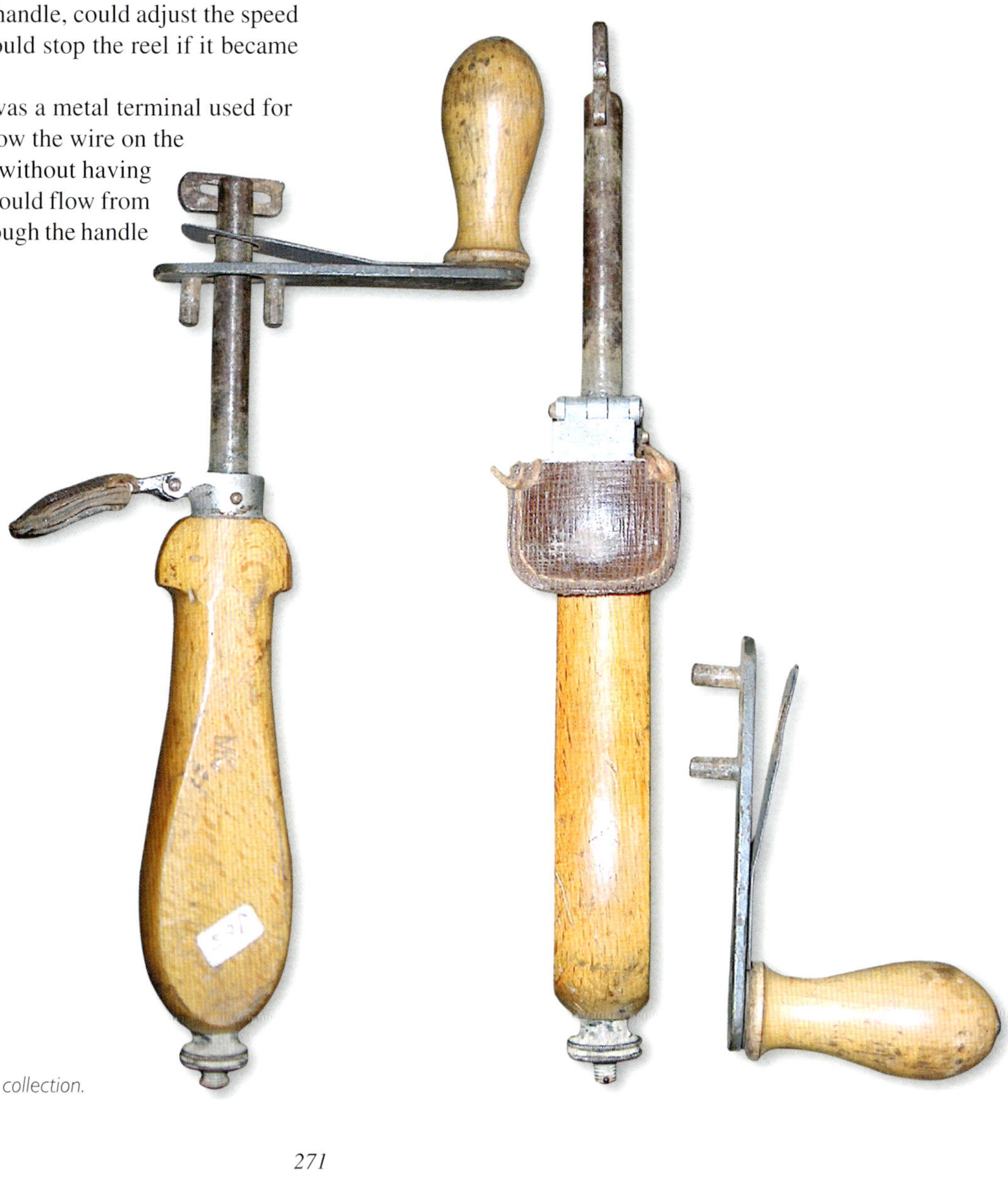

Abspuler and *Kurbel* (crank handle). *Private collection.*

Small Transmission Box (*Vermittlungskästchen*)

The small transmission box (*Vermittlungskästchen*) enabled soldiers to quickly and effectively create a small telephone central exchange, where different lines came together and no permanent central exchange (*Klappenschrank*) existed. The small wooden box had a height of 4.9" (12.5cm), a depth of 3.9" (10cm) and a width of 1.6" (4cm).

Several *Vermittlungskästchen*, one for each incoming line, were connected to each other to create an improvised central exchange. At least one "connector box" (*Übertrageskästchen*) was required as well. The wooden *Übertrageskästchen* had a height of 4.9" (12.5cm), a depth of 3.9" (10cm) and a width of 2.5" (6.3cm) and was connected to the transmission boxes. The idea behind this concept was that each *Telegraphentrupp* carried one small transmission box, which could be connected whenever, required with the boxes of other units. The *Vermittlungskästchen* and *Übertrageskästchen* were connected to each other by wiring the two connector clamps (*Verbindungsklemmen*) together, which were found at the front and rear of the boxes. The assembled central exchange was connected to a field telephone, an army field telephone or a *Zusatzkasten*. Each *Vermittlungskästchen* served an incoming telephone line and if a call came in, a telephone operator would pull a switch on the transmission box (*Abfrageschalter*) and would physically connect the telephone to the *Vermittlungskästchen* with a connecter cable.

Three devices were used on the transmission box, to indicate that a call was coming in:

The *Weckerfallklappe* (*Anruf mit Induktor*) was a small metal box which provided a visible signal using a small white reflector, moved by a magnet, behind a glass.

The *Kugelzeichen* (*Summeranruf*) provided both a visible and audible signal.

A headphone (*Kopffernhörer*) provided a sound signal.

The *Vermittlungskästchen* and *Weckerfallklappe* belonged together and were stored in a black leather pouch that was looped around the belt. *Courtesy of BT.*

Front view of the leather pouch.

Rear view.

A papercloth version of the *Vermittlungskästchen* pouch. The Kugelzeichen can be seen as well on top of the box. *Private collection.*

Telephone, battery and small transmission box (*Vermittlungskästchen*) combination. The *Vermittlungskästchen* is equipped with a small black metal box (*Weckerfallklappe*), which provided a visible signal when a telephone call came in.

The same *Vermittlungskästchen* equipped with a headphone.

Vermittlungskästchen with *Kugelzeichen*. *Courtesy of Eric Siegel.*

Telephone, battery, *Zusatzkasten* and small transmission box (*Vermittlungskästchen*) combination.

A pre-war signal unit using various telegraphers' equipment shows the combination hand tool, the special telegraphers message/map case, the folding wire reel, and the amp meter. The latter was called "*Elementprüfer a.A*" (old model) or "*n.A*" (new model). The old model was able to test batteries one by one, while the new model could test three batteries of a battery box at once.[16] The battery box attached to the pole is probably a "telephone battery model 1913". *Courtesy of Brian Ludwig.*

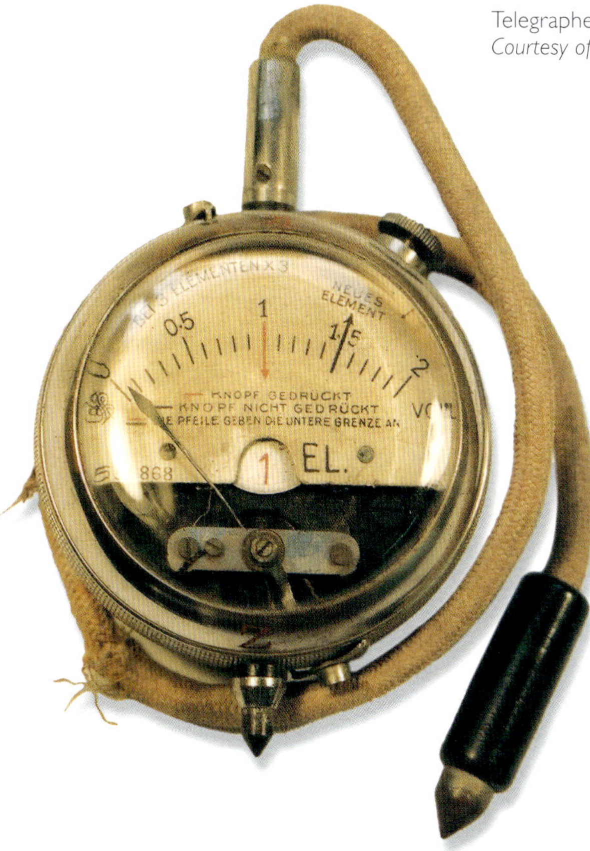

Telegrapher's amp meter for testing electrical and phone line connections. *Courtesy of Brian Ludwig.*

Another example of a *alter Art* (*a.A.*) amp meter and its pouch. *Courtesy of BT.*

The instruction sheet in the pouch indicates that only a single battery element should be tested.

Later battery testers could be switched to test either one single or three batteries at once. When switching between one or three batteries (*Element*), a small round wheel would either display the letters "1EL" or "3EL". The instruction sheet in the pouch for these more advanced testers was as follows: "*Der Elementprüfer darf bei Umschalterstellung 1 EL nur an einzelne Elemente, bei 3 EL nur an ganze Batterien zu 3 Elementen angelegt werden. Zur Prüfung von Taschenlampenbatterien auf 3EL schalten.*" (The tester should only be used to test one element when set to 1EL, or three elements when set to 3EL. For testing trench light batteries, switch to 3EL.). *Courtesy of Eric Siegel.*

Telegraph

Telegraphy was used to connect army and general headquarters. According to "The German Army Handbook, 1918", three devices were used. The *Siemens* telegraph (*Schnelltelegraph*), which could transmit/receive approx. 27,000, words an hour, the Hughes' telewriter (*Fernschreiber*) and a sounder (*Klopfer*). The *Fernschreiber* and the *Schnelltelegraph* produced words directly printed onto paper.

Wireless Communication

Communication, which depended on telephone, or telegraph wires, was extremely vulnerable to artillery fire and difficult to protect. First line communication cables were often destroyed during the first artillery bombardment and as a result, front line infantry commanders were on their own when making tactical decisions and could not easily request supporting artillery fire on new enemy positions. The need for wireless transmission which was achieved for the first time in 1892, soon became very widely accepted in all branches of the Army. The purpose of the early wireless telegraphy was to transmit Morse signals between stations. Most naval vessels, reconnaissance aircraft and ground forces were equipped with heavy and non-portable wireless sets (*Funkentelegrafie*). Pilots would use Morse signals to direct artillery fire to the correct enemy positions.

The German company *Telefunken,* raised in 1903, already supplied large transmitters in 1905 for the new costal radio station of the navy (*Küstenfunkstelle Norddeich Radio*) and in 1906 the first transmitter for the large *Nauen* station with had a transmission range of 300 km.[17] Beginning in 1915, smaller and portable devices (*Funkgeräten*) were manufactured by *Telefunken* and distributed to the front line troops.

Telegraph post *KW 61 E. Royal Army and Military History Museum, Brussels.*

A wireless station. *Courtesy of Faris Siwadi.*

Transmitter/receiver *T.S.F. E. 85. Royal Army and Military History Museum, Brussels.*

Telegraph post *J.D.Flieg S.E.G.* 1916, type D2. *Royal Army and Military History Museum, Brussels.*

Telefunken EV211b. Royal Army and Military History Museum, Brussels.

Message Grenades Fired with a Rocket Launcher (*Nachrichtengeschosse, Signalwerfer*)

In order to transport messages, a message thrower device was constructed. The message was placed in a mortar bomb very similar as the bomb used with the *Granatenwerfer model 16* (see later) but smaller and made of tin and not of cast steel. The upper part of the grenade was empty and could contain a message. A blank cartridge placed at the bottom, between the three wings, fired the rocket.[18]

The launcher was about 32.7" (83cm) long. It has a large spike at the end to fix the thrower into the ground, which was about 4.7"(12cm) long. The middle part contains the firing mechanism in a hollow steel rod of 19.7" (50cm) long and the cylindrical upper part was 8.2" (21cm) long with a diameter of 4.3" (11cm). In addition to messages, the device also could fire small ammunition and light grenades up to a range of 600 yards.

Close up of firing mechanism.

Left: Message grenades could be fired with a small special purpose rocket launcher. *Courtesy of BT.*

Right: Message rocket (*Meldewurfgranate*) with a length of 11.2" (28.5cm). The fins had a width of 1.06" (2.7cm) and were 2.8" (7cm) long. The cylindrical message container was 3.7" (9.5cm) long. The rocket is made from a hollow shaft, which would slip over the rod of the *Signalwerfer. Courtesy of BT.*

Interior view of message grenade.

Different types of grenades. *Courtesy of Eric Siegel.*

Notes

1 Les telephones de l'armee allemande 1914-1918 (1), Eric Siegel.
2 Picture in "*Der Grosses Krieg in Bildern*".
3 Source: http://cedarvalley.virtualave.net/articles/wartimebirds/warbirds.htm.
4 Source home2.planetinternet.be/rice1/military.htm.
5 The German Army Handbook, 1918, p. 121.
6 Source: historische-uniformen.de
7 The article on flare pistols was written by Brian Ludwig.
8 Correspondence with Eric Siegel.
9 Source: http://historische-uniformen.de/Truppen/TB2/Tele2.htm
10 W. Haupt, p. 59.
11 The German Army Handbook, 1918, p. 120.
12 Eric Siegel.
13 *Alter Art* or *a.A.* means 'old model' and is sometimes abbreviated as a.A. *Neuer Art* or *n.A.* means 'new model'.
14 Correspondence with Eric Siegel.
15 The German Army Handbook 1918, p.65.
16 Eric Siegel, Militaria Magazine 192.
17 Source : http://www.telefunken.de/
18 An example of this device can be seen in Woolley, volume 2, page 52.
19 Information: Chip Minx.

Chapter Seven

Weapons

Introduction

Starting in 1915, several techniques and new weapons were being introduced to try to break through the static enemy lines and defenses. Offensive stick grenades, the use of poison gas, digging tunnels under enemy lines and flame-thrower attacks were often tried for the first time. The weaponry used by the individual soldier can be generally categorized into rifles, revolvers, pistols, machine-guns, grenades, bayonets, flame-throwers, knives and trench clubs.

Although many deviations and exceptions exist, the following table shows the different types of rifles and pistols/revolvers issued to the troops depending on their branch of service:

Unit	Officer	NCO	E.M.	Mounted NCO/EM	Other
Infantry	P08	*Gewehr* 98	*Gewehr* 98		Flag bearer P08
Machine-gun troops[1]	P08	*P08*	*Kar* 98		*Hornist, Fahrer* P08
Storm troopers (*Sturm-Bataillone*)	P08	*Kar* 98	*Kar* 98	-	-
Jäger	P08	*Gewehr* 98	*Gewehr* 98	-	Flag bearer P08
Landwehr infantry	-	*Gewehr* 88/05, *Gewehr* 88	*Gewehr* 88/05, *Gewehr* 88	-	-
Landsturm infantry	-	*Gewehr* 88, *Kar* 88,	*Gewehr* 88, *Kar* 88, Captured rifle	- Captured rifle	-
Cavalry[2]	P08	P08	Kar 98	-	Musician P08
Field artillery[3]	P08/Revolver	P08/Revolver	P08/Revolver	P08/Revolver	-
Foot artillery	P08	*Kar* 98/Gew91	*Kar* 98/Gew 91	-	-
Leichte Munitionskolonnen[4]	P08/Revolver	P08/Revolver	P08/Revolver	P08/Revolver	-
Infantry Munitionskolonnen	LP08/Revolver	LP08/Revolver	*Kar* 98/*Kar* 88	LP08/Revolver	-
Artillery Munitionskolonnen	LP08/Revolver	LP08/Revolver	*Kar* 98/*Kar88*	LP08/Revolver	-
Mountain artillery	Lange P08	Lange P08	*Kar* 98	Lange P08	-
Pioneer	P08	*Gewehr* 98	*Gewehr* 98[5]	-	-
Ersatz, Landwehr, Landsturm Pioneer	P08	*Gewehr* 88/95	*Gewehr* 88/95	-	-
Cyclist (*Radfahrer*)	P08	*Gewehr* 98[6]	*Gewehr* 98	-	-
Railway (*Eisenbahn*)	P08	*Gewehr* 98	*Gewehr* 98	-	-
Searchlight (*Scheinwerfer*)	P08	*Kar* 98	*Kar* 98	-	Fahrer P08
Kraftfahrer	P08	*Kar* 98	*Kar* 98	-	-
Communication (*Telegrafentruppen*)	P08	P08	*Kar* 98	P08	Fahrer P08
Luftschiffertruppen	P08	*Kar* 98	*Kar* 98	P08	-
Fliegertruppen[8]	P08	*Kar* 98	*Kar* 98	-	-
Train	P08	*Kar* 98/*Kar* 88	*Kar* 98/*Kar* 88	-	-
Medical (*Sanitätswesen, Veterinärswesen*)	P08	P08	P08	-	-
Police (*Feldgendarmerie*)	P08/Revolver	P08/Revolver	P08/Revolver	-	-
Generals	P08	-	-	-	-
Staff (*Stabsordonanzen*)	-	P08	*Kar* 98[9]	-	-
Stabswachen	-	P08	*Kar* 98	-	-

According to the "*German Army Handbook*" from 1918, the *Gewehr* 98, Pistol P08, *Bergmann*, heavy machine gun 08 and 08/15 all fired the same type of .311" caliber ammunition. Six types of ammunition existed: "S", "R", "K", "L.S.", "L.E." and incendiary ammunition. "S" ammunition (*Spitz-munition* or *S-Patrone*) has a pointed 10 mg bullet made of lead. The entire cartridge has a length of 28mm. The letter "S" was stamped on the base of the cartridge. "R" ammunition (*Rillen-munition*) was a more advanced design and can be recognized because of a 1mm wide groove around the lower edge of the bullet to obviate stoppages caused by loose cases. The third pattern was the "K" ammunition (*Spitz mit Kern munition*) used for armor piercing purposes. It closely resembles the "S" pattern, but had a blunter point and had a red band painted around the cap of the cartridge. The letter "K" was stamped on the base of the cartridge.[10] "L.S." ammunition (*Leucht-spur*) was nearly the same as the previous armor piercing cartridges, but part of the bullet was filled with tracer composition. "L.E." (*Luft-Einschiess*) cartridges produce white smoke on impact and were used for ranging purposes and were slightly larger than the "S" cartridge.

Bayonet (*Seitengewehr*)

The armed forces used a wide variation of bayonets (*Seitengewehr*) patterns before and during the war. These were, among others, the model 71, model 71/84, model 84/98, model 98, model 98/02 and the model 98/05. In addition, Bavaria adopted the "*Infanterie-Säbel 38*". Other dismounted troops of special branches of service often had their own bayonet. During the war, the "short bayonet model 98" (*Kurzes Seitengewehr kS98*) was used by colonial, machine-gun, airship, telegraph and searchlight troops and medical orderlies. This short bayonet was also popular with officers but against 1915 regulations as officers had to replace their swords with the model 98/05 bayonet. Other specialized bayonets included the "*Hirschfänger 71*" for Prussian *Jäger* and *Schützen* and also marine formations, the *Marine-Seitengewehr* model 19[11] (*Entermesser für Torpedo-Bootsbesatzungen*), the "*Pioneer-Faschinenmesser 71*" for *Eisenbahn* and *Landwehr* pioneers, the "*Artillerie-Seitengeweht 71*" for *Landwehr* Foot artillery, the "*Seitengewehr U/M*" for Field artillery and the Bavarian artillery "*Seitengewehr 92*".

Entermesser für Torpedo-Bootsbesatzungen. This special bayonet was used by some Imperial Navy formations and had a total length of 23.2" (59cm), the scabbard was initially made from leather, later from steel and had a length of 17.7" (45cm). *Courtesy of Domein Raversijde -Ostend.*

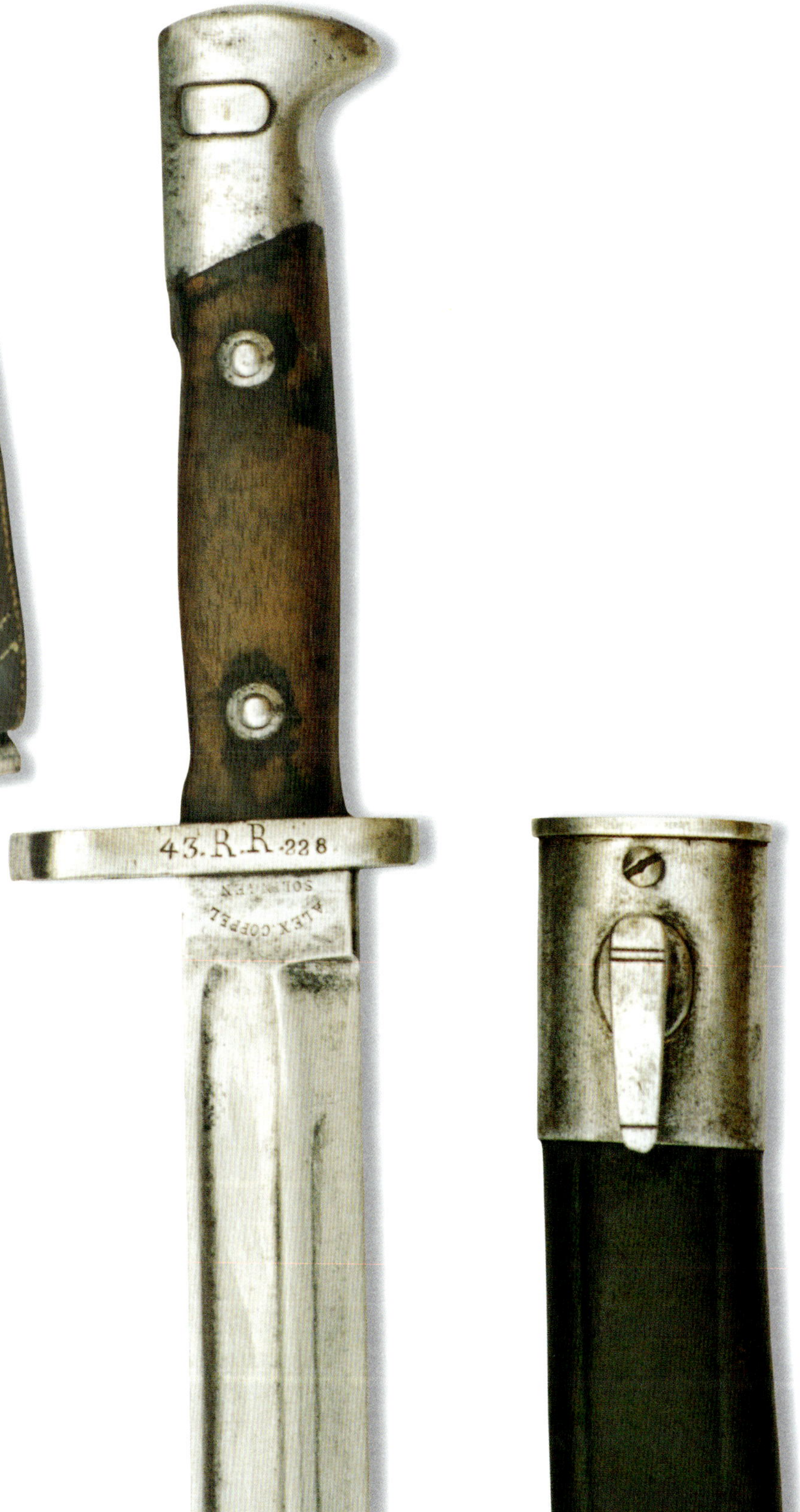

Bayonet model 1871/84, unit marked "43.R.R.228" and made by "*Alex Coppel Solingen*". The bayonet has an overall length of 14.8" (38cm). The scabbard has a leather body. A limited number of these bayonets were issued with saw tooth. *Courtesy of Faris Siwadi.*

This photograph shows the shovel and carrier, bayonet model 98 and blue/red/blue *Troddel of the 8th company. Courtesy of Faris Siwadi.*

The model 98/05 (introduced in 1905 for the rifle *Gewehr* 98) was the most widely issued bayonet within the army when the war broke out. The 98/05 bayonet was produced in two versions, called *a.A* (*Alter Art*) or "old pattern" and *n.A* (*Neuer Art*) or "new pattern" as of 1914. The bayonet had a total length of 20.4" (52cm) with a 15.3" (39cm) steel sawback blade. Later 98/05 scabbards were made entirely of steel. The scabbard was originally made from leather (*Lederscheide*) with metal reinforcements on the throat and tip. The *n.A.* model received a steel protective plate to prevent the wooden handle from becoming damaged when firing the rifle, which was especially severe with the Carbine 98a.

Sawback versions of the 98/05 were issued to pioneer and other technical troops. The sawback was a very effective cutting tool and was not intended to increase the lethal nature of the blade. However, stories were told in the German ranks that the Allied troops considered the sawback bayonet as a devious weapon and that soldier carrying one were shot immediately after being taken prisoner. The War Ministry decided to stop the production of the saw bayonet and soldiers in the field sometimes changed existing bayonets by removing the teeth.

Bayonet model 1884/98 *a.A.*, unit marked "*55.R.6.155*" and made by "*Weyersberg Kirschbaum Solingen*". The bayonet has an overall length of 14.9" (38.2cm). The scabbard has a leather body. *Courtesy of Faris Siwadi.*

Unissued 98/05 bayonet frog made in 1917 by *Dieterlie & Winter, Offenbach A/M.* and ink stamped *BA XVIII. Courtesy of Brian Ludwig.*

During the war, simply designed and quickly manufactured bayonets were issued to troops in the front line, called "Ersatz" bayonets. While existing blades in stock were used with a length of approx. 15.3" (39cm), late-war bayonets can have blades from 9.8" (25cm) to 12.5" (32cm) in length. Not many markings can be found on these bayonets.

This was only a brief introduction to the field of World War I German bayonets. Much more information can be found in several books listed in the reference section. (for example Walter, John. *The German Bayonet*)

Rear view with date and manufacturer markings.

Rear view of bayonet frog.

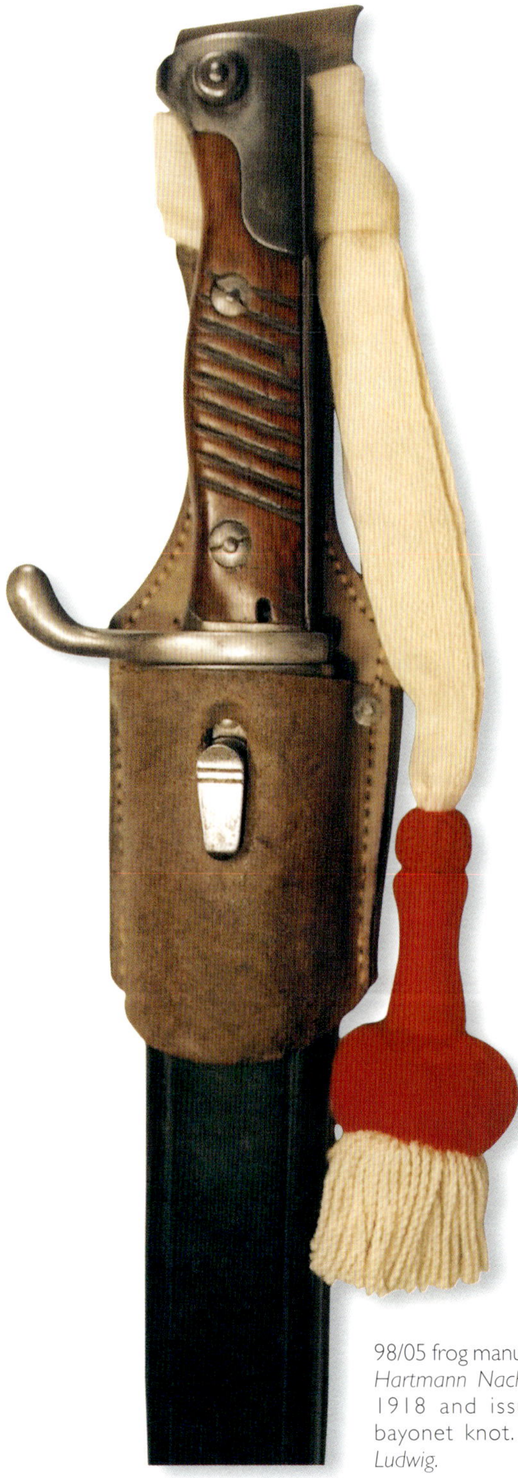

98/05 frog manufactured by *Otto M. Hartmann Nach...,Offenbach a./M.*, 1918 and issue 6th company bayonet knot. *Courtesy of Brian Ludwig.*

Saw bayonet 95/05 with metal scabbard. Marked: *R. Stock & Co and B. Marienfelde. Courtesy of BT.*

Left: Ersatz bayonet marked "*2627*". The total length of the bayonet is 18.1" (46cm) and the blade is 12.2" (31cm). Right: Ersatz bayonet with green paint and marked 4494. Usually, the green paint has worn of, but this nice example still has most of the original finish. The total length of the bayonet is 15.7" (40cm) and the blade is 9.8" (25cm). *Courtesy of BT.*

Regimental markings are only rarely found on ersatz pieces. This bayonet is marked "*R.J.R.91 3.M.G.K.*" *Courtesy of Michael Brennan.*

Ersatz bayonet with carrier and *Troddel* for the 13th MG company. *Courtesy of Michael Brennan.*

Bayonet Knot (*Troddel*)

The *Troddel* or bayonet knot identified the battalion and company that the soldier belonged to in the regiment by means of different color combinations. Having been a mandatory item during the pre-war years, the use of the *Troddel* declined during the war years. The cavalry formation had a different type of bayonet knot, called *Faustriemen*. The *Troddel* and *Faustriemen* consisted of the following components from top to bottom:

A linen strap (*Riband*).
A woolen Slider (*Schieber*). For *Faustriemen*: constructed from woven or plaited leather.
The stem (*Stängel*).
The crown (*Kranz*). For cavalry *Faustriemen*: constructed from woven or plaited leather.
The tassel (*Quaste*).

It's just great if one finds a World War I relic in your own backyard. The following bayonet is a Belgian mod 1889 infantry bayonet,[11] which were frequently used by German *Landwehr* troops as well. It was left by the retreating German Army near a Belgian farm in *Tremelo* (*Veldonckstraat*) (between *Aarschot* and *Leuven*/Brussels), which belonged to the great-grand parents of the author's wife. Unfortunately, the bayonet was used years ago as a tool in the garden and the blade was broken in half.

Troddel, white-blue-white for 13th Machine gun company. *Courtesy of BT.*

Private-purchase 13th Machine gun company bayonet knot. *Courtesy of Brian Ludwig.*

Private-purchase 12th company bayonet knot. *Courtesy of Brian Ludwig.*

The strap and tassels were white and changed to grey to reduce visibility during the war. Non-commissioned officers wore their states colors woven into the slider and the crown. The color scheme within the regiment was as follows:

Company	Stem	Crown and slider
Battalion I		
Company nr. 1	*White*	*White*
Company nr. 2	*White*	*Red*
Company nr. 3	*White*	*Yellow*
Company nr. 4	*White*	*Blue*
Battalion II		
Company nr. 5	*Red*	*White*
Company nr. 6	*Red*	*Red*
Company nr. 7	*Red*	*Yellow*
Company nr. 8	*Red*	*Blue*
Battalion III		
Company nr. 9	*Yellow*	*White*
Company nr. 10	*Yellow*	*Red*
Company nr. 11	*Yellow*	*Yellow*
Company nr. 12	*Yellow*	*Blue*
Machine gun company nr. 13	*Blue*	*White*
Fortress Machine-gun Abteilung nr. 14 (optional)		

Jäger contingents were organized in independent battalions of five companies plus a machine-gun battalion. The bayonet knot was entirely dark green for enlisted men. For *Oberjäger* and re-enlisted men, the *Troddel* was interwoven with colored silk, including the tassel. Commissioned officers wore a sword knot, called *Portepee*, which lacked the tassels. As described in *"Jäger & Schützen, dress and distinction 1910-1914"*, the following color schemes were used for *Jäger* battalions:

Strap	Stem, crown, slider & tassel	State
Enlisted men		
Dark green	Dark green	Prussia
Dark green	Dark green	Mecklenburg
Dark green	Dark green	Saxony
Same as infantry	*same as infantry*	Bavaria
Oberjäger		
Dark green piped with silver silk	Dark green combined with silver silk	Prussia
Dark green piped with golden silk	Dark green combined with golden silk	Mecklenburg
Dark green piped with silver silk	Dark green combined with silver silk	Saxony

White piped light-blue	Crown light blue with white center stripe, tassel white filled light blue, slider and stem white/light-blue	Bavaria
Re-enlisted men		
Dark green	Slider dark-green, tassel white, stem and crown white/black	Prussia
Dark green	Slider dark-green. tassel, stem and crown blue/yellow/carmine	Mecklenburg
Dark green	Slider dark-green, tassel white filled green, stem and crown white/green	Saxony
White	Crown light blue with white center stripe, tassel white filled light blue, slider in battalion color, stem white/light-blue	Bavaria

Rifles

The German Army used six main types of rifles or carbines. The *Gewehr 98*, *Karabinier 98*, *Gewehr 88*, *Gewehr 88/05*, *Karabinier 88* and the *Gewehr 91*. The *Gewehr 98* and *Karabinier 98* were the two main weapons of front line troops during the war. Other rifles captured during battle were used as well. Rifles and weapons in general will not be discussed in detail in this book, as they are already described in length in many excellent reference books. (e.g. Walter, John. *Central Powers Small Arms of World War I*) However, the rifle or carbine was an important and integral part of the appearance of the German soldier, so the most common types will be briefly described. The length and weight of the different German rifles and carbines are as follows[12]:

Weapon	Total length	Weight
Gewehr 98	49.2" (125cm)	9.0 lbs (4.1 kg)
Karabinier 98	43.3" (110cm)	7.7 lbs (3.5 kg)
Gewehr 88	49.2" (125cm)	8.4 lbs (3.8 kg)
Gewehr 88/05	49.2" (125cm)	8.4 lbs (3.8 kg)
Karabinier 88	37.4" (95cm)	6.8 lbs (3.1 kg)
Gewehr 91	37.4" (95cm)	6.8 lbs (3.1 kg)

Although there were standards for marking weapons, these were not always uniformly followed. Most rifles display four different markings. The type of the rifle in Gothic letters, like "*Gew 98*", the serial number usually completely stamped at the left side of the chamber, several inspection marks and finally the name of the manufacturer with the year of production on top of the chamber. Different patterns of inspection marks existed, like a Prussian eagle with outstretched wings or a crowned Bavarian Lion. The most common manufactures were *Erfurt, Danzig, Spandau, Waffenfabrik Oberspree, Amberg, Waffenfabrik Mauser* and *Simson & Sohn Suhl*. A special numbering scheme was used for the serial numbers. The first weapons were numbered 1 to 9999, the second batch 1a to 9999a, then 1b to 9999b and this continued until 1z to 9999z. The next range was 1aa to 9999aa and the entire sequence was repeated with two letters as the suffix.

Bayonet 98/05 with frog and EM *Troddel*. The bayonet is marked "*ERFURT W14*". The "W14" is the *Klingrückenstempel*, indicating the year the bayonet was taken in use. The "W" stands for Wilhelm and "14" stands for 1914. A smaller stamped mark, called *Abnahmestempel* can be seen on top of the bayonet. The *Troddel* is yellow/red/yellow indicating the *II. Batallion 7. Kompanie. Courtesy of BT.*

Gewehr 98

The *Gewehr 98* rifle was the main battle rifle of the infantry, *Jäger*, *Schützen* and pioneers both before and during the First World War. It proved to be a robust and accurate weapon. The 7.9mm caliber rifle was adopted on April 5, 1898, as the *Gewehr 98* and during the early part of 1899 was used in troop trials by various Guard units and a training school. Mass production of the rifle began in 1900 at the government arsenals at *Danzig, Erfurt* and *Spandau* and in subsequent years at *Amberg* and various private arms firms, including *Waffenfabrik Mauser*. The rifle had an internal box magazine, loaded through the action by brass stripper clips holding five rounds. Up to 35 to 40 rounds could be fired per minute. The barrel was of blued steel and the stock and hand guard in light brown wood. The *Gew 98* was sighted to 200 meters and could be increased by 50-meter steps up to 2000meters. Up to three rifles fitted with a telescopic sight were issued per infantry company.[13] A limited number of rifles were adapted with a special detachable magazine holding 25 rounds (*Grabenmagazin* or "*Ansteckmagazin für 25 Patronen*") to increase the firing power of the *Gewehr 98*. Rifles with the *Grabenmagazin* were difficult to handle.

These four soldiers are equipped with rifles with a detachable magazine holding 25 rounds (*Grabenmagazin* or "*Ansteckmagazin für 25 Patronen*"). *Courtesy of Thomas Wictor.*

The rifle had an internal box magazine, loaded through the action by brass stripper clips holding five rounds.

Mauser Gewehr 98 made by *Danzig* in 1905. This weapon has serial number "697a" stamped onto the left side of the chamber. The rifle is equipped with a protective cover, marked with the Imperial Crown (a marine infantry or See-Battalion unit) and the letters "DRP" (*Deutsches Reichs Patent*). These covers were used to prevent dirt and mud from entering the mechanism. The trigger is covered with an ingenious mechanism called *"Winterzieher"* so that the rifle could also be fired when thick gloves were worn. The device is marked *"mod 98"*. A removable cover for the barrel of which a close-up can be seen completes the set. The rifle has a weight of 9 lbs (4.1kg) without the accessories and a total length of 49.2" (125cm). The bayonet could not be put on when the barrel cover was attached. *Courtesy of BT.*

The removable barrel cover.

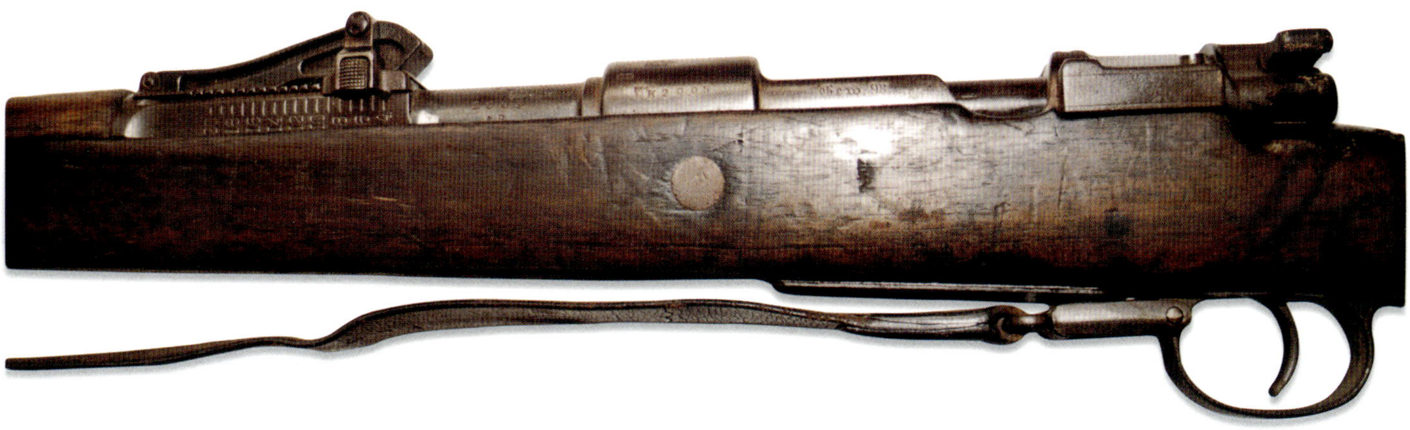

Mauser Gewehr 98 made by *Erfurt* in 1908. This weapon has serial number "2005b". The stock of the G98 displays inspection marks and the unit identification marks appear on the butt disc: "48 R 2 582" with stamps for the *Infanterie-Regiment von Stülpnagel (5. Brandenburgisches)* Nr.48 (Army Corps III), 2nd Company, weapon number 582. *Courtesy of BT.*

Carbine 98 (*Gewehr Karabinier 98 K*)
The second most important rifle was the Carbine 98 (*Gewehr Karabinier 98 K*) used by cavalry, foot artillery, train and *Verkehrtruppen* since 1908. The carbine had a length of 43.3" (110cm) and a weight of 7.7 lbs (3.5kg). It also fired 7.9mm caliber. It had a turndown bolt, which would less likely interfere with the soldier's kit.

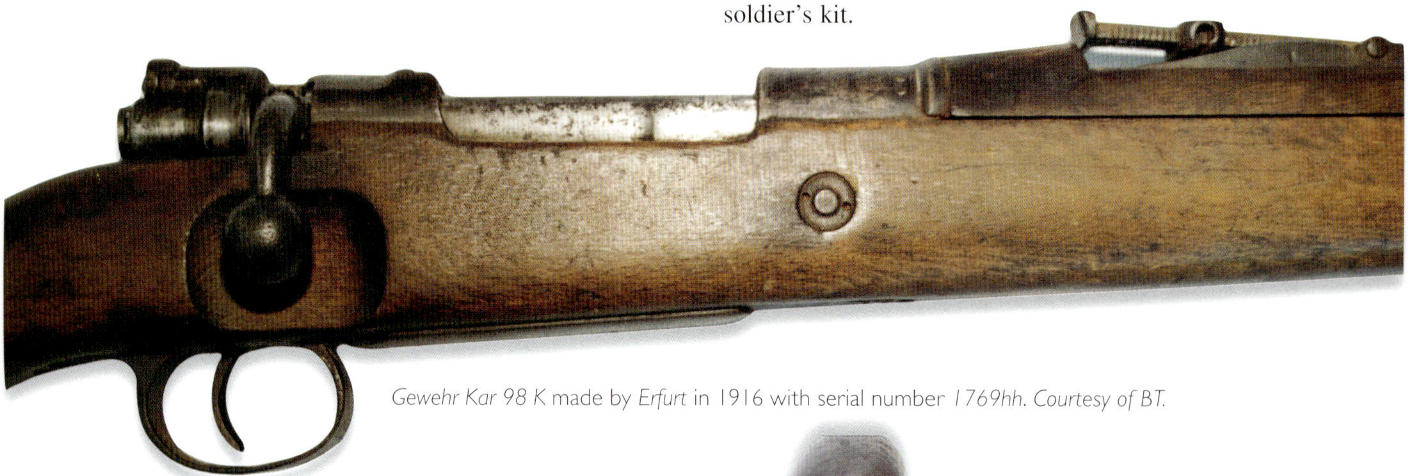

Gewehr Kar 98 K made by *Erfurt* in 1916 with serial number *1769hh. Courtesy of BT.*

Carbine Model 88 (*Karabinier 88*)

The *Karabinier 88* was the predecessor of the *Karbinier 98* and primarily used by cavalry formations before these switched over to the new model. During the war, colonial troops, *Landsturm*, train and munitions supply convoys used the *Karabinier 88*.

Many different types of carbine holsters (*Karabinerfutteral*) were issued to cavalry units. The *Karabiner Futteral* 98 was distributed in 1909 for the *Gewehr Kar 98* and carried at the left side of the saddle. It had an overall length of 42.5" (109cm) and was made from thick brown leather. Prior to 1909, other types existed as well that were shorter in length, such as the one for the carbine model 88. These were, amongst others, the *Futteral* 73, *Futteral* 88 and *Futteral* 96. Mounted soldiers of other contingents, like Train units, had their own specific design of carbine holsters. *Author's early collection.*

Gewehr 91

The *Gewehr 91* was almost identical to the *Karabinier 88* and used by Foot artillery and cyclists (*Radfahrer*).

Gewehr 91 made by *Erfurt* in 1893. This weapon has serial number *4597e* (bolt) and *37e* (left chamber). *Courtesy of BT.*

Gewehr 98 for Cyclists (*Radfahrer*)

The 1913 introduced "*Gewehr 98 für Radfahrer*" was almost identical with the *Gewehr 98*, but specially altered for cyclists. The bolt knob (*Kammerknopf*) was down turned as on the carbines.

Gewehr 88 and Gewehr 88/05

Landsturm units used the obsolete *Gewehr 88* and modified *Gewehr 88/05*.

13mm Tank-Gewehr Model 1918

The 13mm *T-Gewehr* or sometimes called "Elephant rifle" (*Elefantenbüchse*) was developed by the *Mauser-Werke* at *Obendorf* and demonstrated in January 1918. It was specially designed to more easily penetrate the armor of allied tanks. It had an impressive length of 66.9" (170cm) and a weight of 39 lbs (17.7kg) with its bipod. A team of two soldiers handled it during combat. It fired single rounds, one at a time, which was hand loaded via the multi-locking lug bolt. The firm *Polte* in *Magdeburg* manufactured the special cartridges. Penetration was about 8.6" (22cm) of armor plate at 380 yards (304 meters). Approximately 16.000 rifles were produced, but only 1/3rd saw action in the front line.

Close-up of the bolt of a 13mm *Tank-Gewehr*. The rifle was sighted in steps of 50 meters. *Royal Army and Military History Museum, Brussels.*

The cartridges were carried in a special bag, holding 20 rounds. *Royal Army and Military History Museum, Brussels.*

Lance

The lance has a long history on the battlefield and was considered to be a weapon with many advantages. It not only had an effective range of more than 3 meters, it also inflicted severe injury and had an impressive and positive influence on the morale of the troops. It was very much adapted for chasing the enemy running away from the battlefield, but was less suited for close combat. Whilst only the *Uhlans* and *Landwehr* cavalry were initially equipped with the lance (until 1852), and although already discontinued by many other nations, the weapon became standard issue for all German mounted contingents in 1889 for all EM and NCOs.

The wooden lance model 1869 was based on the lances used until 1852 by *Uhlans* and *Landwehr* Cavalry, but they had six instead of three eyes to attach a small lance flag and a larger metal plate on the spear head to better fix the head onto the lance. Originally, the earlier wooden lances (*Lanze 1869*) had a weight of about 1.8kg and a length of 123" (314cm). In 1890 a slightly longer model weighing nearly 2kg with a length of 125" (320cm) was introduced made from a steel tube. The spear head was 20cm in length. A lance flag (*Lanzenflaggen*) was attached to three (until 1852), six (*Lanze* 1869) or four (as of 1869 for steel lances) steel rings below the spearhead. In the middle of the lance was a almost 19.5" (50cm) long ribbed area (*Handgrif*) with brass rings around the edges, for holding the lance. A 2m long brown leather straps (*Lanzenriemen*) was used to carry the lance. These straps were white for Cuirassiers until 1890. According J. Kraus, a number of experimental lances were tried in 1910 made from rolled sheet steel, with a ball behind the head to prevent the lance from penetrating the body of the opponent too far and breaking. This new design did not see widespread use in the German cavalry.

It is of interest to note that the wooden lance had a large bladed head, while the model 1890 steel lance had a smaller pointed spike. Argentine model 1895 lances are often mistaken for the German model 1890 lances, as they were also made of rolled steel but with the older pattern bladed head as found on the German wooden lance. They are usually stamped "MODELO ARGENTINO 1895".

The left and right stirrup irons were both equipped with a 3.5" (9cm) high lance pouch (*Lanzenschuh*). This cylindrical shaped pouch was made from brown leather and had a diameter of 1.2" (3cm) at the bottom and 2.1" (5.5cm) at the top.

Lance flags (*Lanzenflaggen*) were strapped to the steel eyes of the lance, just below the head. The color and design of the flag depended of the state of origin and was also different for EM and NCOs. While EM flags were in the state colors, NCO flags bore the state monogram. The following table shows the colors in use by each of the states:

State or regiment	EM colors	NCO colors
Baden	yellow-red	white base with a yellow griffin
Bavaria	white-blue	white base with a yellow lion on a shield
Brunswick	blue-yellow	yellow base with a white horse in a red circle
Hessen	white-red	white base with a white-red lion
Mecklenburg	yellow-red	yellow base with a red shield
Prussia	white-black	white base with a black eagle
1 Leib Husaren	white deaths head on a black background as of 1892	
2 Leib Husaren	black deaths head on a white background as of 1894	
Oldenburg (until 1895)	red-blue	white base with a yellow star & white eagle
Oldenburg (in 1895)	red-blue	red base with a yellow star & white eagle
Oldenburg (as of 1896)	red-blue	blue base with a yellow star & white eagle
Saxony	white-green	white base with a black lion & yellow shield
Württemberg	black-red	red base with a yellow shield

Pistols and revolvers

Reichsrevolver Model 1879 and 1883

The 10.6mm *Reichsrevolver* was a solid-frame revolver with a single-action trigger and a six round magazine. These guns had no ejection system for the spent shells. It had a safety lever at the left and a square butt cap with a lanyard ring. The first model was issued in 1879. It had an overall length of 13.3" (33.8cm) and was issued to Dragoons, Cuirassiers, NCOs of infantry regiments and Field artillery.[14] It was eventually replaced by the *Pistole 08* but still remained in service during the First World War. The model 1883 was the same in design, but made shorter with an overall length of 10.7" (27.2cm). The butt was rounded and had a lanyard ring.

Close-up of the unit marks *75.A.1.29*, which stands for the 75th Field Artillery Regiment, Battery 1, Weapon number 29 (see p 305).

This short barrel 10.6mm *Reichsrevolver* with rounded butt and lanyard was made by *Erfurt* in 1884. The revolver is numbered *122d* and *1055. Courtesy of BT.*

This photo from the 12th Reserve Field Artillery regiment was taken in October 1915. The soldier wears a spiked helmet with a ball, a helmet cover with *R 12* and a *Reichsrevolver* in a holster holster at his right hip. *Courtesy of Faris Siwadi.*

Mauser C96

The *Mauser Selbstlade Pistole C96* is commonly known as the *Broomhandle Mauser*. It was first developed in 1890 and continuously modified until 1912. Its main competitor was the *Luger* pistol which became the prime side arm in the German army. Nevertheless, during the war, the army contracted with *Mauser* to purchase 150,000 "Red Nine" C96 pistols, chambered for the 9 m/m *Parabellum* (a.k.a. 9 m/m *Luger* cartridge). Approximately 135,000 were delivered before the end of the war. Because original *Mauser* pistols were issued for 7.65mm caliber, a red "9" painted on the grip clearly indicated which type of ammunition to use. The magazine could hold six, ten or twelve rounds. The wooden holster for the *Mauser* also doubles as a shoulder stock.

Model 1914 Mauser

The model 1914 *Mauser* was a fairly common pistol for officers to privately purchase as their sidearm. While not standard issue in the German Imperial Army, the model 1914 was acceptable as a substitute sidearm and those pistols so accepted will generally show an Imperial Army acceptance mark.

Luger P08 (*Pistole 08*)

The German navy adopted the 9mm *Parabellum Luger* in 1904 and the pistol became the standard sidearm used by the German army during the First World War. The LP08 was sighted to 800 meters and was able to penetrate a French steel helmet.[15] *Lugers* were produced by the German government arms factories such as *Erfurt* or the *Deutsche Waffen- und Munitionsfabriken (DWM)*. The pistol could hold 8 cartridges of 9mm ammunition. The P08 pistols were complex in their operation and dirt in the interior parts of the firing mechanism could easily cause the pistol to fail.[16]

According to Jan Still in his book, "Imperial *Lugers* and Their Accessories", German Army unit markings are found on approximately 15 percent of the Army *Lugers* manufactured during the period 1908 through 1914. For most *Lugers* the markings are stamped according to regulations, with slight deviations, into the grip strap. Stamped numbers can be of three sizes. The largest, 4.2mm high Roman numbers, indicates the battalion or corps; the next highest 3.1mm high, indicates the regiment number and the company, battery, squadron, or detachment number; and the smallest 2.1mm high indicates the weapon number. For example: " *36. R.M.G. 52.*" can be decomposed out of: "R." (Infanterie Regiment) and "M.G." (*Maschinengewehr* or Machine Gun). The number marking "36" corresponds to the 36th Fusilier Infantry Regiment and the serial number of the 52nd issued weapon. Since most regiments had only one company, it is assumed that it was the one and only MG company of the 36th Fusiliers. After the war started, fewer *Lugers* were unit marked given the lower priority assigned to accomplishing such work. Also, the German Ministry of War issued a document dated November 2, 1916 that dispensed with the requirement to mark issue weapons. Although the practice did continue to a minor extent, less than one percent of those manufactured during the period 1915 through 1918 have unit marks.[17]

1915 dated 08 *Luger* pistol manufacture by *Deutsche Waffen und Munitions (DWM)*. Courtesy of Brian Ludwig.

Black leather holster (*Pistolentasche* 08) for the *Pistole* 08. The holster is made from stiff brown or black leather and enclosed the pistol completely. A flap secured by a buckle closed the holster. It has a small compartment for a spare magazine and internal storage for a stripper tool. *Courtesy of BT.*

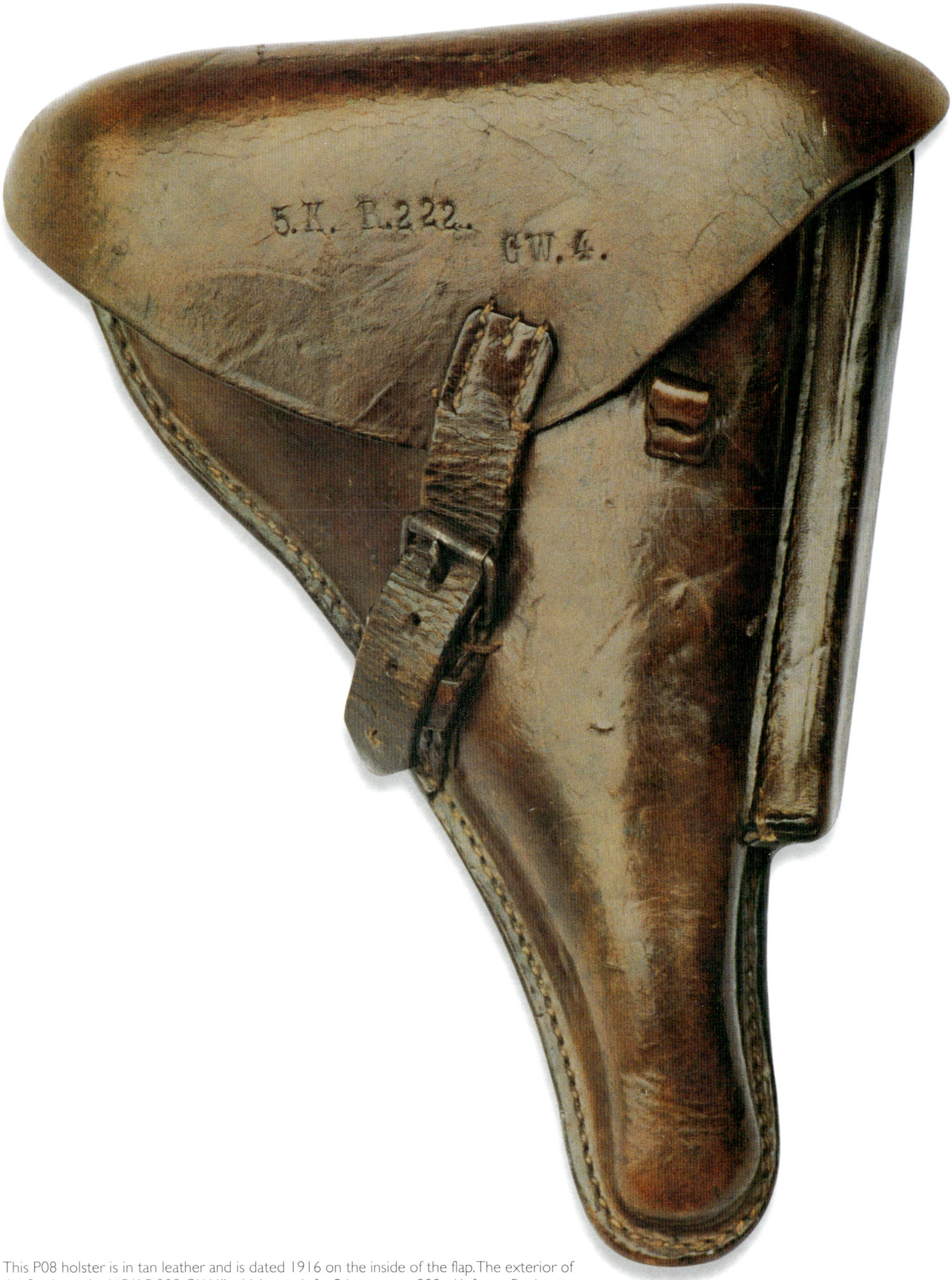

This P08 holster is in tan leather and is dated 1916 on the inside of the flap. The exterior of the flap is marked "*5.K. R.222 G.W.4*", which stands for 5th company, 222nd Infantry Regiment, *Granatenwerfer* Company 4. *Courtesy of Faris Siwadi.*

Lange Pistole 08

Three years after the introduction of the P08, the War Ministry considered a longer pistol with a shoulder stock for the artillery. The *Lange Pistole 08*, also called the "*Artillery Luger*", was officially accepted in 1913.[18] The pistol had an overall length of 12.6" (32cm). Three special leather double pocket spare magazine pouches were introduced for each pistol. These pouches were 5.5" (14cm) long and had a width of 2.4" (6cm) and could contain two spare magazines (*Reservemagazin*).

Black holster (*Pistolentasche*) for the "*Lange Pistole 08*". The holster was attached to a wooden shoulder stock (*Anschlagbrett*), which was carried at the right hip using a long leather strap running over the left shoulder. However, existing holsters were also modified and two leather straps sewn on the back, so it could be worn directly on the belt, like the P08 holsters. The holster had a length of 12.6" (32cm) and was 6.3" (16cm) wide at the top and 1.4" (3.5cm) at the bottom. On the side was a small pouch for a cleaning rod (*Reinigungsstock*). A tiny pouch could be found on the inside flap for a screwdriver (*Schraubenzieher*). *Courtesy of BT.*

A snail drum (*Trommelmagazin* or *Ladenrahmen*) was introduced in 1916. This drum contained 32 bullets and was carried in a cloth pouch on the belt. *Royal Army and Military History Museum, Brussels.*

P08 reserve magazine for two spare magazines. Three of these were issued per "*Lange Pistole 08*". *Royal Army and Military History Museum, Brussels.*

Machine Guns MG08 and MG08/15

The 46kg sledged mounted 1908 heavy machine gun (MG 08) used the same standard cartridge as the rifle, i.e. 7.9mm *S-Patrone*. The sledge mount (*Schlitten 08*) had four legs. In static positions or in the trenches, special smaller trench mounts were manufactured. The gun fired 250-300 rounds per minute using 250 round belts (*Patronengurten*) with a maximum firing distance of 2000 meters.

Several MG08 accessories were available, including a rain cover, a 100 round drum (*Trommel*), water jacket front shield, sledge mount shield and several armor shields (*Schild*), like the *Schild 08* and the *Schild 08/15* issued in 1916. Slings or dragging straps were made in leather or from thick webbing with leather fittings and a metal hook at each end, and were used to drag the sledge when the crew crawled over the ground. Each machine-gun was supplied with four spare barrels. A crew of five operated the gun: an NCO (*Gewehrführer*) and four gunners (*Schützen*) of which two could aim the gun (*Richtschütze*).

The MG08/15 was a portable 30.8 lbs (14kg) water-cooled machine gun sighted to 1400 meters with a bipod, which could be used with the T-rifle as well. The gun was derived from the MG08/15 machine gun, but different in that the diameter of the barrel casing was smaller, a bipod instead of a sledge mount was used and had a rifle but and pistol grip instead of the spade grips. Each MG08/15 was issued with a carrying sling to carry it either over the shoulder during manoeuvres or to use the gun in a standing assault firing position. The model 1911 metal ammunition box could contain two belts of 250 cartridges, while the *Patronenkasten 15* only contained one ammunition belt. The latter was made from metal or wood. One soldier could carry the machine-gun.

For more information on the Maxim machineguns, the reader can refer to the excellent work of *Goldsmith, Dolf, The Devil's Paintbrush.*

A sledge mounted MG08 with crew. An armor shield (*Schild*) is held by the far right soldier. Four cases with two ammunition belts for 250 rounds are standing by. *Courtesy of BT.*

This soldier is equipped with an MG dragging strap, which served to carry the equipment and a P08.

MG08. *Royal Army and Military History Museum, Brussels.*

Carrying case for two 100-round MG-08/15 assault drums. Field gray painted with Imperial proof marks and manufactured by *R. Ö.& Kallmann*. Case measures approximately 16x8x6" (41x20x17cm). *Courtesy of Brian Ludwig.*

MG 08/15 100-round drum. The 100-round belt attached to the interior spool and mounted on the right side of the receiver, just below the feed block. *Courtesy of Brian Ludwig.*

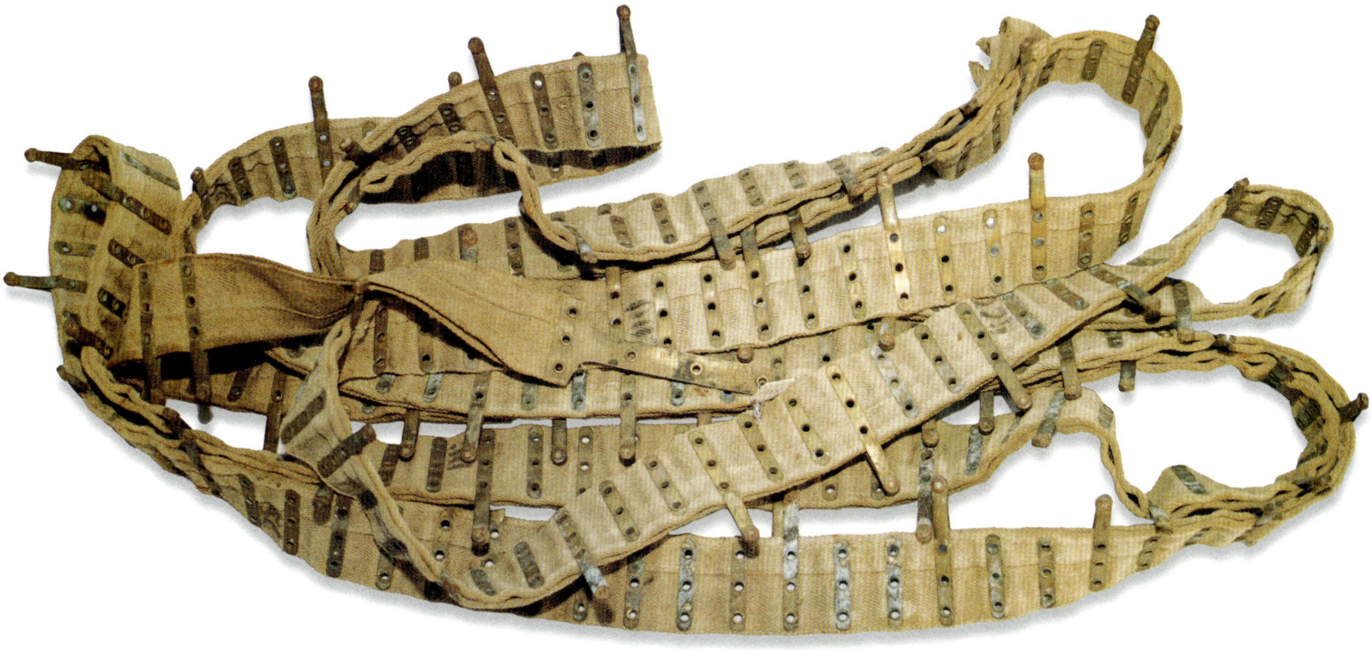

250 round MG ammo belt. The copper end is marked *DWM 9.15*. Belts were issued with 100 or 250 rounds. *Author's early collection.*

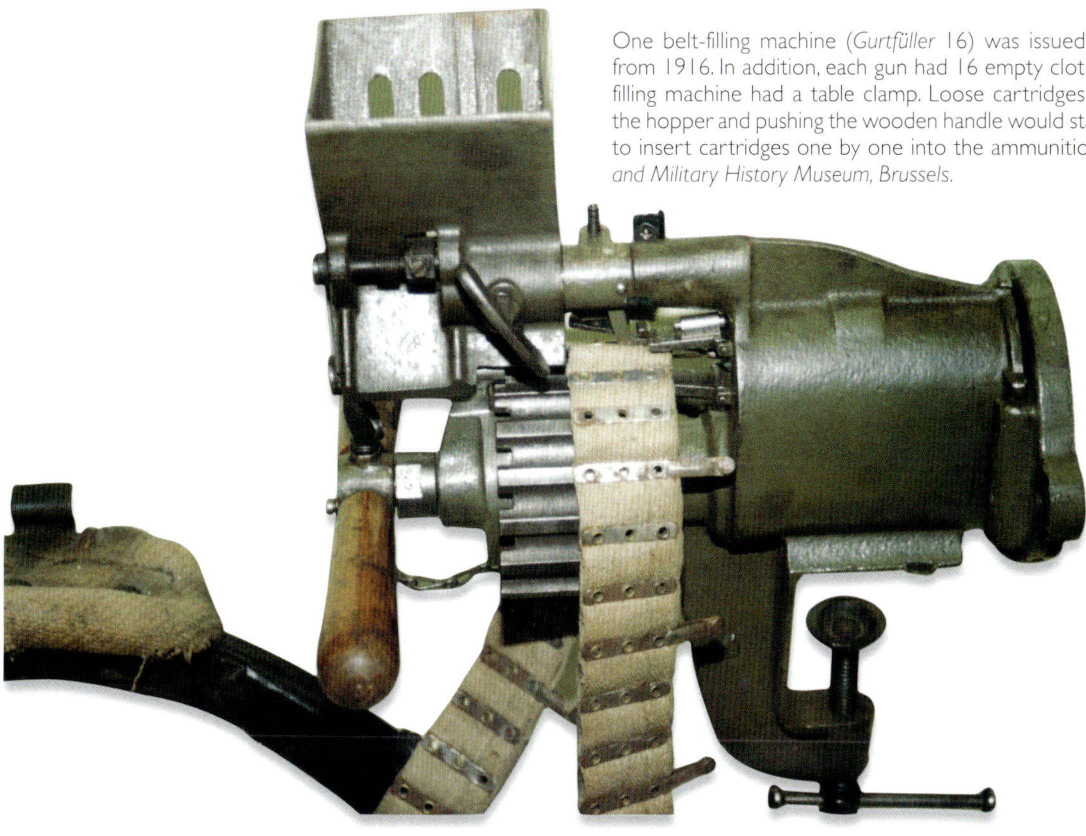

One belt-filling machine (*Gurtfüller* 16) was issued per machine-gun from 1916. In addition, each gun had 16 empty cloth belts.[19] The belt-filling machine had a table clamp. Loose cartridges were placed into the hopper and pushing the wooden handle would start the mechanism to insert cartridges one by one into the ammunition belt. *Royal Army and Military History Museum, Brussels.*

Details.

Another example of the rare early pattern cylindrical MG-08 water can. Courtesy of Eric Siegel.

Early pattern cylindrical MG-08 water can with original field-gray paint and Imperial proof marks. Likely discarded in the field due to several shrapnel holes that punctured the can. Manufactured by *Schutz & SackÖ*, Berlin. *Courtesy of Brian Ludwig.*

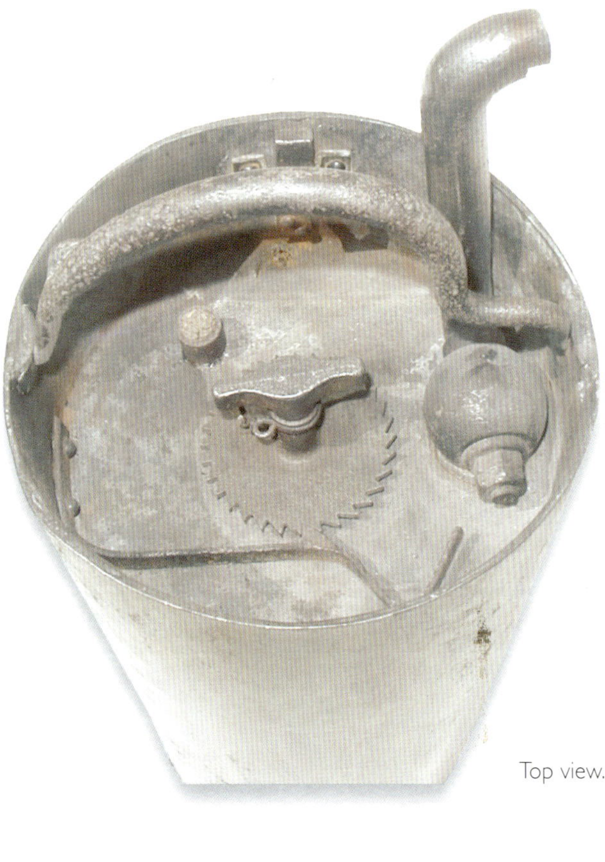

Top view.

Later pattern MG08 water can. *Author's early collection.*

Issue tin oilcan for machine-gun maintenance. *Courtesy of Brian Ludwig.*

The ZF 12 (*Zeilfernrohr 1912*) machine-gun sight with its leather carrying case, manufactured by *Emil Busch A.-G. Rathenow*. The ZF12 and other machine-gun sights were also fitted with ersatz cases often produced from hardened paper cloth. *Courtesy of Brian Ludwig.*

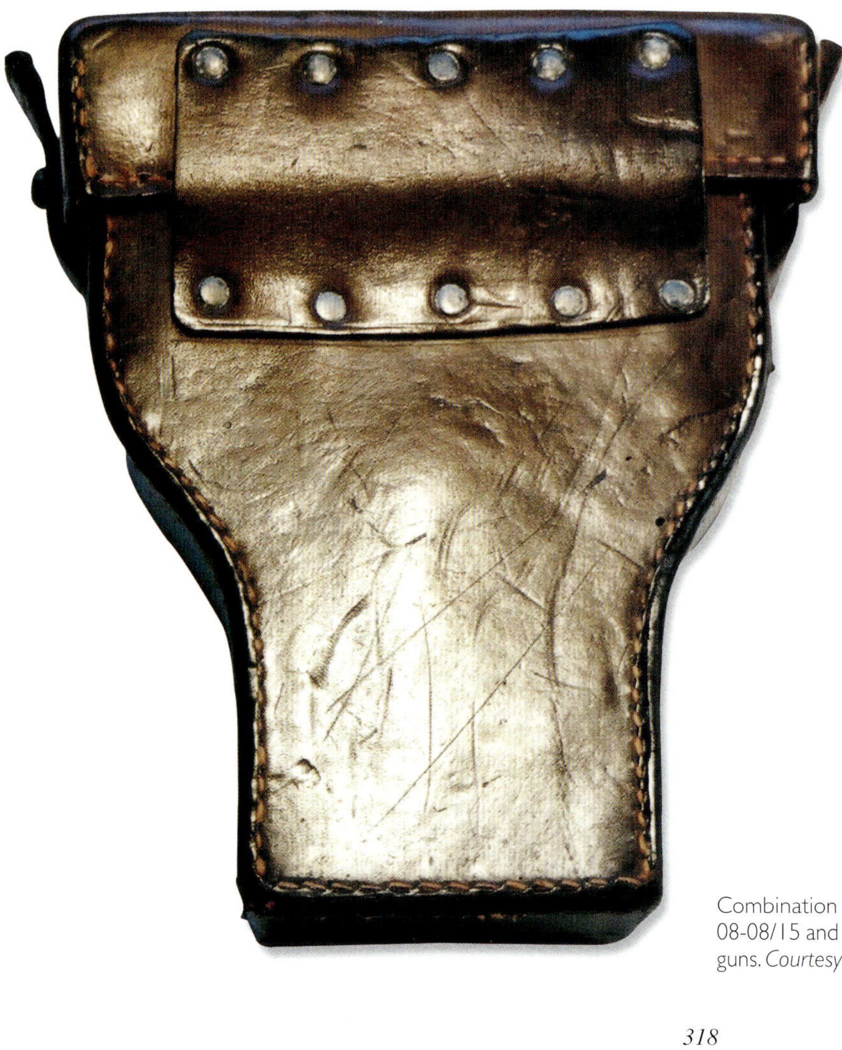

Combination wrench for the 08-08/15 and 08/16 machine-guns. *Courtesy of Brian Ludwig.*

Grenades

This section lists the most common grenades of the German Army. Soldiers were equipped with three types of grenades in 1914. The ball hand grenade model 1913 (*Kugelhandgranate*), the oyster grenade model 1913 (*Diskushandgranate*) and a rifle grenade model 1913.

Ball Grenade (*Kugelhandgranate*)

The ball grenade model 1913 was a segmented cast iron sphere with a copper time fuse. When the fuse was pulled it took seven seconds before the explosion took place. A new model was introduced in 1915. The size and weight was exactly the same, but the cast iron sphere lacked most of the segmentation seen on the model of 1913.

Model 1913 ball grenade. *Author's early collection.*

The ball grenade, here a model 1915, could be carried on the belt using a special metal carrier. *Author's early collection.*

Oyster Grenade (*Diskushandgranate*)

The oyster grenades were percussion models, which exploded on impact. Around the edges of the oyster-like iron shell were six plungers, which were forced against a detonator when striking the ground. A new and larger model was also introduced in 1915 with a thin steel outer shell. Both models had more than one plunger to ensure that at least one would detonate the grenade.

Small model oyster grenade. *Courtesy of Memorial Museum Passchendaele 1917.*

Model 1915 oyster grenade. *Author's early collection.*

Rifle Grenade 1913 and 1914

Two types of fragmentation rifle grenades existed in 1914 of approximately 2.2 lbs (1kg) in weight. They had a large rod, which was inserted into the barrel of the rifle. A blank cartridge was fired which launched the grenade. A range disc could be attached at the nose of the model 1913 grenade or at the base for the model 1914. The grenades lacked accuracy and were quickly replaced.

The conditions of static trench warfare required new and more efficient types of grenades. Three new grenades were introduced starting in 1915. The popular stick grenade (*Stielhandgranate*) in 1915, the egg grenade in 1916 (*Eierhandgranate*) and a new rifle grenade in 1917 (*Wurfgranate*).

Model 1913 rifle grenade. *Author's early collection.*

A model 1914 rifle grenade with range disk and a blank cartridge for launching the grenade. *Courtesy of Memorial Museum Passchendaele 1917.*

Stick Grenade (*Stielhandgranate*)

The offensive stick grenade (*Stielhandgranate B.Z.* or "potato-masher") was introduced in 1915. It was made of a metal cylinder containing an explosive charge, a wooden handle with a time fuse and a pull cord. The cord ran inside the wooden handle and was taped at the base. The soldier would pull the cord, which activated a friction igniter. The fuse was lit and it took 5 1/2 seconds before the detonator went off and the grenade exploded. Some fuses operated within three or seven seconds. The type of the fuse was painted or stamped onto the handle. The cylinder has a metal clip on the side enabling it to be attached to the belt.

A new model appeared in 1916 of which the cord was hidden under a metal screw cap. The cap was unscrewed first and the cord then pulled. This was much safer and protected the mechanism from water and damp. Many different types were issued during the years. Some models exploded on impact while others had a spring ignition mechanism. The exercise grenade had a red painted head with holes drilled into it. It was delivered in wooden supply boxes together with live grenades. The size of the can evolved as well. The first type had a large cylindrical can. As the explosives inside the can were made stronger, it didn't need to be filled up completely. To keep its weight and balance, the upper part of the can was fitted internally with a small wooden block. Later, the size of the can was reduced.

Model 1916 pull cord and metal screw cap.

A group of men in the trenches wearing gasmasks and preparing to throw stick grenades. *Courtesy of Thomas Wictor.*

A very rare variation was a combination of a stick grenade and a ball grenade. A modified *Kügelhandgranate* replaced the metal cylinder and all these models received a spring igniter. Another design was called the *Wilhelm's Handgranate A.Z.*[20] and exploded on impact. Storm troopers sometimes taped six stick grenade cylinders together around a single stick grenade to attack well-defended positions or bunkers.

First model grenade as introduced in 1915. The pull string was taped against the wooden handle. *Courtesy of BT.*

Early model without pull string. A spring mechanism on the exterior of the grenade was used to start the ignition. *Courtesy of BT.*

Left: Late war grenade with a smaller can. The cap is removed and the pull string displayed. The can is repainted green. *Author's early collection.* Right: Exercise grenade with red painted head. *Courtesy of BT.*

Post-war exercise grenade. *Courtesy of BT.*

A rare combination between a stick grenade with external spoon and a ball grenade. *Courtesy of BT.*

The stick grenade heads were stenciled *'Vor Gebrauch Sprengkapsel einsetzen'*, which meant 'Before use insert the detonator'. The paper labels are usually missing. *Courtesy of BT.*

A trench section with a number of soldiers posing with stick grenades. The first person is carrying an early and primitive looking grenade with a wooden handle and a charged head. *Courtesy of Stephen Chambers.*

Egg grenade 1916 (*Eierhandgranate*)

The 350g ovoid shaped egg grenade had an iron body and was introduced in 1916. It was more convenient and easier to throw than the ball grenade and an experienced soldier could throw it 50 yards. During transport, the grenade was closed with a transportation plug, and it received the fuse near the front line. The five or eight second fuses could be screwed into the grenade body using a special tool, the fuse key. The transportation plugs were used with the ball grenade as well. Exercise egg grenades without bursting charge were painted red. Live grenades were filled with black powder, aluminum powder, barium nitrate and potassium perchlorate.[21]

Egg grenade with transportation cap. *Author's early collection.*

A dug fuse key. *Courtesy of BT.*

Courtesy of Eric Siegel.

Rifle Grenade Model 1917 (*Wurfgranate*)

The *Wurf* grenade - also called *jam pot bomb* by the allies[22], was launched with a 1 lb. cylindrical discharger cup fitted on the end of the rifle barrel. The maximum range was approximately 210 yards.[23] Ordinary ball ammunition was fired which passed through a channel in the middle of the grenade, igniting the fuse, which propelled the bomb to its target. The discharger cup had a total length of about 11", and the cylindrical head was 5.1" long with a diameter of 2.3".

Gas and Smoke Grenades

Smoke (or gas) grenades were not used to a great extent, still several models with a different composition existed. Most of these grenades had a spherical iron body of about 4" diameter made of thin sheet metal. The container contained black powder and a liquid in a porcelain container. The explosion would disperse the liquid, which would produce irritant smoke.[24] According to the "German Army Handbook" from 1918, at least four types of gas or smoke grenades were available. These were the *Handgasbombe B*, *Handgasbombe C* and *Reizgasbombe R*, each marked with a red letter "*B*", "*Gas C*" or "*R*" respectively. The fourth version was the *Nebelbombe N*, marked "*Nebel*", a grenade that produced a white cloud of very heavy irritant smoke, which was heavier than air and would stay close to the ground.

The discharger cup was fitted on the rifle barrel and launched the *Wurf* rifle grenade model 1917. The stem of the cup slipped over the muzzle of the rifle and was secured with the steel ring. This device is marked *DWM*, while another similar discharger seen by the author was marked "*DWM 112*". *Courtesy of BT.*

Trench Artillery

Mobile and easy to use trench mortars were introduced in 1915. They projected a finned bomb from a short barrel or tube. Trench artillery can be divided into mortars, grenade launchers and smooth bored mortars. The mortars (*Minenwerfer*) had calibers between 7.6cm and 24.5cm. Grenade launchers like the *Grantenwerfer Modell 16* were small devices, which could easily be moved. Primitive smooth bored mortars were the 91.3mm *Lanz*, the *Ehrhardt*, the *Flügelminenwerfer*, the *Pressluft Minenwerfer* (a pneumatic gun) and the *Albrecht Mörser*.

Soldbuch of a member of the *Minenwerfer Kompagnie 40* with unofficial sleeve insignia. *Courtesy of Sven Kuczyk.*

Minenwerfer Trupp, 2. MW. Batterie II.R.J.R.11. Courtesy of Faris Siwadi.

Granatenwerfer Model 1916

The model 1916 grenade thrower (*Granatenwerfer Gr.W. 16*) was operated by two soldiers and designed to lob grenades of 4 lbs (1.85kg) down into the allied trenches up to a maximum distance of 300 meters (inclination of 45 degrees) and a minimum range of 50 meters (inclination of 80 degrees). This device consisted of two parts: a platform (*Bettung*) of approx. 16kg and a thrower of approx. 24kg. The wooden box with tools and spare parts had a weight of 10 kg.

The spigot contains a firing pin, which is cocked by a lever on the side of the weapon. A lanyard and handle is used to fire the grenade at a safe distance. The 1.85kg grenade (*Wurfgranate 1915*) had either three or four wings and had a propellant charge in the base of the projectile. Late war projectiles had a small charge at the head of the grenade, so it would bounce back after impact and exploded a fraction of a second later in the air- sending shrapnel down on the troops. Exercise grenades were painted red and filled with sand or other materials. Signal rockets could be fired as well with the *Granatenwerfer*. Each launcher came packed in a shipping crate and had many tools and spare parts. Twelve grenade throwers were issued per infantry regiment in 1916 and 24 in 1918.

Granatenwerfer model 1916. *Royal Army and Military History Museum, Brussels.*

Base plate.

Granatenwerfer 16 No. 2712 in the original case with tools and spare parts. This example, manufactured by *Gebruder Bing* of Nuremberg, was captured by American troops and brought back for study by the U.S. military. Items included in the case other than the *Granatenwerfer* are the manual, a rag, spare bolt, tin box with spare firing pins and firing pin springs, a level, various wrenches, oil can, pair of pliers, spare firing toggle, spare arming switch, screw driver and a steel leveling shim. *Gebruder Bing* made numerous items for the Imperial German military including canteens but they were best known as one of Europe's premier metal toy manufacturers. *Courtesy of Brian Ludwig.*

Model and manufacturer markings.

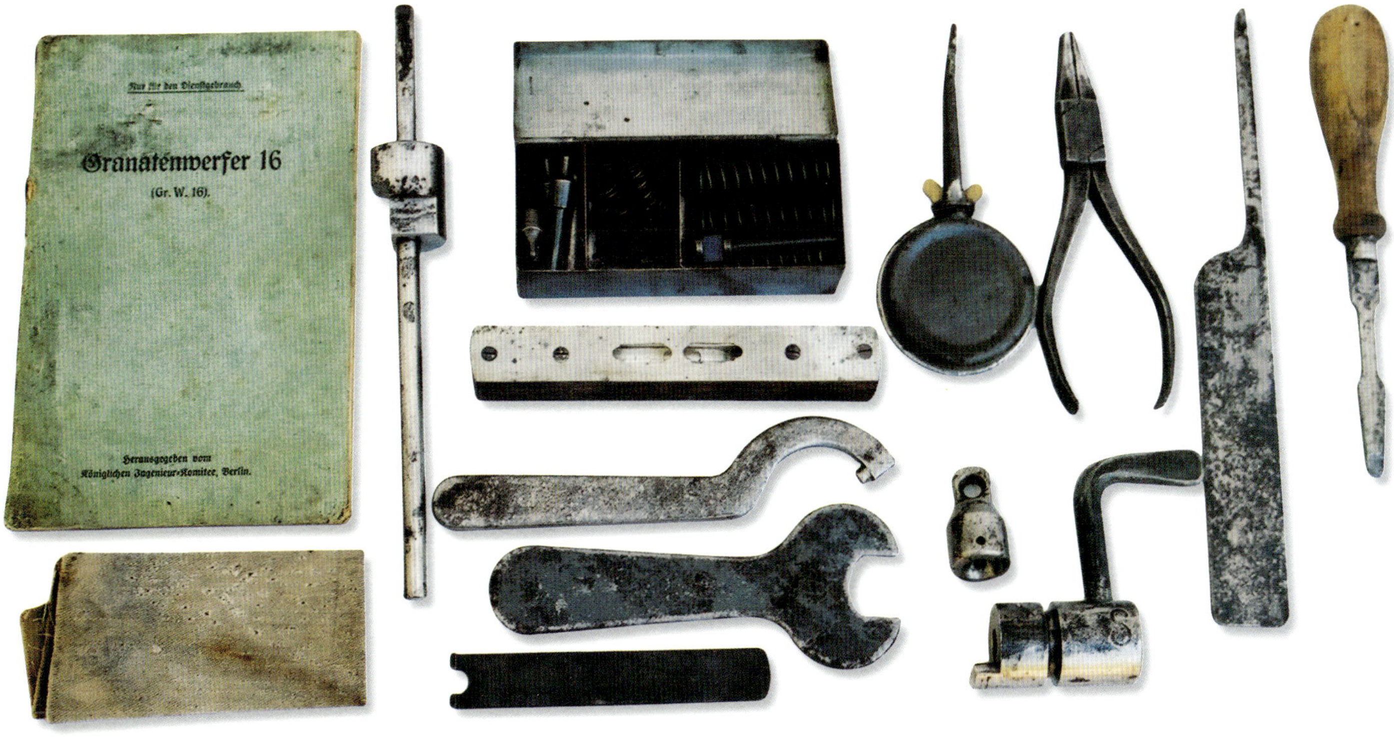

Granatenwerfer 16 instruction book and tools.

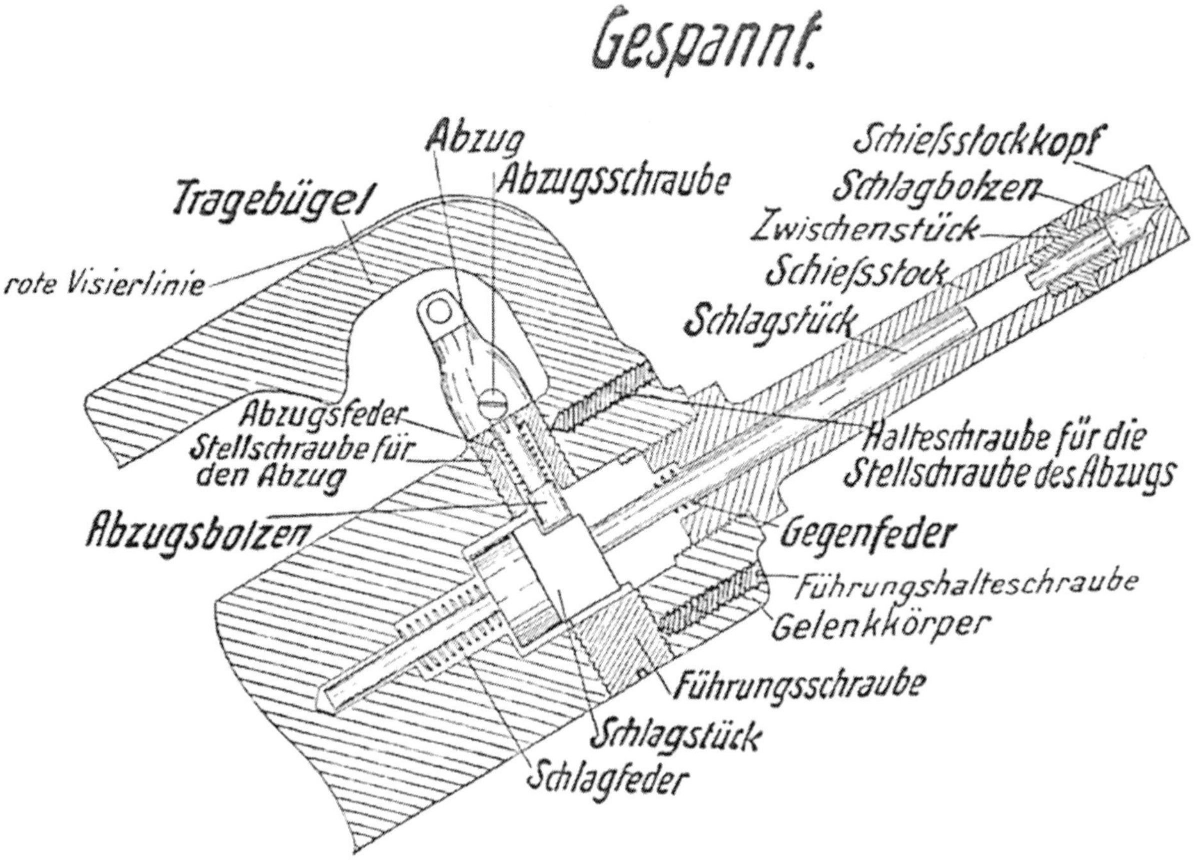

The grenade launcher ready to fire. A large rod (*Schlagstück*) is connected to a spring (*Schlagfeder*) and ready to eject a bolt (*Schiessstockkopf*), which will fire the round (*Patrone*) inside the shaft of the grenade. Drawing from the instruction book: *Granatenwerfer 16 (Gr. W. 16), Königlichen Ingenieur-Komitee, Berlin.*

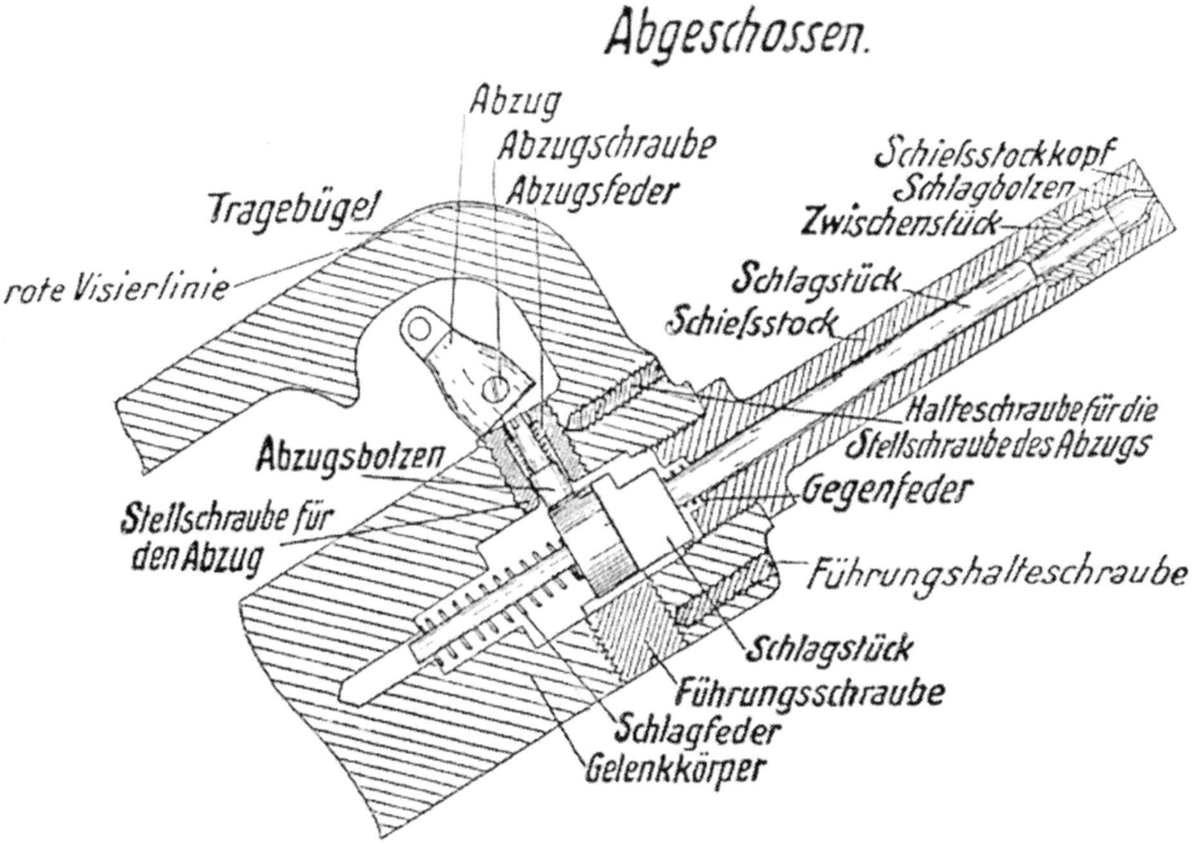

The grenade launcher after firing. Drawing from the instruction book: *Granatenwerfer 16 (Gr. W. 16), Königlichen Ingenieur-Komitee, Berlin.*

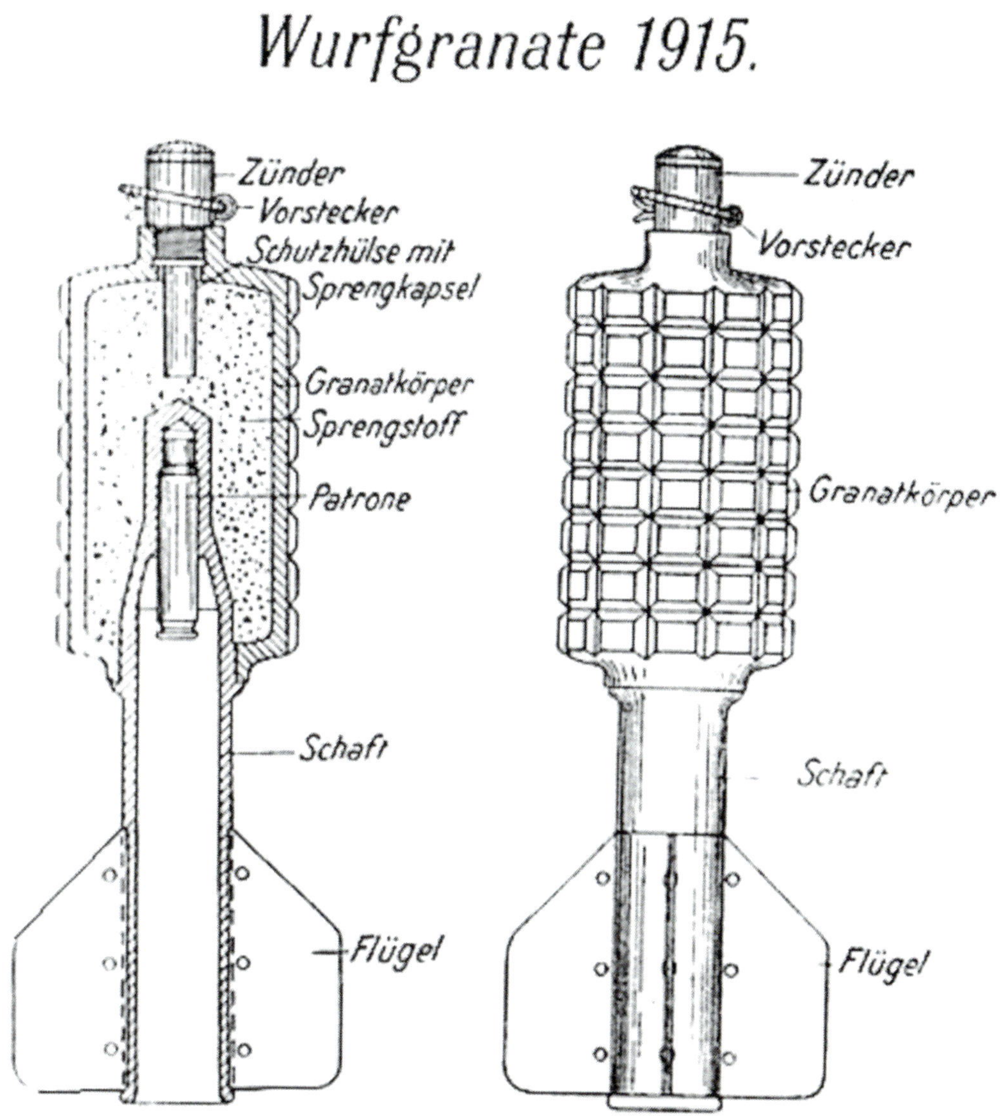

Wurfgranate 1915 diagram. Note the round (*Patrone*) ready to fire the grenade, the igniter (*Zünder*) and the detonator (*Sprengkapsel*). Drawing from the instruction book: *Granatenwerfer 16 (Gr. W. 16), Königlichen Ingenieur-Komitee, Berlin.*

Ammunition box for 10 grenades, model 1915. *Courtesy of Domein Raversijde - Ostend.*

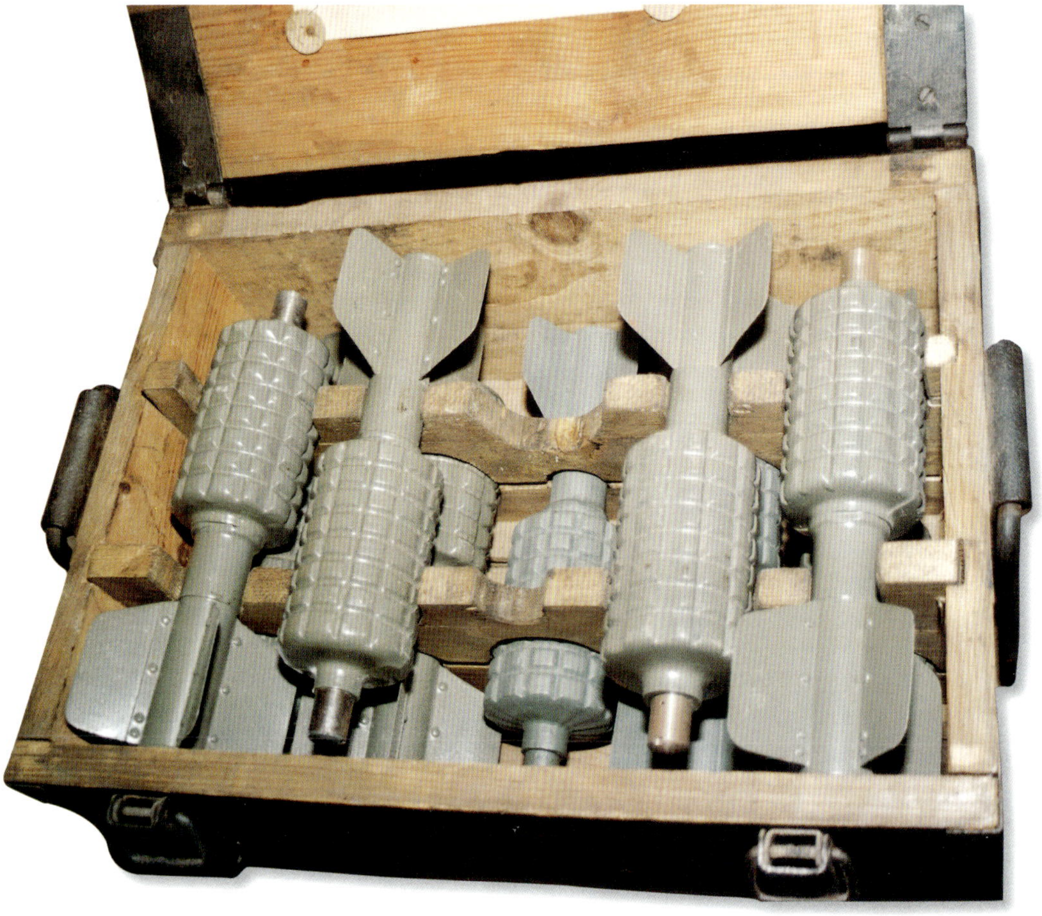

Inside view.

Lanz Minenwerfer

The German 91.3mm *Minenwerfer Lanz* was manufactured in *Mannheim* by *Heinrich Lanz* and put into production in 1915. It fired off grenades (*Glatte Granatenmine H.L.*). The barrel was made of sheet steel and mounted on a folding sledge, fixed onto a wooden plate with iron reinforcements. A striker is installed in a rifle bolt-like system and the gun is cord fired. There was also a special igniter allowing firing with 20 and 35g of black powder. The projectile was loaded into the muzzle and detonated at impact by a special fuse with no delay. At least two variations of this fuse are known. The projectile was filled with *Askallt*, a mixture of *Tolite*, nitroglycerin and sawdust. There is also a bomb projectile containing approximately 375g of explosives. A quick match, which passes through an axial channel, is set alight when the bomb is fired. A very scarce variation is externally fragmented. The range of the *Lanz Minenwerfer* varied between 75 and 450 meters, depending on the type of projectile used.[25]

Left and opposite: Two different types of the *Glatte Granatenmine H.L* for the *Minenwerfer Lanz*. *Courtesy of BT.*

Minenwerfer Lanz. Royal Army and Military History Museum, Brussels.

Flame-throwers (*Flammenwerfer*)

The German Army started to experiment with flame-throwers at the start of the 20th century. The first "*Flammenwerfer Apparate*" were produced in 1911 and supplied to pioneer battalions and pioneer siege trains in 1912. After the start of the war, most flame-throwers were withdrawn from the pioneer battalions and assigned to the Flame-thrower Detachment *Reddemann*, a unit of 48 former firefighters and young war volunteers under the command of Major Bernhard *Reddemann*. Flame-thrower Detachment *Reddemann* first used flamethrowers near Verdun on February 26th, 1915. In March, the unit was enlarged to 800 men and designated the Third Guard Pioneer Battalion. It launched the first mass flame-thrower attack in Belgium around *Hooge* on July 3rd 1915. In April of 1916, the Third Guard Pioneer Battalion became the Guard Reserve Pioneer Regiment, with a strength of 3000 men in twelve field companies, one replacement company, and one experimental company. The Guard Reserve Pioneer Regiment wore the uniform of the Guard Pioneer battalions with white double *Litzen* having red stripes on the collar and cuffs, plain shoulder straps and spiked helmets with a large silver Guard Eagle.

The mechanics of a flame-thrower was very simple. A steel cylinder was filled with a compressed gas (*Nitrogen*) while a mixture of oil and fuel was stored in a separate compartment. Through a valve, the nitrogen was released and ejected the inflammable liquid through a six-foot rubber hose. At the end of the nose was a steel nozzle. The liquid ignited manually on early versions of the flame-thrower. However, manual ignition proved dangerous and later flame-throwers included a springed wick at the nozzle, which lit the fuel mixture automatically.

At least three types of flame-throwers were developed. The first one was a static installation (*Gross, Grosses Flammenwerfer, Großflammenwerfer*), which could operate for 40 seconds and had a range of 40 meters. The large cylinder could contain 100 liters of liquid. Several cylinders could be connected to each other to improve the duration of a flame attack. Although more of a static installation, three pioneers could move it into the battlefield. One soldier would drag the cylinder (*Kessel*) and manipulate the valve to release the contents. A second soldier would carry the 30 m long hose (*Schlauch*) while a third soldier carried and aimed the steel nozzle (*Flammenstrahlrohr*).

Two smaller and more portable flame-throwers existed as well, which proved to be more efficient during mobile operations. They were carried on the back (*Kleines Flammenwerfer*), had automatic ignition and operated for two minutes with a range of 20 to 25 meters. The first mobile design (*Kleif*) consisted of a large metal cylinder with the inflammable liquid and a smaller cylinder with nitrogen (*Stickstoff-Behälter*) at the side or on top of the first one. One member of the crew carried the entire set on the back, while the second person operated the nozzle. Although portable, it was still a heavy and cumbersome device. The second design (*Wex*) was more portable and was shaped like a doughnut with a ball shaped spherical gas-container at the center.[26] This easier to handle flame-thrower was carried at the back as well.

The static model could only be used when the trenches were either very close to each other or when a smoke curtain was required to hide the movements of storm troopers. The portable flame-throwers were used against armored cars, tanks and to clear enemy trenches. The British, American, French and Italian army also used flame-throwers. Today, only a few survive and are on display in museums.[27] The flame-thrower soldiers performed an extremely dangerous task and a special oval insignia with a deaths head (*Totenkopf*) was worn on the left cuff as of July 1917. Members of portable flame-thrower units could wear special equipment on the belt, including a steel cylinder with compressed Nitrogen (*Stickstofflasche*) in a leather carrier, a pouch containing the fuses to ignite the flame-thrower (*Zündertasche*) and a small toolkit (*Werkzeugbeutel*).

An interesting book entitled "*Flammenwerfer und Sturmtruppen*" was published in 1921 by *Hauptmann Theune*, of the former 10th *Flammerwerfer Kompanie* of the *Garde Reserve Pioneer Regiment*, which explains in detail the use and tactics of flame-throwers. *Hauptmann Theune* provides several tactical examples how:

- an enemy trench can be captured with a *Wex* or *Kleif* unit.
- a barricade in an enemy trench can be destroyed with the flame of a double-*Kleif* and how the connecting trenches can be cleared with a *Wex* or *Kleif* unit.
- an attack can be organized on a fortified position, like a block-house with a *Wex* assault unit.
- a trench can be captured in a combined attack from two sides with a *Wex* or *Kleif* assault unit.
- a frontal infantry attack can be supported with flame-thrower assault units (*Flammenwerferstoßtrupp*).
- a frontal infantry attack can be supported with flame-thrower support units (*Flammenwerferbegleittrupps*).
- a reinforced *Wex* assault unit can perform a frontal attack with support of flames from a larger flame-thrower.

This photograph shows a *Kleif* flame-thrower in action. The picture came from a photo album belonging to *Flugzeugführer Otto Mertens*, who was a member of the *Fliegerabteilung A 242. Courtesy of BT.*

Above: The *Wex* flame-thrower. *Reproduced from "Flammenwerfer und Sturmtruppen", 1921.* Right: The *Kleif* flame-thrower. *Reproduced from "Flammenwerfer und Sturmtruppen", 1921.*

Grosses Flammenwerfer. The photograph shows the carriages (*Groflkarren*) used to move the large flame-throwers. The left carriage is loaded with the *Gross* and two Nitrogen bottles (*Stickstoffflaschen*). One pioneer carries a *Zündertasche* and the other a tool kit (*Werkzeugbeutel*). A period pictures also showed a man carrying a *Gross* on his back, which must have been a terrible experience! *Reproduced from "Flammenwerfer und Sturmtruppen", 1921.*

Knifes and Trench Clubs

No work about the Imperial German army would have been complete with at least some pictures of the most typical knives or trench clubs used. The number of different types of personal knives for officers and EM is immense and can hardly be described in a few paragraphs. Trench clubs existed in several forms as well. A popular design can be seen below in which a metal egg could be used to cause severe injuries. Alternative models were the egg was replaced by a cube can be found as well.[28]

Right: Issue trench mace with cast iron spiked ball and spring handle. *Courtesy of Brian Ludwig.*

Left: Storm troopers often carried all sorts of primitive weapons. This mace (*Totschläger*) was made for use in hand-to-hand combat when raiding enemy trenches. The studded ball is attached to the wooden handle by a spring coil, giving it much more leverage in swinging, and a more forceful blow. The egg-shaped metal ball has five metal spikes and is marked 'FKG', which can also be found on the German egg-grenades. *Courtesy of BT.*

Trench-made mace with field-gray painted wood handle. *Courtesy of Brian Ludwig.*

DEMAG (*Deutsche Maschinenfabrik*) bayonet/knife combination. *Courtesy of BT.*

Nahkampfmesser ca 1916. Marked *HUGO KOLLER* and *SOLINGEN*. The wooden grip has nine grooves. The black leather belt loop is attached to the scabbard by two round hollow pop rivets.[29] *Courtesy of BT.*

Private-purchase combination trench knife/bayonet manufactured by *Karl Eickhorn*. Definitive war-time use can be seen in the shrapnel mark which extends from the cross guard onto the scabbard. *Courtesy of Brian Ludwig.*

Detail of the cross guard.

Private-purchase trench knife with checkered black composition grips and a false bayonet stud. *Courtesy of Brian Ludwig.*

Trench knife made from a SG 84/98 bayonet manufactured by GOTTLIEB HAMMESFAHR SOLLINGEN-FOCHE. The total length is 10.1" (26cm). *Courtesy of Sven Kuczyk.*

Unusual trench knife manufactured by *F. Koeller & Co.* using a common ersatz pattern steel bayonet handle. The belt loop is made of papercloth. *Courtesy of Brian Ludwig.*

These medics shelter in a trench. They wear a Red Cross armband, and an Asculpae (*Äskulapstab)* insignia at the left sleeve. Note the trench club hanging at the right of the photo. *Courtesy of Stephen Chambers.*

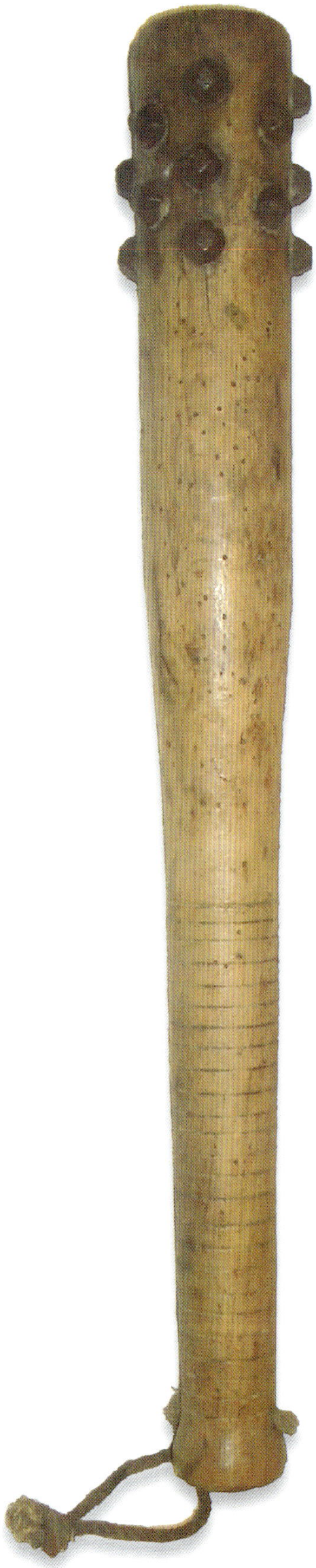

Trench-made mace with wooden handle.
Courtesy of Dirk Theunissen.

Detail of the head reinforced with nails.

The head was made heavier by inserting a steel weight into the wood.

Notes:

[1] J. Kraus, page 507, 509: *Festungs-MG* troops were using the *Gewehr* 88/05.
[2] Hussar, Dragoon, Ulan, Mounted Rifles, Cuirassier, Schwere Reiter.
[3] J. Kraus, page 625: The Lange *Pistole* 08 was introduced with the Field artillery as of August 1914.
[4] Ammunition supply convoys.
[5] J. Kraus, page 665: During patrols, the *Gewehr* 98 was sometimes replaced with a P08.
[6] J. Kraus: *Radfahrer* were using initially the *Gewehr* 98. The "*Gewehr 98 für Radfahrer*" modification was introduced in 1913.
[7] Driver.
[8] J. Kraus, page 713: The Lange *Pistole* 08 was introduced after 1913.
[9] J. Kraus: Stab E.M. Coming from Artillery regiments received a P08.
[10] German Army Handbook, page 49.
[11] *Lubbe* page 109.
[12] J. Kraus: length and weight of the different rifles and carbines.
[13] German Army Handbook, page 49.
[14] Central Powers Small Arms of WW1, John Walter, pages 108 to 110.
[15] Stephun Bull, page 122.
[16] Source: huntingsociety.org.
[17] Correspondance with John Strott.
[18] J. Kraus, page 410: The LP08 was introduced in 1913: Prussia June 1913, Bavaria July 1913.
[19] The devil's paintbrush, page 189.
[20] Stephun Bull, page 126.
[21] The German Army Handbook, page 51.
[22] Stephen Bull, page 126.
[23] The German Army Handboek 1918, page 51.
[24] The German Army Handbook, page 51.
[25] Based on Bulletin 364-2 from C. Kowai.
[26] P.J. Haythorntwhaite, page 73.
[27] It's interesting to know that the flame-thrower of the Finnish Army closely resembled the *Kleif*.
[28] An example of a *Totschläger* can be seen in Woolley, volume 2, page 52.
[29] German military fighting knives, 1914-1945, page 13 n°12, page 51, page 52.

Chapter Eight

Cloth Headgear

Apart from the steel helmet which was first introduced in 1916, the most well-known and very popular headdress in the field of collecting is the spiked helmets and with it, all its variations. Infantry formations wore this type of helmet with a spike, while light infantry (*Jäger*) units wore the shako. Cavalry units had their own distinctive headdress. A fur hat for Hussar units, a lobster tail helmet for *Jäger-zu-Pferde* and Cuirassiers and the Polish inspired *Tschapka* for Uhlan troops. Most foot and field artillery wore the spiked helmet with a ball rather than a spike. Cloth headgear can be divided into two categories: peaked caps and peakless caps. The peaked service cap (*Dienstmütze*) and the peakless field cap (*Feldmütze*) were both made from field-grey or grey-green material.

It is not the author's intention to write an exhaustive description of all the many types of helmets, as this has already been covered in many excellent reference works (like the work of J.A. Bowman). Still, an overview will be given with enough detailed information and photographs to explain and show most types of headgear used before and during the Great War.

A group of infantry and cavalry officers wearing the model 1910 service cap in both the crusher style and the stiff variation. The second person at the right wears a spiked helmet with helmet cover and belonged to the *Füsilier-Regiment Fürst Karl-Anton von Hohenzollern (1. Hohenzollernsches)* Nr.40 (Army Corps XIV). The higher ranking officers have breast pockets with or without flaps. Note the interesting deaths head (Brunswick regiment?) on the spiked helmet cover of officer on the far right. *Courtesy of BT.*

Head-dress State Colors

On the front of the peaked and peakless caps, each state had a circular cockade with its own colors, and was worn below the white-black-red Reich's cockade. The state badges for *Landsturm* or *Landwehr* units usually carried a silver *Maltese Cross.*[1] On the spiked helmet, a circular cockade was worn on the left side of the helmet. On the right side, the Reich's cockade was worn. The following table shows the various cockade color combinations associated with the different states:

Altenburg	green/white/green
Anhalt	green
Baden	yellow/red/yellow
Bavaria	white/light blue/white
Bremen	white /red/white
Brunswick	blue/yellow/blue
Hamburg	white with red iron cross
Lippe	yellow/red
Lübeck	white with red Maltese cross
Mecklenburg	blue/yellow/red
Meningen	green/white/green
Hessen	white/red/white
Oldenburg	blue/red/blue
Prussia	black/white/black
Saxony	green/white/green
Saxe-Coburg	green/white/green
Saxe-Weimar	green/yellow/black
Schaumburg – Lippe	white/red/blue
Schwartzburg- Rudolfstadt	blue/white/blue
Schwartzburg – Sonderhausen	white /blue/white
Waldeck, Reuss	yellow/red/black
Württemberg	black/red/black

Cloth Headgear

Enlisted Men's Field Cap (*Feldmütze*)

The field-cap was a light cap without a visor. Its origins went back to the German War of Independence when it began to replace the heavy caps.[2] During 1907 the peakless cap (*Feldmütze)* was added to the newly introduced field-grey field uniform for both enlisted men and NCOs.

The cap was exactly the same as the pre-1907 field cap, but was made from field-grey or grey-green cloth (*Tuch*) for *Jäger* battalions. NCOs were also issued with the peakless field cap, which was a change from the pre-1907 practice of NCOs having peaked service caps as well. However, NCOs were permitted to buy their own service caps.

The service cap was 3.3" (8.3cm) in height and had a 1.06" (2.7cm) colored cap band (*Besatzstreifen*) and piping around the top. At the front of the cap, two cockades were present. The state cockade (*Landeskokarde*) was attached to the colored *Besatzstreifen*, while the black-white-red German Imperial cockade was attached to the field-grey or grey-green cloth. The design of the cockades was different for enlisted mens field caps, enlisted mens peaked caps and officers. The field cap cockades for enlisted

Soldier wearing a field-grey cap without visor. He wears a tunic with Swedish cuffs, which are piped black along the top. The short *Litzen* on the collar indicates that he probably belonged to a pioneer or artillery unit. *Courtesy of BT.*

Soldiers were issued field caps without a visor, but could privately purchase the more elegant peaked cap. This person belonged to a Brunswick regiment and has a small deaths head insignia between the two cockades of his cap. He is wearing a model 1915 *Feldbluse* with white piped shoulder straps. The photograph was made by *Atelier Spiegel, Braunschweig, Neubau Damm. Courtesy of BT.*

Pre-war dark blue NCO peaked cap. The cap is made from dark blue uniform wool and has a red cap band and piping. A field-grey version was not issued officially for NCOs during 1907. The front is complete with NCO style national and Prussian cockades. *Courtesy of BT.*

men had a diameter of approx. 1" (2.7cm) and were sewn to the body of the cap by means of two visible holes in the cockade. EM peaked cap cockades did not have the two holes visible in the cockade, had a diameter of 0.8" (2cm) but were otherwise the same. The 0.85" (2.2cm) officer's cockade was of better quality and had a raised rim. Saxony used 0.8" (2cm) cockades for both the field caps and peaked caps. As with many German regulations, these were not always strictly adhered to and NCOs or enlisted men sometimes used the more impressive officers cockades.

When the new tunic (*Bluse*) was introduced in 1915 (see later), a universal peaked cap for all ranks was adopted at the same time, but only a few units were equipped with this new headdress before the end of the war.

Enlisted men's Bavarian cockade for the *Feldmütze* with a diameter of approx. 1" (2.7cm). The white paint of the outer circle has worn off over time.

Enlisted men's Imperial cockade for the *Feldmütze* with a diameter of approx. 1" (2.5cm).

A Prussian state cockade for the peaked cap with a diameter of approx. 0.8" (2cm).

Another version of the Imperial officers cockade.

Often, a small piece of cloth was sewn between the cockade and the cap.

High quality Hessen or Bremen state cockade of 0.85" (2.2cm).

Model 1907/10 Branch of Service Field Cap Variations

Different branches of service were distinguished with different cap colors, piping or cap bands:

Unit	Cap color	Cap band	Piping
Infantry	field-grey	red	red
Marine infantry	field-grey	white	white
Jäger & Schützen			
All Jäger units except Bavaria	grey-green	light green	light green
Bavaria	field-green	light green	light green
Schützen	grey-green	black	light green
Artillery			
Field artillery, Reserve field artillery	field-grey	black	red
Foot artillery, Reserve foot artillery	field-grey	black	red
Technical, pioneer, train...			
Zeugpersonal - Feldwebel	field-grey	black	red
Feuerwerkpersonal - Oberfeuerwerker & Feuerwerker	field-grey	black	red
Festungsbau-personal - Festungsbaufeldwebel	field-grey	black	red
Pioneer battalions	field-grey	black	red
Eisenbahn	field-grey	black	red
Telegraph battalions	field-grey	black	red
Luftschiffer	field-grey	black	red

Kraftfahrer, Verkehrstruppen	field-grey	black	red
Train	field-grey	light blue	light blue
Stabsordonanzen	grey-green	light green	citron-yellow
Reitendes			
Feldjägerkorps	grey-green	scarlet	scarlet
Sanitätswesen & Veterinärswesen			
Sanitätswesen[3]	field-grey	dark blue	red
Sanitätswesen - Bavaria	field-grey	light blue	red
Veterinärswesen[4]	field-grey	black	carmine
Sanitätswesen[5]-Sanitätsoffiziere	field-grey	red	red
Cavalry			
Jäger zu Pferde	grey-green	light green	citron-yellow
Cuirassier			
Garde du Corps	field-grey	scarlet	white
Garde Cuirassier	field-grey	cornflower blue	white
1 Cuirassier	field-grey	black	white
2 Cuirassier	field-grey	carmine	white
3 Cuirassier	field-grey	blue	white
4 Cuirassier	field-grey	scarlet	white
5 Cuirassier	field-grey	rose	white
6 Cuirassier	field-grey	Russian-blue	white
7 Cuirassier	field-grey	citron-yellow	white
8 Cuirassier	field-grey	green	white
Cheveauleger			
1, 2 Cheveauleger	field-grey	carmine	carmine
3. Cheveauleger	field-grey	rose	rose
4, 5 Cheveauleger	field-grey	scarlet	scarlet
6. Cheveauleger	field-grey	rose	rose
7, 8 Cheveauleger	field-grey	white	white
Schwere Reiter			
Saxon 1 Schwere Reiter	field-grey	white	light blue
Saxon 2 Schwere Reiter	field-grey	black[6]	light blue
Bavarian 1 Schwere Reiter	field-grey	light red	light red
Bavarian 2 Schwere Reiter	field-grey	light red	light red
Dragoon			
1, 2 Dragoon Guards	field-grey	scarlet	scarlet
1 Dragoon	field-grey	scarlet	scarlet
2 Dragoon	field-grey	black	black
3 Dragoon	field-grey	rose	rose
4 Dragoon	field-grey	light yellow	light yellow
5 Dragoon	field-grey	scarlet	scarlet
6 Dragoon	field-grey	black	black
7 Dragoon	field-grey	rose	rose
8 Dragoon	field-grey	citron-yellow	citron-yellow
9, 10 Dragoon	field-grey	white	white
11, 12 Dragoon	field-grey	carmine	carmine
13 Dragoon	field-grey	scarlet	scarlet
14 Dragoon	field-grey	black	black
15 Dragoon	field-grey	rose	rose
16 Dragoon	field-grey	citron-yellow	citron-yellow
17 Dragoon	field-grey	scarlet	scarlet
18 Dragoon	field-grey	black	black
19 Dragoon	field-grey	white	white
20 Dragoon	field-grey	scarlet	scarlet
21 Dragoon	field-grey	light yellow	light yellow
22 Dragoon	field-grey	black	scarlet
23 Dragoon	field-grey	scarlet	scarlet
24, 25 Dragoon	field-grey	white	white

26 Dragoon	field-grey	citron-yellow	citron-yellow
Uhlan			
1, 2 Guard Uhlan	field-grey	scarlet	scarlet
3.Guard Uhlan	field-grey	golden-yellow	golden-yellow
1 to 8 Uhlan	field-grey	scarlet	scarlet
9 Uhlan	field-grey	white	white
10 Uhlan	field-grey	carmine	carmine
11 Uhlan	field-grey	citron-yellow	citron-yellow
12 Uhlan	field-grey	light blue	white[7]
13 Uhlan	field-grey	white	white
14 Uhlan	field-grey	carmine	carmine
15 Uhlan	field-grey	citron-yellow	citron-yellow
16 Uhlan	field-grey	light blue	white[8]
17 Uhlan	field-grey	white	white
18, 19 Uhlan	field-grey	scarlet	scarlet
20 Uhlan	field-grey	citron-yellow	citron-yellow
21 Uhlan	field-grey	yellow	yellow
1, 2 Bavarian Uhlan	field-grey	scarlet	scarlet
Hussar[9]			
Leib-Garde-Hussar	field-grey	scarlet	citron-yellow
1 Leib-Hussar-Regiment	field-grey	black	white & red
2 Leib-Hussar-Regiment	field-grey	black	white
3 Hussar	field-grey	scarlet	white
4 Hussar	field-grey	brown	golden yellow
5 Hussar	field-grey	madder red	white
6 Hussar	field-grey	dark green	citron-yellow
7 Hussar	field-grey	Russian blue	citron-yellow
8 Hussar	field-grey	dark Blue	white & light blue
9 Hussar	field-grey	cornflower blue	citron -yellow
10 Hussar	field-grey	dark green	citron -yellow & red
11 Hussar	field-grey	dark green	white & red
12 Hussar	field-grey	cornflower blue	white
13 Hussar	field-grey	cornflower blue	white & red
14 Hussar	field-grey	dark Blue	white & red
15 Hussar	field-grey	dark Blue	white & citron-yellow
16 Hussar	field-grey	light blue	white & citron-yellow
17 Hussar	field-grey	black	citron-yellow & red
18 Hussar	field-grey	cornflower blue	yellow & red
19 Hussar	field-grey	cornflower blue	white & purple-red
20 Hussar	field-grey	cornflower blue	white & light blue
Landwehr Cavalry Officers	field-grey	scarlet	scarlet

Model 1910 Military Officials (*Beamte*)

Military officials wore field-grey uniforms and headgear, which were identical in cut to the military officer's uniforms. It is therefore important to understand the color schemes used for non-military personnel. The officer's type field cap was field-grey and was made from *Tuch* or *Doskin*. The colored cap band and the piping identified the type of occupation.

To clearly show the *Beamte* status, a small metal insignia was worn between the two cockades and on the shoulder straps or boards. The insignia varied depending on the state of origin. For example, a Prussian *Beamte* had a Prussian Eagle, Saxony a silver lion with the Saxon coat of arms and Hessen a silver lion. The insignia was often not worn at all, to hide the status of the *Beamte*.

Unit	Cap color	Cap band	Piping
Armee-Musikerinspizienten	field-grey	carmine	carmine
Bekleidungsämter	field-grey	dark blue	red
Blutuntersuchstellen	field-grey	cornflower blue	carmine
Feldgeistliche	field-grey	violet	-
Festungstelegraphen	field-grey	black	red
Garnisonverwaltungsbeamte 1913	field-grey	dark blue	light blue
Generalstabes - Obere Beamte	field-grey	dark blue	bright red
Generalstabes - Rendant 1913 Bavaria	field-grey	cornflower blue	white
Kassenwesen - Obere Beamte	field-grey	dark blue	white

Kriegministerium - Obere Beamte	field-grey	dark blue	carmine
Kriegministerium - Obere Beamte Bavaria	field-grey	dark blue	bright red
Lazarettverwaltung	field-grey	dark blue	cornflower blue
Militärapotheker	field-grey	carmine	carmine
Militär-Baubeamte- Obere Beamte	field-grey	dark blue	carmine
Militärbildungsanstalten	field-grey	dark blue	bright red
Militärjustizverwaltung - Obere Beamte	field-grey	light blue	red
Proviantsamts and Feldmagazinbeamte 1913	field-grey	dark blue	citron-yellow
Reichmilitärgerichts	field-grey	light blue	red
Remotendepots	field-grey	dark blue	bright red
Technische Institute - Obere Beamte	field-grey	dark grey	carmine
Technische Institute - Beamtstellvertreter 1913	field-grey	light blue	light blue
Technische Verkehrtruppen	field-grey	black	red
Telegraphenbauwarte	field-grey	black	red
Unterapotheker	field-grey	carmine[11]	carmine
Waffenmeister	field-grey	black	red
Waffenmeister Bavaria	field-grey	dark grey	red
Zahlmeister-Obere Beamte	field-grey	dark blue	white
Zahnärzte	field-grey	carmine	carmine

Grey-green cloth with light green cap band and piping. This color combination was used by *Jäger* units (except Bavaria which had a field-grey cap). The cockades which are original to the cap still have a piece of red or black cloth behind them. *Courtesy of BT.*

Artillery or pioneer EM cap with black cap band and red piping. The interior is marked "*B.A.IV*", which indicates that the 4th army corps clothing depot issued this cap. Both pioneer and artillery caps have the same colored cap band and piping. The *Magdeburgisches Pionier-Bataillon Nr. 4* belonged to the 4th army corps. *Courtesy of BT.*

NCO *Feldmütze* with dark green cap band and piping for a member of the "*Zivil & Militärverwaltung der besetzten Gebiete*" in use from 1915 onwards. *Courtesy of BT.*

Field-grey model 1910 cap as worn by EM with white cap band and piping. This cap could have belonged to a member of the 7, 8 Cheveauleger, the 9, 10, 24, 25 Dragoon or the 9, 13, 17 Uhlan. *Courtesy of BT.*

Field-grey EM train cap with light blue cap band. The national cockade is missing. Many soldiers removed this cockade from their caps during the revolution of 1918. The cap is dated 1917 and marked with the XVIII army corps stamp, therefore it probably belonged to the *Großherzoglich-Hessisches Train-Bataillon Nr. 18 with garrison* in *Darmstadt. Courtesy of BT.*

This is an EM Dragoon field cap of the 6, 14, 17 or 18th regiment with a field-grey body with black piping around the top and black cap band. The two cockades are present and have been restored with white and black paint. *Courtesy of BT.*

Infantry EM *Feldmütze* with red cap band and piping of the 14th Infantry Regiment, Bavaria. Marked "*JR 14*" and "*B.D.III*". The name of the owner is written in light blue ink: "*Hartmann*". The 14th IR had its garrison in *Nürnberg* and belonged to the 3rd army corps. *Courtesy of BT.*

NCO field cap with the rarely found violet cap band and piping of a *Feldgeistliche*. *Courtesy of BT.*

Infantry EM field cap marked "*K.B.A.G*" (*Kriegs Bekleidungsamt Garde*) 1915. Size 57. *Courtesy of BT.*

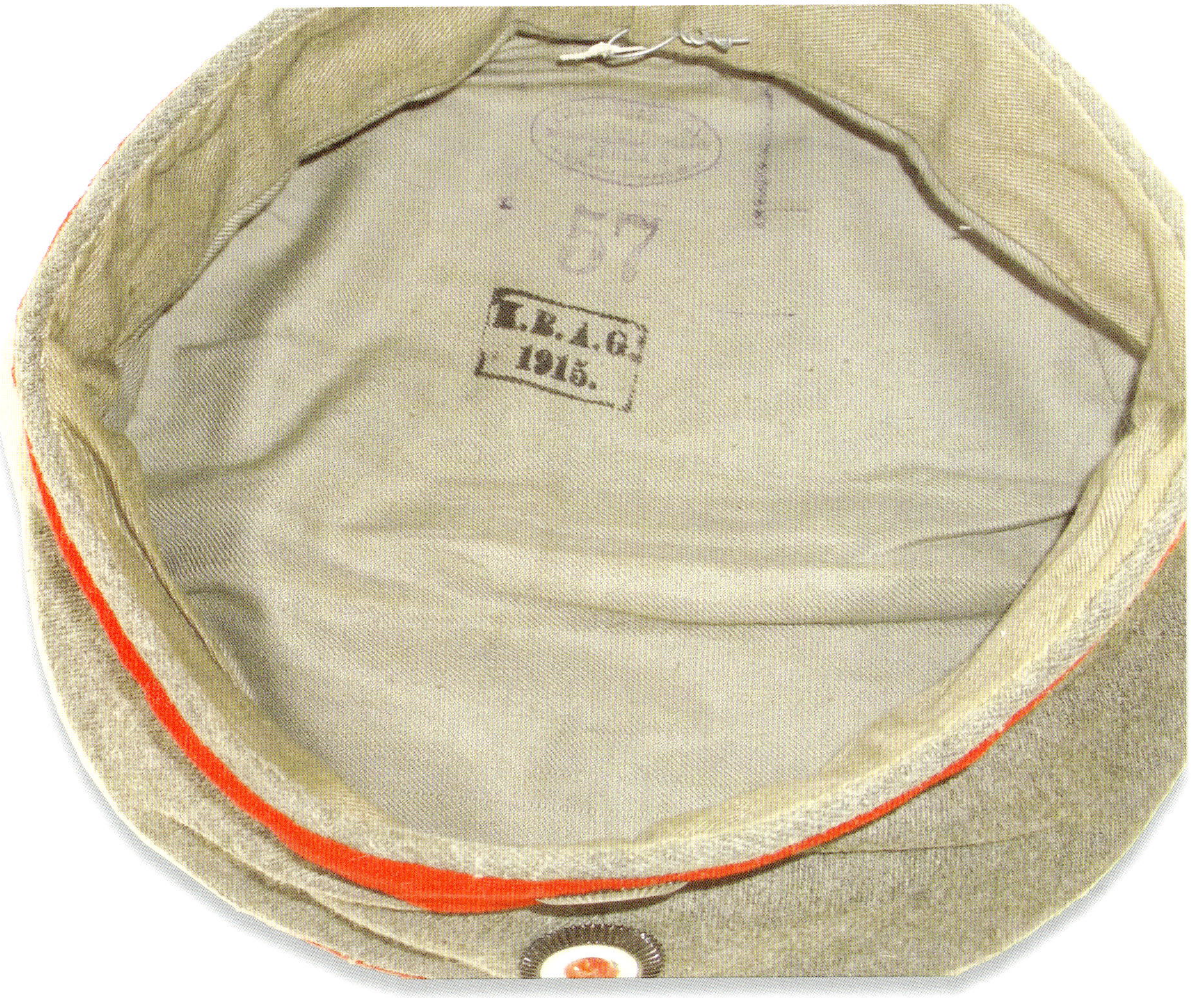

EM field cap with carmine band as worn by the 10, 14 Uhlan, the 11, 12 Dragoon or the 1, 2 Cheveauleger. The band is covered by a camouflage cloth – which is still originally fixed. These cloth bands were first worn from March 1915. *Courtesy of BT.*

Prussian EM field cap with purple cap band, assumed to have belonged to a *Feldgeistliche*, but the violet color is of a different shade to the previous example. *Author's early collection.*

This cap displays the unique *Karpatenabzeichen* issued to the troop in 1917.[12] The Austro-Hungarian Emperor gave the insignia to the 1st and 200th infantry division, which formed the *Karpatenkorps* under the command of the k.u.k. 7th Army.[13] The *Karpatenkorps* was heavily involved in the campaign against Russia in 1916. The EM insignia was made from *Weiflblech* and the officer's insignia from silver. It features deer antlers (*Hirschgeweih*) and fir twigs. A small sword is located in the middle of the insignia. Only a few of these commemorative insignia (*Erinnerungsabzeichen*) were worn in the German Army, although some troops created their own non-official insignia. *Courtesy of Dirk Theunissen.*

Field Cap Cloth Covers

During the war, it was found that the colors of the cap bands (*Besatzstreifen*) were visible from a considerable distance. To prevent identification of units by enemy observers a grey cloth cover was issued for wearing over the cap band. Some cloth covers were sewn permanently on to the caps while others were removable and fitted with a buckle. The grey cloth band had a width of 1.3" (3.2cm). This cloth band was fixed around the cap band and over the front state cockades, by means of a small slit in the band's material.

Small cover to hide the colored cap band of the service cap. This piece is dated 1917. *Courtesy of BT.*

Model 1917 Enlisted Men's Field Caps (*Einheitsfeldmütze*)

A new cap, called *Einheitsfeldmütze* was introduced during the summer of 1917[14] for NCOs and EM. This cap was entirely field-grey, so the need for an additional cloth band, covering the colored cap band (*Besatzstreifen*) was eliminated. Prussia used a darker green cap band and piping, while Bavarian caps were entirely made from the same field-grey wool.

This EM *Einheitsfeldmütze* was the new uniform cap for EM and had green piping and a green cap band. The cap became standard issue in the early post-war *Reichswehr* army and was later outfitted with a cloth visor. The cockades are not correct for this cap. Also, note that the thread of the upper cockade runs horizontally instead of vertically, which is also incorrect. *Courtesy of BT.*

Train reservist field cap with added visor. *Royal Army and Military History Museum, Brussels.*

Prussian field cap with added visor and very wide chinstrap. *Royal Army and Military History Museum, Brussels.*

Model 1908 *Dienstmütze*

A special field cap was introduced in 1908 for train and medical troops (*Sanitätswesen*).[15] These troops did not wear the spiked helmet, but a field cap with visor. The cap was different to the normal cap in that it had a larger visor and a chinstrap. The visor, chinstrap and chinstrap buttons were black. The cap received a new field-grey visor and chinstrap during the new regulations of 1915. When the *Einheitsfeldmütze* was introduced in 1917, a new *Einheits-Dienstmütze* was made available as well without any colored piping or cap band.[16] Many shakos and spiked helmets

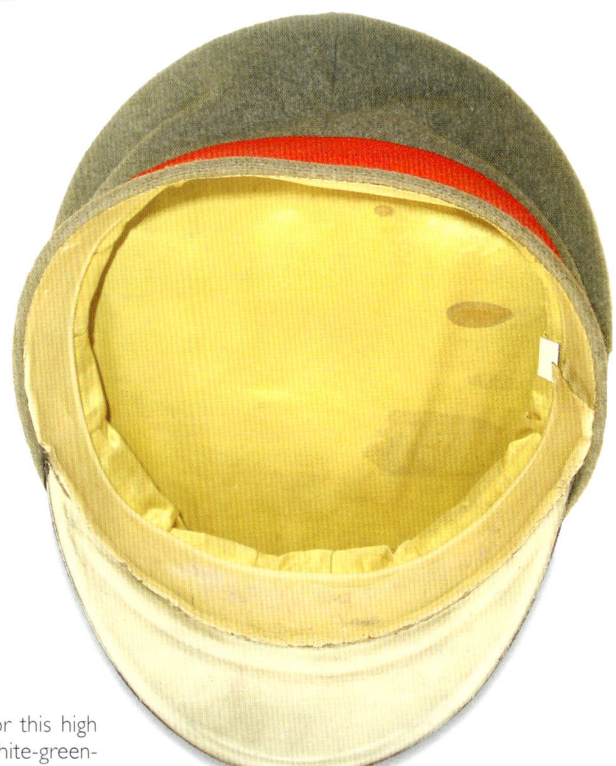

Stiff Saxon infantry service cap. The inside of the black lacquered visor is white for this high quality cap. The front is completed with a national and a Saxon state cockade in white-green-white. *Courtesy of BT.*

became available from front line troops after the introduction of the steel helmet. Because of this, in 1918, the *Dienstmütze* was made obsolete and was replaced by leather headgear. The *Dienstmütze* was to be returned to the clothing depot. (*Bekleidungsamt*). In Prussia, the visor was taken off and the *Dienstmütze* was reworked to become a *Feldmütze*.

Model 1910 Officers Service Cap

The officer's service cap was introduced in 1910[17] and was made from field-grey or grey-green cloth with a black visor. The colored cap band and piping followed the same rules as for enlisted men and NCO field caps. However, the black cloth was replaced by black velvet. The total height of the cap was 4" (10cm) with a 1.6" (4cm) cap band. Two black metal buttons hold the 0.6" (1.5cm) wide chinstrap. Many officers' caps were also issued without a chinstrap.

The special officer cockades are fixed to the colored cap band and on the field-grey crown of the cap. NCOs with *Portepee* were entitled to wear the officer's cap as well. Most caps were soft without the stiffened crown as seen in pre-1910 caps. High-ranking officers still preferred to have stiff caps and privately made caps tend to resemble the older colored designs.

This NCO wears a field-grey *Feldbluse* introduced in 1915 and a cap with EM cockades. *Courtesy of BT.*

Hussar's peaked cap for an officer of the *Husaren-Regiment Kaiser Nikolaus II von Russland (1.Westfälisches) Nr.8.* The cap has a dark blue cap band, white piping and an additional row of light blue piping above the cap band. It is produced in an earlier lighter tone of field-grey wool. *Courtesy of BT.*

Hussar peaked cap of an NCO of the *Kgl. Sächs. 2. Husaren-Regiment Nr.19*. This field-grey cap has a cornflower blue cap band, piping around the cap band and around the top in white. A second row of piping in purple-red can be seen above the cap band. The Saxon *Landeskokarde* is white/green/silver. The cap is made from late war field-grey wool. *Courtesy of BT.*

Crusher style NCO cap of a pioneer featuring black cap band and red piping. The cap shows a good amount of use and has a nice salty look. *Courtesy of BT.*

This special Prussian officer khaki cap was manufactured with a weight of exactly 100g. These caps are rarely found. Some damage is evident at the top of the cap; otherwise it is in good condition. It has a black chinstrap attached by two black smooth buttons. *Courtesy of BT.*

Detail of the manufacturer's label with the 100g weight indication.

This is an officer's cap of the *Alpenkorps* with *Edelweiss* insignia on the left side. This Bavarian infantry cap is field-grey with a carmine cap band and piping. When Italy declared war, Germany decided to send supporting troops, called the *Alpenkorps*, to *Tirol* in 1915 to defend the Austro-Hungarian border. The *Alpenkorps* was composed of the following units:[18]

Field artillery 203 and 204
Gebirgs-Maschinegewehr-Abteilung 201 to 210
Foot artillery batteries 101 and 102
Reserve-Maschinegewehr-Abteilung 4
Pioneer companies 101
Gebirgs-Kanonen-Abteilung 1 and 2
Gebirgs-Minenwerfer-Abteilung 269 to 272
3rd Squadron of the 4th Cheveauleger Regiment
Bavarian Infanterie-Leib-Regiment 1, 2 and 3
Feld-Flieg. Abteilung 9
Bavarian Jäger-Brigade 1, 2 and Jäger-Regiment 1, 2, 3
Bavarian Schneeschuh-Btl.1, 4 and Prussian Schneeschuh-Btl.2, 3
Bavarian Gebirgs-Artillerie-Abteilung 2
Jäger-Bataillon 1, 2, 10
Reserve-Jäger-Bataillon 2, 10, 14
Gebirgs-Fernsprech-Abteilung 29
Funker-Kommando 12

The Alpenkorps was reinforced with other units during 1915, including artillery, pioneers, Jägers and cyclists.

The *K.u.k Landesverteidigung Tirol* made 20.000[19] *Edelweiss* insignia available for the German contingents as a gift for their contribution. The Prussian War Ministry approved this insignia on September 9th 1915[20]. The insignia measured 1.6" (4cm), was cast in metal with a dark silver grey finish. The center of the *Edelweiss* was golden yellow. It was worn on either the shako (at the left over the cockade) or on the left side of the field cap on the colored cap band. *Courtesy of BT.*

This side view shows the Edelweiss insignia on the left side and the chinstrap attachment.

These *Jäger-zu-Pferde* officers wear a field cap with a cloth covered cap band. Similar to the peak less field caps for enlisted men and NCOs, officers used a cover as well to hide the colorful cap band. Observe the cuff lace typical of the mounted rifles. *Courtesy of BT.*

Model 1915 New Regulation Field Caps

Different branches of service could be distinguished by differences in cap color, piping or cap band:

Unit	Cap color	Cap band	Piping
Infantry	field-grey	red	red
Marine infantry	field-grey	white	white
Artillery			
Field artillery, Reserve field artillery	field-grey	black	red
Foot artillery, Reserve foot artillery	field-grey	black	red
Technical, Train, Pioneer			
Train	field-grey	potash blue	potash blue
Bavarian train	field-grey	potash blue	light red
Zeugpersonal - Feldwebel	field-grey	black	red
Feuerwerkpersonal-Oberfeuerwerker & Feuerwerker	field-grey	black	red
Festungsbau-personal - Festungsbaufeldwebel	field-grey	black	red
Pioneer battalions	field-grey	black	red
Eisenbahn	field-grey	black	red
Kraftfahrer, Verkehrstruppen	field-grey	black	red
Luftschiffer	field-grey	black	red
Telegraph battalions	field-grey	black	red

Jäger & Schützen			
All Jäger Units except Bavaria	grey-green	light green	light green
Bavaria	field-grey	light green	light green
Schützen	grey-green	black	light green
Sanitätswesen and Veterinärswesen			
Sanitätswesen[21]- Sanitätsoffiziere	field-grey	dark blue	red
Sanitätswesen[22]	field-grey	red	red
Veterinärswesen[23]	field-grey	black	carmine
Feldgendarmerie	field-grey	dark green	red
Reitendes Feldjägerkorps	grey-green	scarlet	scarlet
Cavalry			
Jäger zu Pferde	grey-green	light green	citron-yellow
Cuirassier			
Garde du Corps	field-grey	scarlet	white
Garde Cuirassier	field-grey	cornflower blue	white
1 Cuirassier	field-grey	black	white
2 Cuirassier	field-grey	carmine	white
3 Cuirassier	field-grey	blue	white
4 Cuirassier	field-grey	scarlet	white
5 Cuirassier	field-grey	rose	white
6 Cuirassier	field-grey	Russian blue	white
7 Cuirassier	field-grey	yellow	white
8 Cuirassier	field-grey	green	white
Cheveauleger			
1. & 2. Cheveauleger	field-grey	orange red	orange red
3 Cheveauleger	field-grey	rose	rose
4, 5 Cheveauleger	field-grey	scarlet	scarlet
6 Cheveauleger	field-grey	rose	rose
7, 8 Cheveauleger	field-grey	white	white
Schwere Reiter			
Saxon 1 Schwere Reiter	field-grey	white	cornflower blue
Saxon 2 Schwere Reiter	field-grey	black	cornflower blue
Bavarian 1 Schwere Reiter	field-grey	citron-yellow	citron-yellow
Bavarian 2 Schwere Reiter	field-grey	citron-yellow	citron-yellow
Dragoon			
1, 2 Dragoon Guards	field-grey	scarlet	scarlet
1. Dragoon	field-grey	scarlet	scarlet
2. Dragoon	field-grey	black	black
3 Dragoon	field-grey	rose	rose
4 Dragoon	field-grey	golden-yellow	golden-yellow
5 Dragoon	field-grey	scarlet	scarlet
6 Dragoon	field-grey	black	black
7 Dragoon	field-grey	rose	rose
8 Dragoon	field-grey	golden-yellow	golden-yellow
9, 10 Dragoon	field-grey	white	white
11, 12 Dragoon	field-grey	carmine	carmine
13 Dragoon	field-grey	scarlet	scarlet
14 Dragoon	field-grey	black	black
15 Dragoon	field-grey	rose	rose
16 Dragoon	field-grey	golden-yellow	yellow
17 Dragoon	field-grey	scarlet	scarlet
18 Dragoon	field-grey	black	black
19 Dragoon	field-grey	white	white
20 Dragoon	field-grey	scarlet	scarlet
21 Dragoon	field-grey	golden-yellow	golden-yellow
22 Dragoon	field-grey	black	scarlet
23 Dragoon	field-grey	scarlet	scarlet
24, 25 Dragoon	field-grey	white	white
26 Dragoon	field-grey	golden-yellow	golden-yellow
Uhlan			

1, 2 Guard Uhlan	field-grey	scarlet	scarlet
3 Guard Uhlan	field-grey	golden-yellow	golden-yellow
1 to 8 Uhlan	field-grey	scarlet	scarlet
9 Uhlan	field-grey	white	white
10 Uhlan	field-grey	carmine	carmine
11 Uhlan	field-grey	golden-yellow	golden-yellow
12 Uhlan	field-grey	light blue	light blue & white[24]
13 Uhlan	field-grey	white	white
14 Uhlan	field-grey	carmine	carmine
15 Uhlan	field-grey	golden-yellow	golden-yellow
16 Uhlan	field-grey	light blue	light blue & white[25]
17 Uhlan	field-grey	white	white
18 Uhlan	field-grey	purple-red	purple-red
19 Uhlan	field-grey	scarlet	scarlet
20, 21 Uhlan	field-grey	golden-yellow	golden-yellow
1, 2 Bavarian Uhlan	field-grey	scarlet	scarlet
Hussar[26]			
Leib-Garde-Hussar	field-grey	scarlet	citron-yellow
1 Leib-Hussar-Regiment Nr. 1	field-grey	black	white & red
2 Leib-Hussar-Regiment Nr. 2	field-grey	black	white
3 Hussar	field-grey	scarlet	white
4 Hussar	field-grey	brown	golden-yellow
5 Hussar	field-grey	madder red	white
6 Hussar	field-grey	dark green	citron-yellow
7 Hussar	field-grey	Russian blue	citron-yellow
8 Hussar	field-grey	dark blue	white & light blue
9 Hussar	field-grey	cornflower blue	citron-yellow
10 Hussar	field-grey	dark green	citron-yellow & red
11 Hussar	field-grey	dark green	white & red
12 Hussar	field-grey	cornflower blue	white
13 Hussar	field-grey	cornflower blue	white & red
14 Hussar	field-grey	dark blue	white & red
15 Hussar	field-grey	dark blue	white & citron-yellow
16 Hussar	field-grey	light blue	white & citron-yellow
17 Hussar	field-grey	black	citron-yellow & red
18 Hussar	field-grey	cornflower blue	golden-yellow
19 Hussar	field-grey	cornflower blue	white
20 Hussar	field-grey	cornflower blue	white

Model 1915 military officials (*Beamte*)

Unit	**Cap color**	**Cap band**	**Piping**
Armee-Musikerinspizienten	field-grey	carmine	carmine
Bekleidungsämter 1915	field-grey	cornflower blue	white
Blutuntersuchstellen 1915	field-grey	black	carmine
Feldgeistliche	field-grey	violet	violet
Festungstelegraphen	field-grey	black	red
Garnisonverwaltungsbeamte 1915	field-grey	cornflower blue	white
Geheime Feldpolizei and Zentralpolizei 1915	field-grey	dark blue	cornflower blue
Generalstabes - Obere Beamte	field-grey	dark blue	light red
Kassenwesen - Obere Beamte 1915	field-grey	cornflower blue	white
Kriegministerium - Obere Beamte	field-grey	dark blue	carmine
Kriegministerium - Obere Beamte Bavaria	field-grey	dark blue	light red
Lazarettverwaltung 1915	field-grey	cornflower blue	white
Militärapotheker	field-grey	carmine	carmine
Militärbildungsanstalten 1915	field-grey	cornflower blue	white
Militärdolmetscher 1915	field-grey	cornflower blue	white
Militärjustizverwaltung - Obere Beamte	field-grey	light blue	red
Militär-Baubeamte - Obere Beamte	field-grey	dark blue	carmine
Proviantsamts and Feldmagazinbeamte 1915	field-grey	cornflower blue	white
Reichmilitärgerichts	field-grey	light blue	red

Remotendepots 1916	field-grey	cornflower blue	white
Technische Institute - Beamtstellvertreter 1915	field-grey	medium blue	medium blue
Technische Verkehrtruppen	field-grey	black	red
Telegraphenbauwarte	field-grey	black	red
Unterapotheker	field-grey	carmine	carmine
Waffenmeister	field-grey	black	red
Waffenmeister Bavaria	field-grey	dark grey	red
Zahlmeister-Obere Beamte 1915	field-grey	cornflower blue	white
Zahnärzte	field-grey	carmine	carmine
Zivil & Militärverwaltung der besetzten Gebiete 1915	field-grey	dark green	dark green

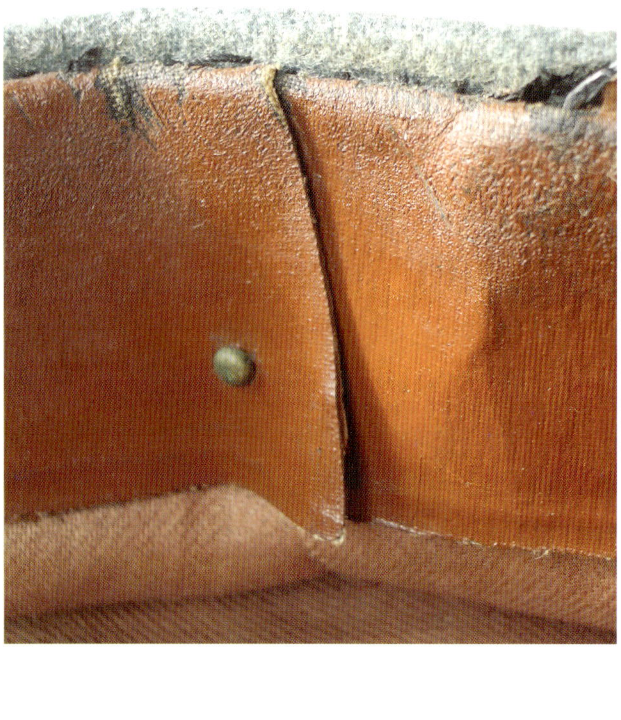

Feldgrau model 1915 officers service cap with dark green velvet cap band and piping. The Oldenburg state cockade is blue/red/blue. This cap was used by the "*Militärverwaltung der Besetztes Gebiete*" or the military administration for the occupied territories in Belgium and Russia. *Courtesy of BT.*

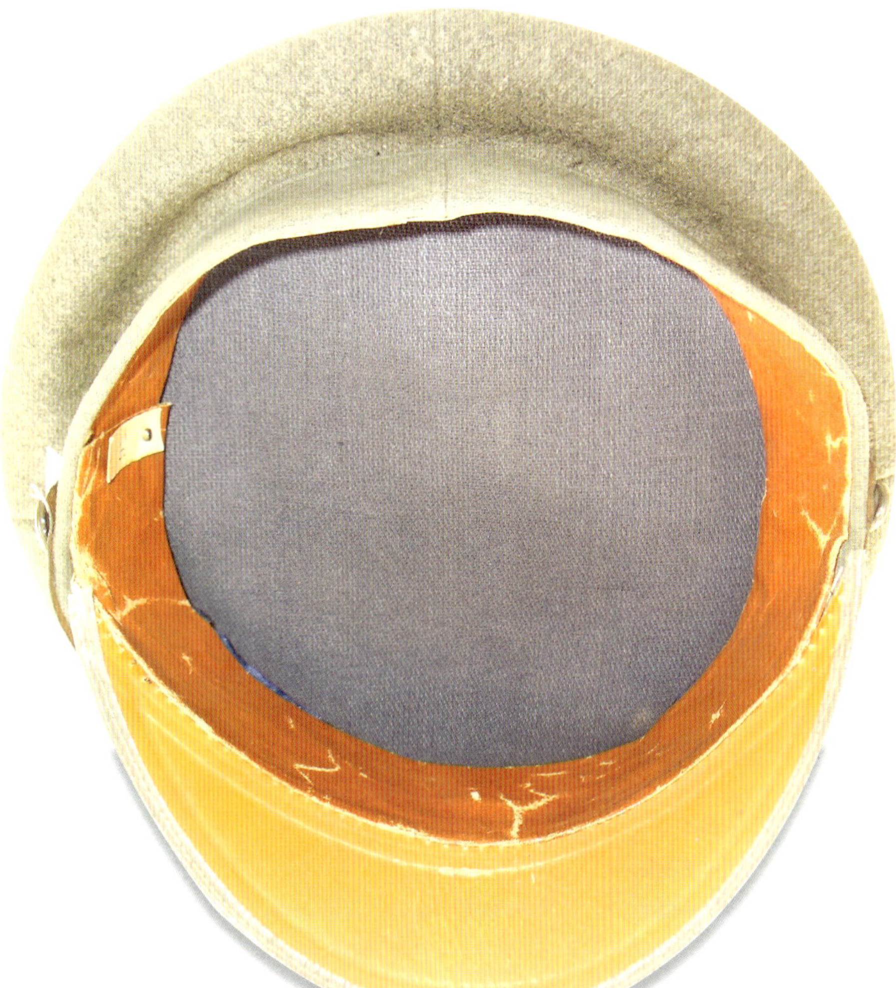

Model 1917 Officers Service Cap (*Einheitsfeldmütze*)

A new officers field-grey or grey-green field cap was introduced in 1917.[27] The officers *Einheitsfeldmütze* had field-grey piping and a field grey cloth cap band and was very similar in appearance to the EM's cap. The Bavarian version was entirely made from field-grey material. The chinstrap and the front peak were field-grey as well. During 1918, because of leather shortages, peaks and liners were made from fiber, paper or other ersatz materials.

Model 1917 officers service cap. *Courtesy of BT.*

Model 1915 Future Peacetime *Schirmmütze*

When the new "future peace-time" uniform was introduced in 1915, the peaked cap underwent a number of changes.[28] The cap was again field-grey or grey-green, having a height of 3.5" (9cm) with a 1.4" (3.5cm) wide cap band. It had a stiff appearance and an oval shape with a field-grey peak 1.6" (4cm) in width and with a 1.8" (4.5cm) liner made from leather. The color of the cap band and piping underwent some changes as well (see table), but the most obvious way to recognize a "future piece-time" cap is to look at the peak, which was now field-grey instead of black. This is particularly useful for Hussar, Cuirassier or Dragoon caps, which were not field-grey, but had the same colorful appearance as their peacetime predecessors.

Model 1915 branch of service field cap variations: different regiments or branch of services could be distinguished by differences in the cap color, piping or cap band:

Unit	Cap color	Cap band	Piping
Infantry	field-grey	red	red
Artillery			
Field artillery, Reserve field artillery	field-grey	black	red
Foot artillery, Reserve foot artillery	field-grey	black	red
Technical, Train, Pioneer			
Zeugpersonal - Feldwebel	field-grey	black	red
Feuerwerkpersonal-Oberfeuerwerker & Feuerwerker	field-grey	black	red
Festungsbau-personal - Festungsbaufeldwebel	field-grey	black	red
Pioneer battalions	field-grey	black	red
Eisenbahn	field-grey	black	red
Kraftfahrer, Verkehrstruppen	field-grey	black	red
Luftschiffer	field-grey	black	red
Telegraph battalions	field-grey	black	red
Train	field-grey	potash blue	potash blue
Train - Bavaria	field-grey	potash blue	light red
Jäger & Schützen			
All Jäger Units except Bavaria	grey-green	light green	light green
Jäger Battalion 14	grey-green	light green[29]	light green
Bavarian Jäger	field-grey	light green	light green
Schützen	grey-green	black	light green
Sanitätswesen & Veterinärswesen			
Sanitätswesen - Sanitätsoffiziere	field-grey	dark blue	red
Veterinärswesen	field-grey	black	carmine
Sanitätswesen	field-grey	red	red
Feldgendarmerie	field-grey	dark green	red
Reitendes Feldjägerkorps	grey-green	scarlet	scarlet
Cavalry			
Jäger zu Pferde	grey-green	light green	citron-yellow
Cuirassier[30]			
Garde du Corps	white	scarlet	scarlet
Garde Cuirassier	white	cornflower blue	cornflower blue
1 Cuirassier	white	black	black
2 Cuirassier	white	carmine	carmine
3 Cuirassier	white	blue	blue
4 Cuirassier	white	scarlet	scarlet
5 Cuirassier	white	rose	rose
6 Cuirassier	white	Russian blue	Russian blue
7 Cuirassier	white	yellow	yellow
8 Cuirassier	white	green	green
Cheveauleger			
1, 2 Cheveauleger	field-grey	orange red	orange red
3 Cheveauleger	field-grey	rose	rose
4, 5 Cheveauleger	field-grey	scarlet	scarlet
6 Cheveauleger	field-grey	rose	rose
7, 8 Cheveauleger	field-grey	white	white
Schwere Reiter			
Saxon 1 Schwere Reiter	white	cornflower blue	cornflower blue
Saxon 2 Schwere Reiter	white	black	black
Bavarian 1 Schwere Reiter	field-grey	citron-yellow	citron-yellow

Bavarian 2 Schwere Reiter	field-grey	citron-yellow	citron-yellow
Dragoon			
1, 2 Dragoon Guards	cornflower blue	scarlet	scarlet
1 Dragoon	cornflower blue	scarlet	scarlet
2 Dragoon	cornflower blue	black	black
3 Dragoon	cornflower blue	rose	rose
4 Dragoon	cornflower blue	golden-yellow	golden-yellow
5 Dragoon	cornflower blue	scarlet	scarlet
6 Dragoon	cornflower blue	black	black
7 Dragoon	cornflower blue	rose	rose
8 Dragoon	cornflower blue	golden-yellow	golden-yellow
9, 10 Dragoon	cornflower blue	white	white
11, 12 Dragoon	cornflower blue	carmine	carmine
13 Dragoon	cornflower blue	scarlet	scarlet
14 Dragoon	cornflower blue	black	black
15 Dragoon	cornflower blue	rose	rose
16 Dragoon	cornflower blue	golden-yellow	golden-yellow
17 Dragoon	cornflower blue	scarlet	scarlet
18 Dragoon	cornflower blue	black	black
19 Dragoon	cornflower blue	white	white
20 Dragoon	cornflower blue	scarlet	scarlet
21 Dragoon	cornflower blue	golden-yellow	golden-yellow
22 Dragoon	cornflower blue	black	scarlet
23 Dragoon	dark green	scarlet	scarlet
24 Dragoon	dark green	white	white
25 Dragoon	cornflower blue	white	white
26 Dragoon	cornflower blue	golden-yellow	golden-yellow
Hussar			
Leib-Guarde Hussar	red	dark blue	yellow
1 Hussar	black	red	white
2 Hussar	black	black[31]	white
3 Hussar	red	dark blue	white
4 Hussar	brown	brown	yellow
5 Hussar	dark red	black	white
6 Hussar	dark green	red	yellow
7 Hussar	Russian blue	red	yellow
8 Hussar	dark blue	cornflower blue[32]	white
9 Hussar	cornflower blue	cornflower blue	yellow
10 Hussar	dark green	deep pink	yellow
11 Hussar	dark green	red	white
12 Hussar	cornflower blue	white	white
13 Hussar	cornflower blue	red	white
14 Hussar	dark blue	red	white
15 Hussar	dark blue	yellow	white
16 Hussar	light blue	red	white
17 Hussar[33]	black	red	yellow
18 Hussar	cornflower blue	red	yellow
19 Hussar	cornflower blue	crimson	white
20 Hussar	field-grey	light blue	white & light blue
Uhlan			
1, 2 Guard Uhlan	field-grey	scarlet	scarlet
3 Guard Uhlan	field-grey	golden-yellow	golden-yellow
1 to 2 Uhlan	field-grey	orange-red	orange-red
3 to 8 Uhlan	field-grey	scarlet	scarlet
9 Uhlan	field-grey	white	white
10 Uhlan	field-grey	carmine	carmine
11 Uhlan	field-grey	golden-yellow	golden-yellow
12 Uhlan	field-grey	light blue	white
13 Uhlan	field-grey	white	white
14 Uhlan	field-grey	carmine	carmine

15 Uhlan	field-grey	golden-yellow	golden-yellow
16 Uhlan	field-grey	light blue	white
17 Uhlan	field-grey	white	white
18 Uhlan	field-grey	purple-red	purple-red
19 Uhlan	field-grey	scarlet	scarlet
20, 21 Uhlan	field-grey	golden-yellow	golden-yellow
1, 2 Bavarian Uhlan	field-grey	scarlet	scarlet

Model 1916 military officials (*Beamte*)[34]

Unit	**Cap color**	**Cap band**	**Piping**
Armee-Musikerinspizienten	field-grey	carmine	carmine
Bekleidungsämter 1915	field-grey	cornflower blue	white
Blutuntersuchstellen 1915	field-grey	black	carmine
Feldgeistliche	field-grey	violet	violet
Festungstelegraphen	field-grey	black	red
Garnisonverwaltungsbeamte 1915	field-grey	cornflower blue	white
Geheime Feldpolizei and Zentralpolizei 1915	field-grey	dark blue	cornflower blue
Generalstabes - Obere Beamte	field-grey	dark blue	light red
Kassenwesen - Obere Beamte 1915	field-grey	cornflower blue	white
Kriegministerium - Obere Beamte	field-grey	dark blue	carmine
Kriegministerium - Obere Beamte Bavaria	field-grey	dark blue	light red
Lazarettverwaltung 1915	field-grey	cornflower blue	white
Militärapotheker	field-grey	carmine	carmine
Militärbildungsanstalten 1915	field-grey	cornflower blue	white
Militärdolmetscher 1915	field-grey	cornflower blue	white
Militärjustizverwaltung - Obere Beamte	field-grey	light blue	red
Militär-Baubeamte - Obere Beamte	field-grey	dark blue	carmine
Proviantsamts and Feldmagazinbeamte 1915	field-grey	cornflower blue	white
Reichmilitärgerichts	field-grey	light blue	red
Remotendepots 1916	field-grey	cornflower blue	white
Technische Institute - Beamtstellvertreter 1915	field-grey	medium blue	medium blue
Technische Verkehrtruppen	field-grey	black	red
Telegraphenbauwarte	field-grey	black	red
Unterapotheker	field-grey	carmine	carmine
Waffenmeister	field-grey	black	red
Waffenmeister Bavaria	field-grey	dark-grey	red
Zahlmeister - Obere Beamte 1915	field-grey	cornflower blue	white
Zahnärzte	field-grey	carmine	carmine
Zivil & Militärverwaltung der besetzten Gebiete 1915	field-grey	dark green	dark green

Landsturm cap (*Wachstuchmütze*)

Armed *Landsturm* units were generally performing guard duties for prisoners of war, for communication lines, frontiers and coast defenses. They only performed front line service at the Eastern front. In 1917, 942 *Landsturm* infantry battalions existed of which 120 were grouped in 40 *Landsturm* infantry regiments.

Landsturm units wore over their field cap a shiny black cap made from wax cloth (*Glanzwachstuch*). The cap was approx 2.8" (7cm) in height with a 1.2" (3cm) black cap band and a 1.6" (4cm) black front visor. At the back, two eyes and hooks enabled the cap to be tightened around the field cap. Each side had one air ventilation hole, which was increased to three at each side in Bavaria.[35]

The yellow metal *Landwehr* cross was sewn with eight threads to the cap body and measured 1.8" (4.5cm) by 1.8" (4.5cm) and had the motto of the state. These were:

Bavaria	*In Treue Fest*
Hessian	*Gott, Ehre, Vaterland*
Hansa	*Mit Gott fürs Vaterland*
Prussia	*Mit Gott für Konig und Vaterland 1813*
Saxony	*Providentiae memor*
Württemberg	*Furchtlos und trew*
Other states	*Mit Gott für Fürst und Vaterland*

A state cockade (*Landeskokarde*) was fixed below the cross. As of July 1915, *Landsturm* units were equipped with a helmet, but the *Landsturm* cap continued to be used with units in the home country. Starting in 1914, the cap was also issued in field grey wax cloth.[36] The cap was used until mid 1918.

Great looking Prussian *Landsturm* cap with the state motto: *"Mit Gott für König und Vaterland 1813". Royal Army and Military History Museum, Brussels.*

A 1915 dated picture taken in Antwerp, Belgium of the *Bayerischer Landsturm, Fussartillerie Batl 1.AK, 4.Batterie.* The men are equipped with obsolete rifles, ammo pouches and the M71 bayonet.

1st *Landsturm* infantry battalion, January 15th 1915.

Notes:

1 F.J. Stephen, page 17.
2 European Military Uniforms, a short history, Paul Martin, Spring Books 1967, page 64.
3 Unterärtze, Feldunterärtze, Feldhilfsärtze, Sanitärtsoffiziere (only peaked cap).
4 Unterärtze, Feldunterärtze, Feldhilfsärtze, Veterinärsoffiziere (only peaked cap).
5 Kränkenträger, Krankenwärter, K^che, Apothekerhandarbeiter (cap with peak).
6 Schwere reiter cap band: Black velvet for officers.
7 The 12th and 16th Uhlan had a light-blue cap band, but white piping around the top and above the cap band.
8 The 12th and 16th Uhlan had a light-blue cap band, but white piping around the top and above the cap band.
9 The Hussar field cap had often two rows of piping above the cap band only.
10 The cap band of Beamte was made from velvet (*Samt)* (pre-1915) or cloth (*Tuch*).
11 Before 1915, the cap band was made from velvet for *Militärapotheker* and from cloth (Tuch) for *Unterapotheker.*
12 Militärische Kopfbedeckungen der Kaiserzeit, Reiner Hermann, page 27: The *Karpathenabzeichen* was issued on 11.7.1917.
13 Militärische Kopfbedeckungen der Kaiserzeit, Reiner Hermann, page 27: For actions during August 1916 and July 1917.
14 Stephen Bull, page 75: The *Einheitsfeldmütze* was adopted in July 1917.
15 Die grauen Felduniform der deutschen armee, Moritz Ruhl, and J. Kraus: A special field cap was introduced in 1908 for train and medical troops (*Sanitätswesen*): Prussia February 1908, Bavaria, Saxony and Württemberg March 1908.
16 J. Kraus: A new *Einheits-Dienstmütze* was made available as well without any colored piping or cap band: Prussia and Bavaria October 1917.
17 J. Kraus: The Officers service cap was introduced in 1910: Prussia February 1910, Bavaria November 1910, Saxony April 1910, Württemberg March 1910.
18 Status 26.5.1918
19 Militärische Kopfbedeckungen der Kaiserzeit, Reiner Hermann, page 26: 20.000 Edelweiss insignia were distributed.
20 J. Kraus: The Prussian War Ministry approved the Edelweiss cap insignia on 9.9.1915: Bavaria 11.9.15, Württemberg 20.9.15.
21 Unterärtze, Feldunterärtze, Feldhilfsärtze, Sanitärtsoffiziere (only peaked cap).
22 Kränkenträger, Krankenwärter, Köche, Apothekerhandarbeiter (cap with peak).
23 Unterärtze, Feldunterärtze, Feldhilfsärtze, Veterinärsoffiziere (only peaked cap).
24 The 12th and 16th Uhlan had a light-blue cap band, but white piping around the top and above the cap band.
25 The 12th and 16th Uhlan had a light-blue cap band, but white piping around the top and above the cap band.
26 The Hussar field cap often had two rows of piping above the cap band only. The model 1915 piping for Saxon regiments now only had a single row of piping.
27 J. Kraus: A new officers field-grey or grey-green field cap was introduced in 1917: Prussia July 1917, Bavaria August 1917.
28 J. Kraus: When the new "future peace-time" uniform was introduced, the peaked cap underwent a number of changes: Prussia on April 1916.
29 With red piping above and below the cap band.
30 Same colors as the piece-time field cap, but with a field-grey peak.
31 Black velvet for officers.
32 Turquoise blue for officers.
33 The 1st , 2nd and 17th Regiments had small death's head badges worn between the two cockades.
34 Source J. Kraus.
35 J. Kraus, page 116: Each side of the *Wachstuchmütze* had one air ventilation hole, which was increased to three at each side in Bavaria: June 1915.
36 J. Kraus, page 116: As of November - December 1914, the *Wachstuchmütze* was also issued in field grey wax cloth.

Disclaimer